Constitutional Faiths

Constitutional
Faiths Felix Frankfurter,
Hugo Black, and the Process of

Judicial Decision Making

MARK SILVERSTEIN

Cornell University Press

Ithaca and London

First published 1984 by Cornell University Press.
Published in the United Kingdom by Cornell University Press Ltd., London.

International Standard Book Number 0-8014-1650-7
Library of Congress Catalog Card Number 83-45946

Printed in the United States of America

*Librarians: Library of Congress cataloging information
appears on the last page of the book.*

*The paper in this book is acid-free and meets the guidelines
for performance and durability of the Committee on Production
Guidelines for Book Longevity of the Council on Library Resources.*

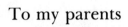
To my parents

Contents

Acknowledgments   9

Introduction   13

1
Liberalism, Democracy, and the Supreme Court   24

2
Felix Frankfurter: Politics as Education   51

3
Hugo Black: Politics as Conflict   90

4
Due Process and the Fourteenth Amendment:
The Limits of Judicial Decision Making   127

5
From *Bridges* to *Dennis*: Free Expression
and the Needs of a Democratic State   174

Conclusion   207

A Note on the Archival Sources   221

Selected Bibliography   223

Index of Cases   231

General Index   233

Acknowledgments

The most pleasurable stage in the completion of a manuscript is the opportunity to thank those who made it possible. First and foremost, I owe much to David J. Danelski of Stanford University. Without his encouragement, friendship, and counsel this enterprise would never have come into being. Benjamin Ginsberg, Theodore Lowi, Isaac Kramnick, William Haltom, Wendy Mink, William Tetreault, Nancy Love, James Curtis, and Thomas Dumm gave generously of their time in reading portions of the manuscript. A very special thanks is owed Aline Kuntz.

The staff of the Manuscript Division of the Library of Congress and Erika Chadbourn of the Harvard University Law School Library aided me in researching the archival sources. Elizabeth Black has kindly granted me permission to use the Hugo L. Black Papers at the Library of Congress. The Brookings Institution provided the funds and opportunity for a year of research in Washington, D.C. Lawrence Malley of Cornell University Press provided expert counsel on the preparation of the manuscript.

Most of all, I owe a profound thanks to the students in my classes at Cornell University Law School and Colgate University. Their contribution to this work is far greater than they might ever believe.

Mark Silverstein

Ithaca, New York

Constitutional Faiths

O Mortal men! be wary how ye judge
Dante, *Paradise*, Canto 20

Introduction

The more I study the deliberative process—the materials to be examined and the time and free thought for deliberation—the more deeply troubled I am by what is more important than a particular decision or series of decisions, and that is by the nature of the process and the temper of mind that brings them to pass.

Felix Frankfurter to Harlan Fiske Stone
February 3, 1936

In April 1962, Felix Frankfurter, then eighty years old, suffered a debilitating stroke. After twenty-three years of distinguished service on the Supreme Court, he was forced to face the inevitable and tender his resignation. Nevertheless, although ill and confined to a wheelchair, he remained in spirit a member of the Court. Often he communicated with his former colleagues, offering advice and commentary on troublesome problems. One such problem was the increasing number of cases arising out of the Negro protest movement in the South. The "sit-in" cases posed difficult legal as well as emotional issues as the Civil Rights Movement shifted from the litigation strategy of the NAACP to the direct action tactics of CORE, SNCC, and other groups. The Court, unanimous at first in striking down the criminal convictions of demonstrators, began to divide when the number of cases, as well as the tactics of the demonstrators, appeared to escalate.[1] During the 1964 term, the Court, in a 5–4 decision, over-

1. For a review of the cases see A. E. Dick Howard, "Mr. Justice Black: The Negro Protest Movement and the Rule of Law," 53 *Virginia Law Review* 1030 (1967).

turned the trespass convictions of participants in a sit-in demon-
stration, holding that the 1964 Civil Rights Act, which became law
while the cases were pending, served to abate the criminal convictions.[2] One of the dissenters was Hugo Black, Frankfurter's longtime adversary on the Court. Following the announcement of the
opinion, Frankfurter wrote Black expressing his "pride" in Black's
forceful dissent. Several days later, while vacationing in Florida,
Justice Black replied:[3]

> It was good to get your letter of Dec. 15th which my office for-
> warded to me here. Your agreement with the dissenting views I ex-
> pressed in the "sit-in" cases was not surprising. More than a quarter
> of century's close association between us in the Supreme Court's ex-
> acting intellectual activities has enabled both of us, I suspect, to an-
> ticipate with reasonable accuracy the basic position both are likely
> to take on questions that importantly involve the public welfare and
> tranquility. Our differences, which have been many, have rarely
> been over the ultimate end desired, but rather have related to the
> means that were most likely to achieve the end we both envisioned.
> Our years together, and these differences, have but added to the
> respect and admiration that I had for Professor Frankfurter even
> before I knew him—his love of country, steadfast devotion to what
> he believed to be right, and to his wisdom. Feeling this way you can
> understand what I mean by saying to you "it was good to get your
> letter."

Black's reply was more than simply sympathetic words for a
dying and respected colleague. Black and Frankfurter truly did
share common goals. United in a distaste for special privilege and
concentrations of wealth and power, both believed in a paternalis-
tic government responsive to the needs and sympathetic to the
plight of the common man. Both directly challenged a constitutional jurisprudence which vested in courts, through the "vague
contours" of the due process clause, the power to inhibit social
and economic reform. Both sympathized with the growing labor
movement and warmly supported the humanitarian goals of the
New Deal. Both passionately believed in the leadership of Franklin Roosevelt. Both were, in short, "liberals" in the twentieth-century sense of the term.

2. *Hamm* v. *City of Rock Hill*, 379 U.S. 306 (1964).
3. The letters are found in HLBLC 59.

Nevertheless, as Black noted, this broad agreement rested on substantial differences over means. Hugo Black and Felix Frankfurter understood the American polity in very different ways and, as a result, spoke for two different conceptions of the role of the Supreme Court. The "rule of law" for Hugo Black meant more than merely restrictions upon the freedoms of the citizenry. Ultimately it meant law based on clear and concise rules, which would check the discretion and will of the judiciary. His reading of history as well as the experience of his own life taught him that men, regardless of temperament and expertise, were incapable of exercising power in a disinterested manner. His conception of the role of the judiciary was founded on a fear of power exercised by the few at the expense of the many, and thus he sought continually to decrease the sphere of judicial judgment. The Court, unaccountable directly to the people, must, in Black's view, remain accountable to the supreme written emanation of the popular will—the text of the Constitution.

Whereas Black sought to confine judicial judgment, Frankfurter, despite protests to the contrary, sanctified it. A fear of power, even judicial power, was alien to his philosophy of government. His faith in expertise and professionalism led him to conceive the role of judges as that of quintessential experts, restrained neither by rigid rules nor constitutional absolutes but by a deep understanding and appreciation of American traditions and democratic principles. Men were capable of the disinterested application of power, and the judge, freed of rigid restrictions, could, like the scientist freed from unverifiable dogma, become an important agent of progress in the modern state. Frankfurter, like Black, was deeply conscious of the undemocratic nature of judicial review; unlike Black, his remedy was to place extraordinary faith in the element of *self* in the doctrine of judicial self-restraint.

The most revealing insights regarding judges and judicial behavior come not from the published opinions but from a study of what Frankfurter once termed the individual judge's idealized political picture of the social order. Of all our political actors, judges are most in need of a political philosophy because, unlike elected representatives, they are constantly in the position of having to justify their authority. This quest for legitimacy forces judges perpetually to confront the ambiguity of their role in a nation with a strong commitment to majority rule. In this search to locate and establish their own authority, judges become America's political philosophers.

Thus a study of the constitutional decision making of Felix Frankfurter and Hugo Black has significance on several levels. Their political experience and thought symbolize the dilemma of American liberalism and the dynamic tensions within the "liberal-democratic" tradition. To the American liberal of the early twentieth century, the trusts and monopolies of the Gilded Age signaled the apparent demise of the Horatio Alger ideal which powered so much of liberal thought. The control of private concentrations of wealth and power demanded a growth in public power, which in turn triggered the classic liberal distrust of the state. To a generation of reformers shaped by Jeffersonian ideals and values, the inevitable antinomy between public and private power constituted the major predicament of modern American life.

Felix Frankfurter responded to the growth of a new America with a deep-seated faith in the administrative state. At the core of his political vision was a belief that scientific training and expertise would allow men to employ public power in a disinterested fashion to control private power. The liberal fear of the state was displaced by a new liberal confidence in science and management. Power was a means to progress, and Frankfurter welcomed the emergence of a strong, independent state as democracy's inevitable response to a changing world.

Whereas Frankfurter was confident of the uses of state power, Black was fearful and skeptical. Aided by a study of history, his political education was shaped by a Populist understanding of the continuing conflict between the few and the many, the rich and the poor, the forces of Alexander Hamilton and those of Thomas Jefferson. History, he believed, proved that men could not be trusted with power, and to assume that power could be employed in a disinterested fashion for the benefit of the many was naive. As suggested in Chapter 3, Hugo Black was a man of Jeffersonian instincts confronted by the reality and the necessity of the New Deal.

A central thesis of this work is that these political values shaped each man's understanding of the role of courts and judges in America and ultimately found expression in the process of decision making they brought to bear in constitutional cases. The study of public law and judicial decision making has been a fertile, if frustrating, subject of inquiry for political scientists. Less disposed than their law school counterparts to accept the traditional doctrinal approach to the study of public law, political scientists have sought to develop a scientific approach to judicial decision making. From the pioneering works of C. Herman Pritchett and Glendon Schubert[4] the principal paradigm developed by political scientists for the scientific study of decision making has centered upon the impact of individual values and attitudes upon judicial votes. Despite methodological limitations,[5] the works of Schubert, Pritchett, and others[6] do appear to confirm the perhaps intuitively obvious fact that values and attitudes influence judicial decisions. The problems of delineating these values, as well as describing how and at what stage they operate in the decision-making process, still remain. This study of Hugo Black and Felix Frankfurter is intended to shed some light on this aspect of the judicial process.

The initial task is to develop an understanding of the core political values of the two men. In the case of Felix Frankfurter, his correspondence now on file at the Library of Congress and the Harvard Law School Library constitutes the primary source material. This material has been available to the public for more than a decade and used by scholars in many diverse projects[7] but is used

4. See, e.g., C. Herman Pritchett, *The Roosevelt Court* (New York: Macmillan, 1948), and Glendon Schubert, *The Judicial Mind* (Evanston: Northwestern University Press, 1965).

5. The methodological technique has been mainly cumulative scaling and factor analysis. For a critique, see Joseph Tanenhaus, "The Cumulative Scaling of Judicial Decisions," 79 *Harvard Law Review* 1583 (1966); Lon Fuller, "An Afterword: Science and the Judicial Process," 79 *Harvard Law Review* 1604 (1966).

6. See, e.g., David Rohde and Harold Spaeth, *Supreme Court Decision Making* (San Francisco: W. H. Freeman, 1976); David Danelski, "Values as Variables in Judicial Decision Making: Notes toward a Theory," 19 *Vanderbilt Law Review* 721 (1966).

7. Compare, e.g., the biographical use of the Frankfurter material in Michael E. Parrish, *Felix Frankfurter and His Times: The Reform Years* (New York: Free Press, 1982), with the use of the same material for psychobiographical purposes in H. N. Hirsch, *The Enigma of Felix Frankfurter* (New York: Basic Books, 1981).

here primarily to illustrate how Frankfurter's faith in science and expertise shaped his understanding of democracy as well as the role of the judge. The Hugo Black files are now available to scholars at the Library of Congress on a restricted basis, and thus much of the Black material appears in print here for the first time. In addition, Chapter 3 contains substantial excerpts from Black's marginal notes found in the volumes of his personal library currently housed at the United States Supreme Court. Black was an avid reader and a self-taught historian, and his marginal comments and indexing of the great works of political theory and history constitute a priceless resource for the study of his political thought. Indeed, from these sources emerged the conflict theory of history that would play a critical role in the development of his constitutional jurisprudence.

In delineating the core political values of both men, I have emphasized their pre-Court writings and careers. The second half of this study, however, attempts to describe the influence of their values on judicial decision making, and hence the focus is on the period from Black's appointment to the Court in 1937 to approximately the *Dennis* decision in 1951. Here again, the private papers of the justices provide an important source of research material. Opinion writing, particularly in the case of majority opinions, is a product of group dynamics. Solitary dissents and concurrences are shaped and constrained by institutional and professional norms. The private memorandums, draft opinions, and notes of the justices reveal far more than does the public record of how individual justices perceived and decided cases.[8] A careful study of this material will help to illuminate the impact of political values and theory on judicial decision making.

Hugo Black and Felix Frankfurter were deeply troubled by the tension between judicial review and majority rule. They sought to ease this tension through the use of highly developed, individualized norms of judicial decision making which would work to define the judicial role and screen decision making from the vaga-

8. Many of the cases discussed in Chapters 4 and 5 are undoubtedly familiar to students of constitutional law. The point of using such cases is to illustrate that well-known, oft-cited cases take on added meaning and significance when one attempts to understand the process of decision making which produced them.

ries of personal preference. These role expectations and norms were the product of the differing political beliefs held by the two men. For Frankfurter and Black, critical differences in political values found expression in different role expectations for judges.[9]

Judging, particularly at the level of the Supreme Court, is a complex undertaking. Institutional norms constrain judges, but these norms range from the relatively inflexible to those in which discretion and personal values come into play.[10] A judge's role orientation is a synthesis of inflexible norms and the judge's perception of the expectations of others as well as his own values in defining more open-ended norms.[11] The norm of judicial restraint provides an important example. As Chapter 1 illustrates, this norm is a necessary response by judges to the perception of courts as countermajoritarian institutions by a people with a strong attachment to the value of majority rule. Nevertheless, despite the apparent necessity for a norm of restraint, its definition varies according to each judge's political philosophy.[12] Frankfurter and Black were firm in their belief in restraint as a standard for judging; they differed substantially, however, over what

9. Role theory has played an important part in judicial research. See, e.g., J. Woodford Howard, *Courts of Appeals in the Federal Judicial System* (Princeton: Princeton University Press, 1981); Theodore Becker, *Political Behavioralism and Modern Jurisprudence* (Chicago: Rand McNally, 1964); Kenneth Vines, "The Judicial Role in the American States: An Exploration," in Joel B. Grossman and Joseph Tanenhaus, eds., *Frontiers of Judicial Research* (New York: Wiley, 1969); James Gibson, "Judges' Role Orientations, Attitudes and Decisions: An Interactive Model," 72 *American Political Science Review* 911 (1978).

10. For example, when Jerome Frank wrote Black suggesting it was a bit foolish for judges to wear black robes, Black agreed but concluded that this was a norm of behavior that was so firmly accepted it could not be breached (HLB to Frank, 10/17/45, HLBLC 28). A more flexible norm is that of judicial independence; the value of an independent judiciary is universally accepted. See Dorothy B. James, "Role Theory and the Supreme Court," 30 *Journal of Politics* 160 (1968). As Bruce Allan Murphy illustrates in *The Brandeis/Frankfurter Connection: The Secret Political Activities of Two Supreme Court Justices* (New York: Oxford University Press, 1982), Frankfurter's interpretation of that norm permitted wide-ranging involvement in extrajudicial affairs. Although Hugo Black was an important force in the Democratic party in his pre-Court years, his interpretation of judicial independence led him to a far more cloistered life as a judge.

11. James Gibson, "The Role Concept in Judicial Research," 3 *Law and Policy Quarterly* 291 (1981).

12. James, "Role Theory and the Supreme Court," p. 177.

that standard required in actual practice. Restraint, of itself, places few limits on judicial behavior; it is only when individual judges attempt to give meaning to restraint that it becomes a critical norm with significant impact on political behavior.

Thus in the case of Frankfurter and Black political values primarily entered the judicial process in the formation of their role orientation.[13] This conclusion, however, does not simply confirm the work of scholars who find in personal value judgments the explanatory variable in voting behavior or the realist assumption that legal reasoning serves merely as a rationalization of personal choice.[14] Constitutional adjudication is far more than the sum total of judicial likes and dislikes. The quest for a scientific model of judicial behavior was premised on the assumption that judges behaved in a manner similar to other political actors and concluded that nonlegal elements of decision making dictated the outcome of cases. The present study suggests that judges are different because for judges the operation of key personal values tends to limit rather than expand the range of discretion. Phrased another way, judicial values, operationalized through role conceptions, serve to define the judicial universe. Role restricts the stimuli a judge may properly consider in deciding cases and normatively weighs those deemed appropriate.[15] In short, for Felix Frankfurter and Hugo Black personal values were the foundation of individualized role orientations designed to shield decision making from personal choice.

For at least the past decade, judicial research on role orientation has been based on interview or questionnaire responses of sitting judges. The result has been an emphasis on trial court and appellate court judges other than the justices of the U.S. Supreme Court. Although the scholarly interest in lower courts is an impor-

13. Recent empirical work by J. Woodford Howard, Jr., on judges of the U.S. courts of appeals indicates a strong link between political orientations and role perceptions (*Courts of Appeals in the Federal Judicial System*, chap. 6).

14. See, e.g., Glendon Schubert, *The Judicial Mind Revisited* (New York: Oxford University Press, 1979); Reed Lawlor, "Personal Stare Decisis," 41 *Southern California Law Review* 73 (1967). On legal realism in general see Wilfred E. Rumble, *American Legal Realism: Skepticism, Reform and the Judicial Process* (Ithaca, N.Y.: Cornell University Press, 1968).

15. Gibson, "Role Concept in Judicial Research," considers the effect of role in a similar fashion.

tant development in judicial research, the Supreme Court, because of its unique institutional setting, can be a fertile area for role research. Moreover, a preoccupation with current judges may be a constraint upon the use of role as a tool of judicial research. If the linkage described here between political values and role orientation stands the test of further investigation—and existing empirical data suggest it will[16]—then the private papers, diaries, notes, and other personal writings of deceased judges constitute an extraordinary resource for the study and understanding of a judge's political values and the resulting impact on judicial behavior. Nor is such research time-bound; an appreciation of the development of role orientations for judges of the past will inevitably aid in fashioning the interview and questionnaire techniques for the study of the judges of the present.

In Chapters 2 and 3 the political values of Frankfurter and Black are examined in detail. Each was influenced by the ideas of the reform movements in the late nineteenth and early twentieth centuries. To understand these ideas as well as their impact upon Frankfurter and Black, it is necessary to place them within the social setting in which each man found them. In doing so, I am not attempting to describe the psychological factors that may have impelled these men to embrace certain values.[17] There may well be, for example, psychological reasons why Frankfurter was an avid defender of the provisions of the Fourth Amendment. The inquiry here is, however, the manner in which ideas and strains of American thought shaped the political understanding of the two men. The goal of these chapters is to develop a richer, more detailed picture of the political values of the two justices than is possible through the interview or questionnaire technique employed in macrojudicial role studies.

In Chapters 4 and 5 the constitutional decision making of the two men is examined from the perspective developed in the pre-

16. See note 13, above.

17. In this respect, Chapters 2 and 3 resemble intellectual histories of the two men. See Morton White, *Social Thought in America* (New York: Oxford University Press, 1976), particularly pp. ix–xxviii. I do not mean to suggest that psychobiography has no place in the study of the judiciary—see Hirsch, *Enigma of Felix Frankfurter*—but, as I hope to make clear in the following pages, its primary value is in understanding judicial behavior and not ideology.

vious chapters. In each constitutional case presented to the Court, two distinct issues appear. One is simply the issue posed by the litigants. The other is the legitimacy of the exercise of the power of judicial review in the particular instance before the Court. The traditional doctrinal study of constitutional law, as well as the behavioral studies of the past two decades, focus, in different ways, upon the first issue. The study of judicial role orientations necessarily requires a greater appreciation of the second. Hence the focus of these two chapters is less on output (votes) than on what lawyers refer to as "work product" (notes, drafts, memorandums), which reveal far more of how judges perceive and understand cases. Although the categories of cases discussed is limited (Chapter 4 centers on cases construing the impact of the Fourteenth Amendment upon state criminal procedures and Chapter 5 focuses on freedom of expression), I shall argue in conclusion that the role conceptions illustrated by these cases are at work for these men on an extensive basis.

Chapter 1 begins with a review of the judicial tradition inherited by Frankfurter and Black. Because both men found the apparent contradiction between judicial review and democracy to be the central problem defining the role of the Court in American government, they sought in the norm of restraint a means of reconciling that tension. The theme of Chapter 1 is that restraint has indeed been a longstanding norm of judicial behavior, but one that gathers meaning only through individual interpretation.

At least since the work of James Bradley Thayer in the 1890s, the Court's role in the American political system has been the subject of much scholarly debate. The apparent contradiction between judicial review and democracy has remained an enduring issue of American political thought and has captured the imagination of scholars of diverse backgrounds and disciplines.[18] This issue of political theory, however, is not confined to the halls of

18. James Bradley Thayer, "The Origin and Scope of the American Doctrine of Constitutional Law," 7 *Harvard Law Review* 129 (1893). See also Henry Steele Commager, *Majority Rule and Minority Rights* (New York: Oxford University Press, 1943); Leonard Levy, ed., *Judicial Review and the Supreme Court* (New York: Harper & Row, 1967); Louis Lusky, *By What Right?* (Charlottesville, Va.: Michie, 1975); John Hart Ely, *Democracy and Distrust* (Cambridge, Mass.: Harvard University Press, 1980).

academia; it is a theoretical problem which serves to define the court as a political institution and which every justice of the Supreme Court must confront. From this confrontation develops a constitutional jurisprudence. Role orientation and jurisprudence are thus inextricably linked, for both constitute the judicial response to the theoretical contradiction that lurks below the surface in constitutional decision making. What follows is, in essence, a study of how Felix Frankfurter and Hugo Black sought to resolve this continuing theoretical dilemma.

1 Liberalism, Democracy, and the Supreme Court

> The Judge should never be the Legislator: Because then the Will of the Judge would be the Law: and this tends to a State of Slavery.
>
> Massachusetts Chief Justice Thomas Hutchinson, 1767

> We are under a Constitution but the Constitution is what the judges say it is.
>
> Charles Evans Hughes, 1907

Neither FORCE nor WILL

On May 18, 1937, Justice Willis Van Devanter announced his retirement pursuant to the terms of the newly enacted Supreme Court Retirement Act.[1] For Franklin Roosevelt, Van Devanter's retirement presented a long-awaited opportunity. The New Deal had fared poorly before the Court; between January 1935 and June 1936 the Court had ruled against Roosevelt in eight of ten cases in which New Deal measures were at issue.[2] His

1. This act permitted justices to retire without submitting their resignation. A previous act passed in 1869 allowed justices with ten years of service to resign at age seventy with a pension equal to the salary at time of resignation. The amount of the pension, however, was always subject to congressional reduction yet judicial salaries were constitutionally protected. The effect of the Retirement Act was to permit justices to retired on a fixed salary. See *Congressional Quarterly, Guide to the Supreme Court* (Washington: Congressional Quarterly, 1979), p. 661.

2. C. Herman Pritchett, *The Roosevelt Court* (New York: Macmillan, 1948), pp. 1–7, describes the cases.

Court Reorganization Plan—announced in February 1937 as a means of relieving judicial work load but defended a few months later as a plan to save the Constitution from "hardening of judicial arteries"[3]—touched off widespread and bitter debate in the country and appeared doomed for defeat in the Congress. Van Devanter's retirement, however, coupled with the decisions in *West Coast Hotel* v. *Parrish* and *NLRB* v. *Jones and Laughlin Corp.*, appeared to herald a new era.[4] Within two years, Roosevelt had appointed Hugo Black, Stanley Reed, Felix Frankfurter and William O. Douglas—all stalwart supporters of the New Deal—to the Court. By 1943 he had elevated Harlan Fiske Stone to the chief justiceship and named eight associate justices. At least in terms of personnel, the judicial "revolution" had begun.

To understand the impact and significance of a revolution, even a judicial revolution, it is important to consider the *ancien regime*. In many ways the nominations of Felix Frankfurter and Hugo Black to the Court were a reaction against a constitutional jurisprudence which reached its zenith during the first third of the twentieth century. The aim of this chapter is twofold: to chronicle briefly the development of that jurisprudence and to highlight the extent to which the norm of judicial restraint serves both as a source of and a constraint upon judicial power in America.

The liberal and democratic traditions in America often form an uneasy alliance. Louis Hartz has described the power of liberal thought in America, but this liberal tradition exists in a nation with a strong democratic ethos.[5] Liberalism has been the dominant strain of social thought ordering our basic understanding of social and economic relations within the polity.[6] Democratic prin-

3. The words are those of Franklin Roosevelt. See *Congressional Quarterly, Guide*, p. 243.

4. *West Coast Hotel* v. *Parrish*, 300 U.S. 379 (1937), upheld a state minimum wage act similar to one held unconstitutional ten months earlier in *Morehead* v. *New York ex rel Tipaldo*, 298 U.S. 587 (1936). *NLRB* v. *Jones and Laughlin Steel Corp.*, 301 U.S. 1 (1937), upheld the National Labor Relations Act.

5. Louis Hartz, *The Liberal Tradition in America* (New York: Harcourt, Brace and World, 1955).

6. Liberalism does not demand a particular form of government. Many of our institutions reflect liberal values; for example, the adversary system of the common law with individuals asserting rights before a neutral judge obviously reflects

ciples, however, shape the institutions and processes of government.[7] These two strains of thought are not necessarily compatible; the product of a democratic political process may be liberal or
illiberal legislation. Conversely, an electorate of John Lockes
would hardly need an institutional check on majority rule to ensure the protection of property.

From this perspective, the Court, as an institution, is neither liberal nor illiberal; it is, however, not democratic. It can proceed
consistent with democratic values, as when it validates the acts of
popularly elected branches, but it remains our most obvious
hedge against majority rule, and this fact has served as a substantial constraint upon the judiciary throughout American history.
Thus Hamilton's classic defense of the judiciary in *Federalist* 78 as
an institution devoid of both force and will rings true. Unlike the
other "coequal" branches, the judiciary lacks the legitimacy conferred by popular sovereignty. When liberal values and the democratic process are in harmony, the judiciary, even one vested with
the power of judicial review, fits easily within the American political system. When the two are at odds, however, the conflict inevitably finds expression in the workings of the Supreme Court.

As a countermajoritarian institution in a nation whose basic political values are shaped by democratic principles, the Court is in
the difficult position of exercising extraordinary power while at
the same time denying the very existence of that power.[8] Restraint in the imposition of judicial will over that of the popularly
elected branches has been a fundamental norm of judicial behavior since the founding of the republic. The true test of judicial
statesmanship throughout the Court's history, however, has been

---

certain core liberal values. Liberalism could, however, flourish in a civil law society.
Thus as used here, liberalism represents a social theory concerned with freeing
men from a hierarchical world in which an individual's place is determined by external rules. Liberalism defines the relationship between individuals in terms of
equality and the freedom to succeed in the marketplace. See C. B. McPherson, *The
Real World of Democracy* (New York: Oxford University Press, 1966); Isaac Kramnick, "Equal Opportunity and 'The Race of Life,'" *Dissent*, Spring 1981, p. 178.

7. For example, excluding the eighteenth and twenty-first amendments—the
latter repealed the former—six of the last ten amendments increased popular
control of government. Four of these explicitly extended the right of suffrage.

8. This theme runs throughout Robert McCloskey, *The American Supreme Court*
(Chicago: University of Chicago Press, 1960).

the ability to make this disclaimer convincingly while continuing to play a fundamental and positive role in shaping the development of the American state. The norm of restraint is thus an important source of judicial power with its actual operation continually subject to individual differences over the role of the Court and the relative importance of liberal and democratic values within the American polity.

Americans have always had an ambivalent attitude toward lawyers and judges, at once revering a government of law and not men and yet fearing rule by an unelected and unrepresentative elite. In the late eighteenth and nineteenth centuries a strong strain of antilegalism in American thought viewed law and judges as a conspiracy against the newly founded republic.[9] On one level, Americans responded to a classical image of the new nation as one of men living in idyllic simplicity in a land of plenty. On another level, particularly as mercantile interests increased, they embraced an image of man freed from imposed moral and ethical considerations and able to pursue his own interests, subject only to consistent application of sharply defined laws. One result of both of these impulses was a determined effort to restrict the independent will of judges. "Relieve the judges of the rigor of text law," wrote Jefferson at the close of the revolutionary war, "and the whole legal system becomes uncertain. Chancery is a chaos, irreducible to a system, insusceptible to final rules and incapable of definition and explanation. Were this true, it would be a monster whose existence would not be suffered one moment in a free country wherein every power is dangerous which is not bound up by general rules."[10]

One source of general rules to restrict the "monster" of unrestrained judicial power was the common law. The lawyer and judge in nineteenth-century America inherited the British common law and natural rights tradition modified by the particular conditions of the American continent. The common law was inextricably linked to natural rights; indeed, by the mid-eighteenth

9. Maxwell Bloomfield, *American Lawyers in a Changing Society* (Cambridge, Mass.: Harvard University Press, 1976), chap. 2.

10. Jefferson to Mazzei, quoted in John T. Noonan, *Persons and Masks of the Law* (New York: Farrar, Straus, Giroux, 1979), p. 59.

century the common law was considered to be the expression of the natural law. To reach practical results consistent with natural rights, a judge need not exercise his independent will; his task was simply to find the applicable common law rule and apply it to the facts. The cornerstone of the common law appeared to be the strict application of precedent, and it was this attribute of common law judging that its defenders pointed to in response to those who expressed fear of rule by judges.[11] Thus as stout a defender of the judiciary as Chancellor James Kent of New York could warn that without the common law "the Courts would be left to a dangerous discretion to roam at large in the trackless field of their own imagination."[12]

Following the revolutionary war and into the eras of Jeffersonian and Jacksonian democracy, the common law came under increasing attack. Many believed that the common law, with its attachment to precedent, brought to the New World the corruption of English practice and experience.[13] Moreover, the common law was considered the product of a professional elite; to understand, find, and assert the rules of the common law required professional training and thus ran afoul of the democratic impulses of the times. One result was added impetus to the codification movement, which would permit any man to find and understand the law as well as to restrict the will and discretion of judges.[14] With codification, William Sampson concluded, "the law will govern the decisions of judges and not the decisions the law."[15] The code would become the primary basis of all future adjudications. To Kent, Joseph Story, and others who saw in the judiciary and the reality of the flexible standards imposed by the common law the

11. Morton Horwitz, *The Transformation of American Law, 1780–1860* (Cambridge, Mass.: Harvard University Press, 1977), pp. 4–16.

12. James Kent, *Commentaries on American Law*, 4th ed. (1840), V.I Lec. 16.

13. See Horwitz, *Transformation of American Law*, pp. 4–9. Even such stalwart champions of the common law as Kent and Joseph Story agreed that only those common law rules applicable to American conditions should be "received" in the New World.

14. On codification, see Perry Miller, *The Life of the Mind in America* (New York: Harcourt, Brace and World, 1965); and Roscoe Pound, *The Formative Era of American Law* (Boston: Little, Brown, 1938.)

15. William Sampson, "An Anniversary Discourse," in Perry Miller, ed., *The Legal Mind in America* (Garden City, N.Y.: Anchor, 1962), p. 132.

means for shaping the development of America, the codification movement posed a serious threat.

Thus throughout the first half of the nineteenth century, as Morton Horwitz puts it, "the problem of fitting the common law into an emerging system of popular sovereignty became the central task of judges and jurists."[16] The judge, of course, knew he made law; the common law process could be creative, as evidenced by Lord Mansfield in England and Kent, Story, and others in the United States.[17] By the 1820s, judges envisioned the common law as a means of social change equally responsible with legislation for promoting socially desirable conduct.[18] To accomplish this task within the American political setting, however, required a politically astute judiciary skilled at fashioning its decisions as the inevitable result of the application of principles of the common law. Nevertheless, as Robert Cover has illustrated, a popular understanding of the judicial role as one devoid of independent will served both to generate and to constrain judicial lawmaking.[19] The judicial role was ambiguous, and the creativity of the common law process did not make judges legislators. The rhetoric of abnegation masked judicial creativity, but it also was an expression on behalf of judges in America of the tenuous nature of their power.

Louis Hartz has described this period of American history as one in which the two national impulses of democracy and capitalism manifested themselves.[20] Judges, in turn, responded to these impulses. The legal historian Willard Hurst described the law's aiding the economic development of the nation's resources by middle-class entrepreneurs as a "release of energy."[21] As Hurst and other scholars have noted, the liberal tradition in America did not forestall the positive use of the law to encourage mercan-

16. Horwitz, *Transformation of American Law*, p. 20.
17. G. Edward White illustrates this creativity in his chapter on Kent, Story, and Shaw in his *The American Judicial Tradition* (New York: Oxford University Press, 1978).
18. Horwitz, *Transformation of American Law*, p. 30.
19. Robert Cover, *Justice Accused: Antislavery and the Judicial Process* (New Haven: Yale University Press, 1975).
20. Hartz, *Liberal Tradition in America*, p. 89.
21. Willard Hurst, *Law and Conditions of Freedom in Nineteenth Century United States* (Madison: University of Wisconsin Press, 1958), pp. 1–39.

tile development.[22] Because these liberal values were in harmony with the output of the democratic process, judges, even within role conceptions as will-less discoverers of the law, were freed to find in the common law and natural law traditions the tools for shaping the economic development of a nation.[23]

The early development of public law reflected similar impulses. During the chief justiceship of John Marshall, the substantive doctrines of constitutional law were anchored in a judicial respect for the vested right of property and nationalism.[24] Marshall established a theory of judicial role which emphasized constraints on judicial will and discretion as the source of the judiciary's power; he thus, as G. Edward White puts it, "developed a technique of decision making that retained an oracular style but grounded decisions on appeals to first principles of American civilization."[25] Judges were to interpret the law and decide only legal issues, but they were not bound by the written text; to decide great issues of state, judges could go beyond the text of documents to the great and fundamental principles that shaped the founding of America. The genius of Marshall was in his ability to undertake this task while maintaining that "judicial power is never exercised for the purpose of giving effect to the will of the judge, always for the purpose of giving effect . . . to the will of the law."[26] Judicial craftsmanship in the hands of Marshall meant resting decisions in particular cases on broad, generalized principles with which few could argue. "Wrong, all wrong," commented John Randolph of a Marshall opinion, "but no man in the United States can tell why or wherein."[27]

22. Calvin Woodward, "Reality and Social Reform: The Transition from Laissez-Faire to the Welfare State," 72 *Yale Law Journal* 286 (1962).

23. Thus Roscoe Pound could write of an American "variant" of natural law based not on the nature of man but on the nature of the American polity and experience (*Formative Era of American Law*, pp. 3–30; *An Introduction to the Philosophy of Law* [New Haven: Yale University Press, 1922], pp. 1–25).

24. McCloskey, *American Supreme Court*, p. 57.

25. White, *American Judicial Tradition*, p. 9. The oracular style of judging was one in which judges merely found the law "mechanically applying existing rules to new situations." See ibid., pp. 8ff.

26. *Osborn v. Bank*, 22 U.S. (9 Wheat.) 738, 886 (1824).

27. White, *American Judicial Tradition*, p. 33.

To Further the Health, Welfare, and Safety of the Community

Marshall's greatness was not attributable simply to his stature as a man or to his legal acumen, but to his presiding during a period in which, for the most part, Americans shared allegiance to common principles. As long as liberal values and the democratic process were in relative harmony, the Marshall technique of asserting judicial subservience to the law while actively furthering liberal values could succeed. His task was eased because during this period the protection of vested property rights was broadly identified with the public welfare. During the period of Roger Taney's chief justiceship (he succeeded Marshall in 1836) these values began to diverge. When judicial protection of vested property rights appeared to conflict with the legislation of popularly elected branches to further the general welfare, conflict over the role of the Court intensified.

The rise of the police power of the state is illustrative. The basic judicial approach to the protection of property was to measure legislation by its effect on property; if property rights were impaired, any legislation had to be supported by a clear constitutional command. If no constitutional provision could be found in support of the legislation, it was the task of the judiciary to hold the legislation null and void.[28] By the mid-nineteenth century, however, this liberal approach was tempered by a growing realization that the people, through the legislative process, might provide for the general welfare despite the impact on an individual's property rights. The doctrine of the police power became a justification recognized by the judiciary for legislation that appeared to infringe personal property rights.[29] First articulated by Marshall, the police power expressed the continuing viability of the prerogatives of sovereignty which the states had retained through the Tenth Amendment.[30]

28. Edwin Corwin, *Liberty against Government* (Baton Rouge: Louisiana State University Press, 1948), p. 72.
29. Edwin Corwin, *The Twilight of the Supreme Court* (New Haven: Yale University Press, 1934), p. 65.
30. Laurence Tribe, *American Constitutional Law* (Mineola, N.Y.: Foundation Press, 1978), pp. 303, 323.

The Taney years can be viewed as a period in which the Court vacillated between the increasingly conflicting demands of liberal values and the democratic process. Taney's opinion in the *Charles River Bridge* case[31] is an indication of the growing significance of the police power. The owners of a state-chartered bridge contended that the legislature could not authorize competing bridges. Taney concluded that the state had the power to promote the welfare of the populace and in the process restrict the property rights of private individuals. Surrender of this power was possible through grants of absolute monopolies, but unless the legislatures clearly and unequivocally stated this purpose the Court would interpret public grants and charters to permit reasonable regulations under the police power.

Although the Court's recognition of the police power was a response to the public will, the notion of an inalienable, vested right of property still found powerful judicial support. The initial source of the judiciary's power to review state legislation was Article I, Section 10, the contract clause of the Constitution. In the hands of Chief Justice Marshall, this provision became a valuable tool in the protection of private property from state regulation.[32] Although in general the Taney Court continued this trend, albeit with somewhat less vigor,[33] the contract clause proved a transient source of judicial power, particularly as state legislatures reserved the right to modify public grants and charters. If the Court was to continue as the guardian of liberal values in America, a more enduring constitutional foundation for the exercise of judicial authority had to be developed.

The origin of that new authority was the words "due process of law" and "liberty" found in the Fifth Amendment to the United States Constitution and in many of the constitutions of the individual states. During the early stages of American law, these words referred only to lawful procedure and not to the substance

31. *Charles River Bridge* v. *Warren Bridge Co.*, 36 U.S. (11 Pet.) 420 (1837).
32. See *Fletcher* v. *Peck*, 10 U.S. (6 Cranch) 187 (1810); *Dartmouth College* v. *Woodward*, 17 U.S. (4 Wheat.) 518 (1819); *Sturges* v. *Crowinshield*, 17 U.S. (4 Wheat.) 122 (1819); *Ogden* v. *Saunders*, 25 U.S. (12 Wheat.) 213 (1825) (dissenting opinion).
33. Compare *Piqua Branch of the State Bank* v. *Knoop*, 57 U.S. (16 How.) 369 (1854), with *Charles River Bridge*.

of legislation.[34] In the years before the Civil War, the judiciary made a tentative effort to invest in these words a sufficient substantive content to permit judicial protection of property against the rising tide of the police power. In *Wynehamer* v. *New York*[35] the New York Court of Appeals held a state prohibition statute unconstitutional as violating the due process clause of the state constitution. The statute, defended as a valid exercise of the police power, was held to violate the vested property rights of liquor owners protected by the due process clause. A year later, in 1857, Chief Justice Taney in the infamous *Dred Scott* case suggested a substantive content in the due process clause of the Fifth Amendment sufficient to void the Missouri Compromise.[36] A majority of the Court refused to accept Taney's reasoning on this point just as a majority of the state courts refused to follow the lead of the New York Court of Appeals. Nevertheless, the first tentative steps to substantive due process had been taken.

As the values of liberalism and the products of the democratic system began to diverge, the Court developed two seemingly contradictory responses. The doctrine of the police power appeared to signify judicial recognition of the sublimation of the judiciary to popular sovereignty. The slowly emerging doctrine of substantive due process, however, permitted judicial protection of individual property rights despite the judgment of popularly elected branches. Moreover, this latter view, because it rested on judicial interpretation and enforcement of the constitutional text—and the Constitution could be seen as the supreme emanation of the popular will—allowed the judiciary to proceed on this course while continuing to maintain its role as a mere declarer of the written law, ultimately subservient to the popular will.

"rights which are the gift of the Creator"

The movement to find in the words "due process of law" the means to continue judicial control over economic devel-

---

34. Raoul Berger, *Government by the Judiciary* (Cambridge, Mass.: Harvard University Press, 1977), pp. 193ff.
35. 13 N.Y. 378 (1856).
36. *Dred Scott* v. *Sanford*, 60 U.S. (19 How.) 393 (1857).

opment was limited both by its infancy and because the Fifth
Amendment applied only to acts of the national government.[37]
Because state governments were the source of most legislation
during this era, a broad reading of the Fifth Amendment did not
substantially increase judicial power. Although most state constitutions contained a due process clause, the rulings of state supreme courts are limited by a jurisdiction defined by state boundaries. Other state supreme courts, for example, were not bound
by the decision in *Wynehamer*.

The passage of the Fourteenth Amendment in 1868 altered this
situation dramatically. Not only did it contain broad phrases such
as "due process of law" and "privileges or immunities" that would
ultimately require judicial definition, but it also unquestionably
applied to the states. Almost immediately the Court was asked to
construe the new amendment so as to ensure continued judicial
protection of vested property rights. In 1869, the Louisiana legislature passed a statute prohibiting slaughterhouses in the city
of New Orleans save for an exclusive grant to the Crescent City
Company. Rival operators brought an action challenging the
grant in the state courts. Failing there, the operators petitioned
the Supreme Court for relief, contending that the grant violated
the newly enacted amendment. Their argument was that the
Fourteenth Amendment encompassed the "natural rights of
man," including the right to hold and acquire property. The right
to pursue a lawful occupation was a natural appendage to the
vested right to acquire and hold property. The argument of the
petitioners, if accepted by the Court, would place the "natural
rights of man" under federal judicial protection. Fragmentary
state court rulings would be unified and federal review of limited
national legislation would be extended to include that of the
states.[38]

That the majority of the Court refused to accept the petitioners'
argument obscures the importance of the case for it was the dissents of Justices Stephen J. Field and Joseph P. Bradley that
proved to be a turning point in American law.[39] Field aimed his

37. *Barron* v. *Baltimore*, 32 U.S. (7 Pet.) 243 (1833).
38. *The Slaughterhouse Cases*, 83 U.S. (16 Wall.) 36 (1873).
39. Robert McCloskey, *American Conservatism in the Age of Enterprise, 1865–1910*

dissent at the majority's narrow construction of the privileges or immunities clause. The majority held that this clause was limited to rights described in the Constitution or implicit in the citizen's relationship to the federal government. Field, however, looked to the common law of England, the Declaration of Independence, and the natural rights that belonged to every free man to define this phrase:

> No privilege was more fully recognized or more completely incorporated into the fundamental law of the country than that every free subject in the British empire was entitled to pursue his happiness by following any of the known established trades and occupations of the country, subject only to such restraints as equally affected all others. The immortal document which proclaimed the independence declared as self-evident truths that the Creator had endowed all men "with certain inalienable rights and that among these was life, liberty and the pursuit of happiness. . . ." That amendment [14] was intended to give practical effect to the declaration of 1776 of inalienable rights, rights which are the gift of the Creator which law does not confer, but only recognizes.[40]

If less eloquent, Justice Bradley was more direct in his dissent:

> In my view, a law which prohibits a large class of citizens from adopting lawful employment, or from following a lawful employment previously adopted, does deprive them of liberty without the due process of law.[41]

The potential impact of Field's and Bradley's interpretations of the Fourteenth Amendment was enormous. Taken together, the Fifth and Fourteenth Amendments would place all regulatory legislation under the supervision of the federal judiciary. Moreover, it was clear that Field intended the judiciary to have the final word over what constituted "rights which are the gift of the Creator."[42] In the final analysis this interpretation was to ensure that

---

(New York: Harper & Row, 1951), p. 1. See also Walton Hamilton, "The Path of Due Process of Law," in Leonard Levy, ed., *American Constitutional Law: Historical Essays* (New York: Harper & Row, 1966).

40. 83 U.S. at 105.
41. 83 U.S. at 122.
42. Carl Swisher, *Stephen J. Field: Craftsman of the Law* (Hamden, Conn.: Archon, 1963), p. 420.

the political, economic, and social beliefs of the men who sat on the federal bench would, through the power of judicial review, play a substantial role in shaping the social and economic development of America.

The opinions of Field and Bradley in *Slaughterhouse* and subsequent cases recalled the decision-making technique of John Marshall. Like Marshall, Field used broad, generalized principles to decide concrete cases while describing the role of judges as will-less expounders of the law. In the mind of Stephen Field, inalienable rights were at the foundation of organized society, and Field found in the vague phrases of the Fourteenth Amendment the constitutional basis by which he could enforce these views. The "rights which are the gift of the Creator" were the liberal values of an entrepreneurial society.[43] Respect for the popular will was rationalized through constant reference to an oracular concept of the judicial role. In effect, through the contours of the Fourteenth Amendment, Field sought to fuse America's faith in Lockean principles to judicial decisions in specific cases.[44]

Despite a general attachment to the myth of Horatio Alger, Americans soon divided over the means to realize that ideal. During the latter part of the nineteenth century, the stirrings of reform movements were beginning in state legislatures. Inevitably these movements called for increased emphasis on the police power to further the general welfare at the apparent expense of individual rights. For a majority of the Court the Fourteenth Amendment did not alter the line that had existed before the amendment's ratification between the police powers of the state and federal judicial authority. Thus in the two decades following the Civil War, state regulatory efforts generally survived a due process challenge despite powerful dissents from the pen of Justice Field.[45] By the 1890s, however, the tide had turned.[46] Dur-

43. This is at least Swisher's opinion; see ibid., pp. 413–434. A review of Field's opinions emphasizing his respect for the police power appears in Charles W. McCurdy, "Justice Field and the Jurisprudence of Government-Business Relations: Some Parameters of Laissez-Faire Constitutionalism, 1863–1897," 61 *Journal of American History* 970 (1975).

44. Hartz, *Liberal Tradition in America*, pp. 208–209.

45. The most significant example is *Munn* v. *Illinois*, 94 U.S. 113 (1877), in which the Court, through Chief Justice Morrison Waite, upheld an Illinois statute limiting the charges permitted for grain storage against the claim that it violated

ing the period from 1888 to 1895, seven new justices were appointed, each the product of a legal profession steeped in laissez-faire economics and the Social Darwinism of the day. Although Field was seventy-eight years old and in declining health, the new members of the Court shared his distrust of a political system that appeared to surrender control of fundamental rights to the populace. Like Field, they looked to the past for immutable, liberal principles and found in the due process clause the means for judicial enforcement of those principles.[47] Thus in 1890 the Court invalidated a Minnesota statute creating a railroad commission with exclusive and unreviewable power to establish rates on both procedural due process grounds and the assertion that due process vested in courts the power to review the reasonableness of rates.[48] In *Smyth* v. *Ames* the Court held as a matter of constitutional law that the judiciary could review the reasonableness of rate regulations and even proposed a formula for evaluating all rate schedules.[49] From the date of *Smyth* through the constitutional crisis of 1936, the Court held state legislation unconstitutional in 401 cases; in 212 of these cases, the operative constitutional provision was the Fourteenth Amendment. By way of comparison, from 1789 to 1898, under all the provisions of the Constitution, the Court had held state legislation invalid in 171 cases.[50] By the turn of the century the early stirrings in *Wynehamer* and *Dred Scott* had developed into the means by which ju-

---

the due process rights of grain storage operators. "The principle upon which the majority proceeds," wrote Field in dissent, "is in my judgment subversive of the rights of private property heretofore believed to be protected by constitutional guarantees against legislative interference" (94 U.S. at 125).

46. For a scholarly review of the Court's move from procedural to substantive due process see Edwin Corwin, "The Supreme Court and the Fourteenth Amendment," 7 *Michigan Law Review* 643 (1909), and Hamilton, "Path of Due Process of Law."

47. Gary Jacobsohn, *Pragmatism, Statesmanship and the Supreme Court* (Ithaca, N.Y.: Cornell University Press, 1977), p. 26, describes the dominant influences on the Court during this period.

48. *Minnesota Rate Case*, 134 U.S. 418 (1890). The company challenging the statute had no notice of a hearing nor the opportunity to appear and present evidence to the commission. Despite these apparent procedural deficiencies, the Court proceeded to find in the judiciary substantive powers previously thought to be exclusively within the legislative domain.

49. 169 U.S. 466 (1897).

50. Levy, *American Constitutional Law*, p. 130.

dicially enforced liberal values were imposed on the democratic process.

James Bradley Thayer and the Rule of Reason

Perhaps the foremost academic spokesman against the emerging judicial supremacy was James Bradley Thayer of the Harvard Law School. A friend and colleague of Oliver Wendell Holmes, Thayer influenced a generation of Harvard law students, among them Learned Hand and Louis Brandeis. Felix Frankfurter, who arrived at the law school a year after Thayer's death, later wrote to Hand: "It is one of the tragedies of my life that he was gone by the time I entered the Law School."[51] Thayer's article, "The Origin and Scope of the American Doctrine of Constitutional Law,"[52] published in 1893, remains a seminal statement of the limited power and role of courts in a democratic state.[53]

In his article, Thayer posited a "rule of administration" to guide courts in the application of the power of judicial review. A court, Thayer wrote, was free to strike down legislation as unconstitutional only when "those who have the right to make laws have not merely made a mistake but have made a very clear one—so clear that it is not open to rational question." This rule recognized

> that, having regard to the great complex, ever unfolding exigencies of government, much that will seem unconstitutional to one man or body of men may reasonably not seem so to another; that the Constitution often admits of different interpretations; that there is often a range of choice and judgment; that in such cases the Constitution does not impose upon the legislature any one specific opinion, but leaves open this range of choice; and that whatever choice is rational is constitutional.[54]

51. FF to Learned Hand, 10/21/40, FFLC 64-1233.

52. 7 *Harvard Law Review* 129.

53. "I am of the view that if I were to name one piece of writing on American Constitutional Law—a silly test maybe—I would pick an essay by James Bradley Thayer. . . . I would pick that essay . . . because from my point of view it's the great guide for judges and therefore, the great guide for understanding by nonjudges of what the place of the judiciary is in relation to constitutional questions" (Frankfurter in Harlan Phillips, ed., *Felix Frankfurter Reminisces* [New York: Reynal, 1960], pp. 299–300).

54. 7 *Harvard Law Review* at 144.

Although Thayer asserted that this rule was based on firmly established precedent, it was shaped by his belief that it represented the only permissible role for a court and judicial review in a democratic society. He was quick to remind judges that they must always assume that the representatives of the people were virtuous, sensible, and competent. Democracy was founded upon a responsible and educated citizenry, and when the courts substituted judicial will for majority will, the people were ultimately denied the critical experience of self-rule necessary to ensure the workings of a successful democratic state. The ultimate virtue of his rule of administration was that it fixed the responsibility of governing "where it belongs"—with the people.

Thayer understood that holding a statute unconstitutional was more a political than a judicial act. He maintained that it was simplistic to believe that judges merely "ascertain the meaning of the text of the Constitution and of the impeached Act to determine, as an academic question, whether in the Court's judgment the two are in conflict." The task was far more difficult (and political) because the issue was not merely constitutional interpretation but "what judgment is permissible to another department which the Constitution has charged with the duty of making it." Hence Thayer characterized the question of judicial review as one of "political administration," that is, "taking part in the political conduct of government." Thayer believed that decisions of "political administration" in a democracy must be made by the elected representatives of the people. The judiciary held the secondary task "of fixing the outside border of reasonable legislative action."[55] The appropriate question in constitutional decision making was not whether legislative action was affirmatively sanctioned by the Constitution but whether the document clearly prohibited the choice made by the legislature. The entire thrust of Thayer's argument rested on the understanding that the primary political —and hence constitutional—choice remained with the elected branches and a court was not free to act unless palpable error had been made.

Thayer did not seek to eliminate judicial review but rather to

55. Ibid. at 143, 144, 148.

confine its scope. Judicial judgment was ultimately inescapable.[56] Judges could, and would, differ over what constituted reasonable legislation. A reasonableness test, no matter how confined by an understanding of the limited role of the judiciary, requires standards by which to measure a challenged act; in a moral vacuum any piece of legislation is reasonable. Thus the Thayer rule implicitly recognized a judiciary enforcing principles and values existing outside the text of the written law. On the major issue of the day—the extent of the police power—Thayer wrote:

> If a legislature undertakes to exert the taxing power, that of eminent domain or any part of that vast, unclassified residue of legislative authority which is called, not always intelligently, the police power, this action must not degenerate into something different and forbidden—e.g., the depriving people of their property without due process of law; and whether it does so or not, must be determined by judges.[57]

Field and Bradley would find little to disagree with in this statement. They would be further pleased by an exception Thayer carved from his rule of administration:

> But when the question is whether state action be or not be conformable to the paramount Constitution, the Supreme Law of the land, we have a different matter in hand. Fundamentally it involves the allotment of power between two governments—where the line is to be drawn. True the judiciary is still debating whether a legislature has transgressed its limits; but the departments are not coordinate and the limit is at a different point. The judiciary now speaks as representing a paramount constitution and government whose duty it is, in all its departments, to allow to that constitution nothing less than its just and true interpretation; and having fixed this to guard it against inroads from without.[58]

To except review of state court decisions in general and specifically those construing the extent of the police power was to permit

---

56. Sanford Gabin, *Judicial Review and the Reasonable Doubt Test* (Port Washington, N.Y.: Kennikat Press, 1980), pp. 27–46.

57. 7 *Harvard Law Review* at 148.

58. Ibid. at 154–155.

the exception to control the rule.[59] Indeed, the Thayer "rule of administration" hardly qualifies as a rule at all; rather, it is a plea to judges to remember the very limited scope of judicial review in a democracy by a man who saw the drift of Supreme Court decisions earlier than did most other commentators. The message, however, had never been forgotten; judges as diverse as Marshall, Taney, Field, and Holmes had sought to reconcile judicial decision making to their understanding of the democratic process, as is illustrated by the famous case of *Lochner* v. *New York*.[60]

Decided just twelve years after the appearance of Thayer's article and two years after Holmes assumed his seat on the Court, *Lochner* remains one of the most widely cited examples of the evils of substantive due process. Under what it believed to be a valid exercise of the police power, the New York legislature passed a statute forbidding employment in a bakery for more than sixty hours a week or ten hours a day. The New York courts affirmed Lochner's conviction for violating the statute. On appeal to the U.S. Supreme Court, Lochner contended that because the bakery trade was "innocuous" it could not be regulated under the police power and thus the statute was an arbitrary and irrational abuse of power, void under the due process clause of the Fourteenth Amendment.

In finding the regulation invalid, Justice Rufus Peckham first acknowledged the scope of the police power left undisturbed by the passage of the Fourteenth Amendment:

> There are, however, certain powers existing in the sovereignty of each state of the Union, somewhat vaguely termed police powers, the exact description and limitation of which have not been attempted by the courts. Those powers . . . relate to the health, morals and general welfare of the public. Both property and liberty are held on such reasonable conditions as may be imposed by the governing power of the state in the exercise of those powers, and with

59. Gabin posits that Thayer meant by this exception only to exempt state decrees that conflict with the exercise of national power. Given the expanse in the concept of national power, this exception becomes almost meaningless. Moreover, Gabin concedes that what Thayer meant by this limitation remains "a continuing source of puzzlement" (*Judicial Review and the Reasonable Doubt Test*, pp. 40–41).

60. 109 U.S. 45 (1905).

such conditions the Fourteenth Amendment was not designed to interfere.[61]

The key word for Peckham, as for Thayer, was "reasonable." He went on to state the following test:

> In every case that comes before this Court . . . where legislation of this character is concerned and where the protection of the Federal Constitution is sought, the question necessarily arises: Is this a fair, reasonable and appropriate exercise of the police power of the state, or is it an unreasonable, unnecessary and arbitrary interference with the individual to his personal liberty or to enter into those contracts in relation to labor which may seem to him appropriate or necessary for the support of himself and his family.[62]

The test was not markedly different from that proposed by Thayer. The Court was reviewing the action of the New York legislature and, under the Thayer doctrine, was entitled to a stricter standard of review. Furthermore, the reviewed action was that of the police power, which Thayer acknowledged must be carefully scrutinized to avoid "irrational excess." Employing this test, Peckham and four other members of the Court found the statute to be arbitrary and unreasonable. Holmes, in dissent, also applied a test similar to that of Thayer: "I think the word 'Liberty' in the Fourteenth Amendment is perverted when it is held to prevent the natural outcome of dominant opinion, unless it can be said that a rational and fair man necessarily would admit that the statute proposed would infringe fundamental principles as they have been understood by the tradition of our people and our law."[63] Clearly Holmes shared a similar understanding with Thayer of the Court in a democratic system, but the tests proposed by Thayer, Peckham, and Holmes were remarkably similar. For each of these men, the final test of the reasonableness of legislation remained with the judiciary and, notwithstanding the rhetoric of restraint, each man's understanding of the needs of the polity played a critical role in the operation of judicial review.

61. Ibid. at 54.
62. Ibid. at 56.
63. Ibid. at 76. Justice Harlan dissented at length in an attempt to show the necessity of such legislation.

Holmes and Brandeis Dissenting

By the initial years of the twentieth century, American values were in flux. A revolt against formalism, evidenced in the social sciences by the rise of scientific naturalism and in law by sociological jurisprudence, proceeded on the assumption that immutable, untested principles could no longer serve as the means for ordering social and economic life. If Americans still clung to the myth of Horatio Alger, there were now substantial differences over the conditions necessary to ensure the reality of such a dream. Old liberal values were challenged by a new liberalism which found the positive intervention of the state necesssary to ensure progress. The jurisprudence of Field and Bradley, carried into the twentieth century by men such as William Howard Taft, Willis Van Devanter, and Pierce Butler, reconciled the tension between judicial review and democracy by restricting judicial will through what they believed were undisputed first principles of American civilization. As these principles came under increasing attack and American liberalism began its transformation, the oracular concept of the judiciary was thrown into direct conflict with the democratic system.

The appointments to the Court of Holmes in 1903 and Louis Brandeis thirteen years later are critical events in American constitutional history. Seen in retrospect as the proponents of a modern judicial liberalism that would become the guiding light of the Roosevelt Court, these men also evidenced the ambiguities and contradictions that beset an institution that seeks to satisfy both liberal and democratic values.

"Holmes," Grant Gilmore writes, "is a strange, enigmatic figure. Put out of your mind the picture of the tolerant aristocrat, the great liberal, the eloquent defender of our liberties, the Yankee from Olympus. All that was a myth concocted principally by Harold Laski and Felix Frankfurter, about the time of World War I. The real Holmes was savage, harsh and cruel, a bitter and lifelong pessimist who saw in the courts of human life nothing but a continuous struggle in which the rich and powerful impose their will on the poor and weak."[64] It is perhaps one of the great iro-

64. Grant Gilmore, *The Ages of American Law* (New Haven: Yale University Press, 1977), pp. 48–49.

nies of American history that Oliver Wendell Holmes was the first and perhaps only, Supreme Court justice viewed as a folk hero.[65] Holmes, in fact, was skeptical of even the most basic attempts at reform, believing that struggle and competition were inevitable and that human attempts to alter the natural order were bound to fail. In *The Common Law* he gave voice to this belief: "The first requirement of a sound body of law is that it should correspond with the actual feelings and demands of the community, whether right or wrong."[66] In 1919 he wrote Brandeis: "Generally speaking I agree with you in liking to see social experiments tried, but I do so without enthusiasm because I believe it is merely shifting the place of pressure and so long as we have free propagation Malthus is right in his general view."[67]

This fatalism, however, produced America's most "democratic" justice. In Holmes's mind, the judicial role was significantly and unalterably limited by majority rule. Unless beyond the pale of reason, courts must defer to the legislative efforts shaped by majority sovereignty. Francis Biddle recounted an incident which, though humorous, tells much about Holmes. Encountering John W. Davis, then solicitor general, after he had argued an antitrust case before the Court, Holmes asked how many more antitrust cases were on the solicitor general's docket. When Davis replied quite a few, Holmes commented, "Well bring 'em on and we'll decide 'em. Of course I know, and every other sensible man knows, that the Sherman law is damned nonsense, but if my country wants to go to hell, I'm here to help it."[68]

If Holmes's concept of judicial restraint was the product in part of extreme skepticism, Brandeis's was the result of a passionate belief in the necessity and wisdom of reform efforts. The difference was evidenced in many of the dissents written by each man.[69] The typical Holmes dissent was a short, eloquent state-

---

65. Holmes is certainly the only justice to be the subject of a Broadway musical, "The Magnificant Yankee."

66. Oliver W. Holmes, *The Common Law* (Boston: Little, Brown, 1963), p. 36.

67. Quoted in Samuel Konefsky, *The Legacy of Holmes and Brandeis: A Study in the Influence of Ideas* (New York: Macmillan, 1956), p. 9.

68. Quoted in Francis Biddle, *Justice Holmes, Natural Law and the Supreme Court* (New York: Macmillan, 1961), p. 9.

69. Compare, e.g., their dissents in *Quaker City Cab* v. *Pennsylvania*, 277 U.S. 389 (1928).

ment that the Court must not substitute its judgment for that of the legislature, whereas a Brandeis dissent was often a long, detailed statement illustrating the wisdom of the challenged legislation.[70] For Holmes, like Thayer, the primary question was whether the Constitution forbade the choice made by the legislature. Brandeis assumed a more overtly political position in his attempt to prove a statute not only affirmatively sanctioned by the Constitution but necessary for social justice.

Like many Progressives at the turn of the century, Brandeis believed that reform was necessary to ensure the continued viability of the democratic state. In this view he personified the new American liberalism. He believed reform must lead to a return to a small market economy; his enemies were the trusts and monopolies of the Gilded Age. Notwithstanding the furor over his nomination to the Court, he was hardly a radical: like many, he retained faith in the Horatio Alger myth, arguing that it was disappearing as the result of trusts and bosses.[71] The Brandeis liberal sought sufficient government control to restore the competitive conditions in which an Alger could flourish. Upon his nomination, the *New York Times* complained that "Mr. Brandeis is essentially a contender, a striver after changes and reforms."[72] Compared to the apolitical Holmes, who prided himself on not reading newspapers, Brandeis appeared to lack the detachment essential to the judicial role.

In his first dissent on the Court, Brandeis established the tone of what was to follow. The majority in *New York Central Railroad* v. *Winfield*[73] held that Congress, in passing the Federal Employee Liability Act, intended to preempt the field and preclude additional state remedies. Dissenting, Brandeis considered not merely legal precedent but the "world experience" with industrial accidents. This examination exposed "many an assumption upon

70. Brandeis's technique was drawn from his days as an advocate; the famous Brandeis brief in *Muller* v. *Oregon*, 208 U.S. 412 (1908), consisted of a handful of pages citing legal authority and more than one hundred pages of statistics and data proving the need for the challenged legislation. See also Alpheus Mason, *Brandeis: A Free Man's Life* (New York: Viking, 1946), p. 574.

71. Hartz makes this point, *Liberal Tradition in America*, p. 207.

72. Quoted in Mason, *Brandeis*, p. 465.

73. 244 U.S. 147 (1917).

which American judges and lawyers rested comfortably" and contended that "our individualistic conception of rights and liability no longer furnish an adequate basis for dealing with accidents in industry."[74] The passion and fervor found in his *Winfield* dissent appeared in stark contrast to the lofty detachment of Holmes in *Lochner*.

An intensive examination of Holmes and Brandeis is beyond the scope of this study, but even a cursory review suggests the contradictions within "Holmes and Brandeis dissenting." To the new liberal of the twentieth century, Holmes was the epitome of judicial technique. In the hands of Holmes, the judiciary was subservient to majority will and, in the hands of the reform-minded legislatures, that will became the agent of social change. To these same liberal reformers, Brandeis was a hero as a judge who consistently reached the correct results. Social engineering for Brandeis was both a legislative and a judicial task; his independent review and study of the facts more often than not placed him in agreement with legislative determinations. The method of Holmes, however, did not guarantee the correct substantive results, and the Brandeis conception of the role of judges, in the hands of another man, could easily be used to thwart reform. Neither Holmes nor Brandeis provided the new liberal reformer with a jurisprudence that successfully linked correct judicial methods with correct substantive results.

This absence is further evidenced by the problem of personal rights. Both Holmes and Brandeis anticipated that legislative acts might infringe upon minority rights. For Holmes this outcome was the inevitable consequence of majority rule; for Brandeis it was a possible result of legislation furthering the common good. With the coming of World War I and its aftermath, the problem of individual rights took on sharper focus. If the presumed hallmark of Holmes and Brandeis liberalism was deference to legislative reforms under the police power, what was the appropriate response to legislative attempts to restrict free speech, press, and assembly in the name of that same power? To an extent perhaps unforeseen by Holmes and Brandeis, it was precisely this question

74. See also *Adams v. Tanner*, 244 U.S. 590 (1917).

that would serve to define the relationship of the Supreme Court, liberalism, and democracy in the following decades.

Not surprisingly, Justice Holmes's initial free speech decisions emphasized the power of the majority to restrict the speech of the minority.[75] The words, "I see no meaning in the rights of man except what the crowd will fight for," expressed his general attitude.[76] Indeed, the famous clear and present danger test originally was used by Holmes to rationalize the power to restrict free expression. Nonetheless, his belief in the power of the majority rested in part on the free play of competing ideas within the marketplace. A tension appears in all of Holmes's free speech decisions, and the clear and present danger test can be viewed as an attempt to accommodate these conflicting demands. In effect, the test was to place in the courts the power to determine the reasonableness of legislative exercises of the police power touching on free speech. It was not a position that Holmes was necessarily comfortable with, but, given his view of democratic values, the judiciary had to assume that task.

Brandeis gave the clear and present danger test added meaning. The task of a judge in applying that test was not markedly different from his task in an economic policy case; the careful, independent scrutiny of the facts would lead to an inevitable conclusion. Whereas Holmes concentrated on the imminence of the alleged evil in free speech cases, Brandeis added to the equation an independent, more subjective judgment concerning the seriousness of that evil. Brandeis was confident that judges were capable of determining the value or threat of any speech to the democratic system.[77]

Perhaps the best illustration of the difficulties presented to Holmes and Brandeis liberalism by the free speech cases is *Gitlow* v. *New York*.[78] A New York statute made it a felony to advise or

75. See *Patterson* v. *Colorado*, 205 U.S. 454 (1907); *Fox* v. *Washington*, 236 U.S. 273 (1915).

76. Holmes to Laski in Mark DeWolfe Howe, ed., *Holmes-Laski Letters*, vol. 1 (New York: Atheneum, 1953), p. 8, n. 19.

77. See *Pierce* v. *United States*, 252 U.S. 239 (1920). Needless to say, Justices Field, Bradley, et al. had the same faith in their ability to ascertain the dangers of certain economic legislation.

78. 268 U.S. 652 (1925).

teach the duty, necessity, or propriety of overthrowing the government by force. Benjamin Gitlow, a member of the left-wing section of the Socialist party, was charged with violating the statute by publishing sixteen thousand copies of the *Left Wing Manifesto*, which advocated a communist-socialist takeover of the state. At his trial, no evidence was introduced to show that the publication endangered the government of the state of New York. Nevertheless, Gitlow was found guilty, and he sought relief in the U.S. Supreme Court.

Justice Edward T. Sanford, writing for the Court, conceded that the freedom of speech guaranteed by the First Amendment against federal infringement applied to state actions through the Fourteenth Amendment. Yet *Gitlow* presented a significantly different issue than previous free expression cases. The Espionage Acts, under which the previous cases had arisen, were directed at a general evil, and the issue before the courts was whether the accused's speech constituted such an evil. The New York criminal anarchy statute, however, was directed at a particular type of speech which the legislature had determined to be inherently dangerous. Sanford held that only in the former were the courts to apply the clear and present danger test. In the situation presented by *Gitlow* "the state has determined, through its legislative body, that utterances advocating the overthrow of organized government by force, violence and unlawful means, are so inimical to the general welfare and involve such danger that they may be penalized in the exercise of the police power. That determination must be given great weight. Every presumption is to be indulged in favor of the validity of the statute. Mugler v. Kansas, 123 US 523, 661."[79]

Sanford thus struck directly at the heart of the liberal dilemma. Comparing the use of the police power by New York with that of Kansas in *Mugler* posed the question in the starkest terms. In *Mugler*, the Court, though slowly losing ground to the arguments of Justice Field, nevertheless found sufficient votes to uphold a Kansas prohibition statute against the claim that the exercise of the police power violated liquor manufacturers' due process

79. Ibid. at 660.

rights. If the Court was to concede the liberal values of vested property rights to the democratic process, why should not the same concession be made to the equally liberal values of individual rights?

Neither Holmes nor Brandeis provided a workable response. Their dissent, authored by Holmes, rested on a determination that Gitlow's writings "had no chance of starting a present conflagration." Unquestionably this conclusion was correct, but neither Holmes nor Brandeis could maintain that the action of the legislature was irrational and beyond the pale of reason. Caught between the tension of liberal values and democratic processes, the liberalism of Holmes and Brandeis was forced to sacrifice the correct method to achieve the correct result.

Hugo Black, Felix Frankfurter, and the Judicial Revolution

Justice Sanford's challenge would remain for the next generation of justices headed by Felix Frankfurter and Hugo Black. The retirement of Holmes in 1932 brought Benjamin Cardozo to the Court, but arrayed against Brandeis, Cardozo, and Harlan Fiske Stone were Pierce Butler, James C. McReynolds, Willis Van Devanter, and George Sutherland, men who stood firm in the tradition of Justice Field. With the swing votes of Charles Evans Hughes and Owen Roberts, the fate of liberal reform legislation appeared precarious at best.

A majority of the Court often formed behind the oracular tradition, continuing to invoke older liberal values in response to an emerging new consensus. Legal realism and the social science emphasis on human behavior, however, had destroyed the intellectual foundations of that view of decision making. A deepening depression and economic dislocation gave increasing impetus to a liberal movement that called upon the active intervention of the state to ensure the conditions necessary to ensure progress. Thus by the time of the New Deal, this concept of the judiciary was out of joint. Liberalism was not dead—the New Deal still embraced an image of social and economic relations based on competitive individualism—but a process of decision making keyed to vested property rights as a first principle ran directly counter to the spirit of experimentation which marked the New Deal.

The breakdown of consensual, liberal assumptions concerning the role of the state ultimately produced a new Court. Black and Frankfurter came to that Court as the heirs to the tradition of Holmes and Brandeis. In their view, this tradition required judicial deference to the economic and social decisions of popularly elected branches; such a view fit nearly within their own conception of the role of the Court and the democratic process as well as the liberalism of the New Deal. Within a few years of Black's appointment in 1937, however, such issues played a secondary role on the Court's docket; World War II and the ensuing Cold War brought the issues of personal rights and liberties to the forefront. These issues, particularly those involving freedom of expression, exposed the contradiction inherent in the judicial liberalism of Holmes and Brandeis. Furthermore, such issues required the justices of the Roosevelt Court to reexamine and redefine the role of the Court in the American political system. As Black and Frankfurter were soon to appreciate, a faith in judicial restraint neither significantly limited judicial will nor provided a coherent standard to guide judicial decision making.

2 Felix Frankfurter: Politics as Education

> Tomorrow they might easily knock out the Minimum
> Wage Law. . . . The price we pay for this judicial ser-
> vice is too great. . . . A Court *dominantly* composed of
> Holmes and Brandeis and Learned Hand and Car-
> dozo—that's one thing, but taking the judicial fish
> as they run, we have no business to build our insti-
> tutions on such problematic and unlikely happen-
> ings.
> Felix Frankfurter, 1921

> It would be comfortable to discover a Procrustean
> formula. . . . If such were the process of Consti-
> tutional adjudications in this most sensitive field,
> it would furnish an almost automatic task of applying
> mechanical formula and would hardly call for the
> labors of Marshall or Taney, of Holmes or Cardozo. To
> look for such talismanic formula is to assume that
> the broad guarantees of the Constitution can fulfill
> their purpose without the nourishment of history.
> Felix Frankfurter, 1941

The "idealized political picture"

Just as the constitutional jurisprudence of the early
twentieth century appeared to vacillate between the legacy of Justice Field's formalism and the relativism expounded by Justice
Holmes, a similar tension appeared to engulf the social science
and legal scholarship of the era. In the first decades of the twenti-

eth century such scholars as Arthur Bentley and Frank Goodnow sought a new orientation in the social sciences based upon scientific examination and objective descriptions of institutions and human behavior. Previous scholarship, in the view of these men, suffered from deductive, value-laden reasoning based often on the observation and study of documents rather than human behavior.[1] In legal scholarship, Roscoe Pound challenged the rigid formalism of Justice Field. Pound strongly argued against a jurisprudence founded upon immutable first principles and sought in the social sciences and related fields a means for making the law responsive to a changing world. By the 1930s Pound was attacked in turn by a new school of legal realists, who derided any notion of continuity and formalism in the legal system and sought to reduce the study of law to an empirical science. In psychology, the works of Freud and Jung called into question the traditional democratic faith in rational man, concluding that human behavior was largely irrational, particularly in such areas as politics.

The rise of scientific investigation produced a crisis in democratic theory, challenging ethical and moral truths as the basis for democracy and questioning the rationality of human behavior and the possibility of establishing a government based on the rule of law and not men.[2] Science was introduced into the study of politics at the turn of the century and eventually would transform the discipline. This transformation was not without its critics; some scholars took an almost Thomistic approach, imploring their colleagues to a discipline dedicated to a study and understanding of the ethical and moral values in American life. At its inception this debate was confined largely to college campuses and scholarly journals. By the early 1930s, with the country facing economic trauma at home and the rise of totalitarian regimes abroad, the debate took on wider scope and ramifications.

This chapter will examine the pre-Court writings and experiences of Felix Frankfurter to understand his political "education"

1. Arthur Bentley, for example, characterized any scholarship based upon moral and ethical presuppositions as "soul-stuff" (*The Process of Government* [Cambridge, Mass.: Belknap Press of Harvard University Press, 1967], p. 19).
2. See Edward Purcell, *The Crisis of Democratic Theory* (Lexington: University of Kentucky Press, 1973).

and the core political values that shaped his view of the polity. The conflict in the social sciences and legal scholarship provides the backdrop because Frankfurter found value in both camps. He saw in the rise of scientific naturalism and the early stages of legal realism the means to shatter the "myth of the robe," which in the early twentieth century had resulted in judicial control of legislative experimentation and reform. At the same time, so great was his "democratic faith" and his unabashed patriotism that he was unable and unwilling to accept the moral relativism that seemed the inevitable outcome of realism. His task was to merge a faith in the scientific method with a belief in enduring values and principles.

The goal of this chapter is not to make another addition to the recently growing body of biographical work on Frankfurter.[3] A central thesis of this work is that core political values of judges ultimately find expression in the individual process of decision making they bring to bear upon cases. This chapter attempts to illuminate these values in the development of Felix Frankfurter, placing them in the context of the intellectual movements and the social setting in which they took place. Frankfurter recognized the significance of such an investigation; in 1930 he wrote: "It is most revealing that members of the court are frequently admonished by their associates not to read their economic and social views into the neutral language of the Constitution. But the process of constitutional interpretation compels the translation of policy into judgment, and the controlling conceptions of the justices are their 'idealized political pictures' of the existing social order."[4] By the time of his appointment to the Court in 1939, Frankfurter had a firmly developed "idealized political picture" of the American polity. The political world was divided into three groups. To the scientifically trained expert fell the task of administering the democratic state. Frankfurter understood the fiction of the traditional democratic assumption that government was simple and that each citizen had the innate ability to govern. Acknowledging the ex-

3. E.g., Michael E. Parrish, *Felix Frankfurter and His Times: The Reform Years* (New York: Free Press, 1982); H. N. Hirsch, *The Enigma of Felix Frankfurter* (New York: Basic Books, 1981).

4. 14 *Encyclopedia of the Social Sciences* 480 (1930).

traordinary complexity of the modern world, Frankfurter believed that the basic responsibility for governing must be placed in the hands of scientifically trained, disinterested social engineers, who would direct the progress of the modern, democratic state.

The second group consisted of statesmen, who would serve as the critical link between the social engineer and the citizenry. Based upon his strongly held belief that politics was ultimately a process of education, Frankfurter saw the statesman as educator: the conduit through which the citizenry was taught the wisdom of the work of the social engineer.

The third group, the "masses," held ultimate political power. Although many in the social sciences grew increasingly skeptical of anything but the most minimal role for the public in a democratic state, Frankfurter maintained his faith in the populace. The complexity of modern government made it naive to assume that the wisdom of the people could generate the needed reforms, but Frankfurter passionately believed that, with the proper leadership, the masses were capable of setting aside self-interest and sanctioning acts to further the public interest. Always suspicious of groups and particularized interests, Frankfurter viewed politics not as the clash of different interests or the mere election of leaders but as a continual process by which the body politic could be moved in the direction of public interest.

At the center of this political vision was an appreciation of power as an instrument of progress. To the eighteenth-century liberal, a fear of the power of the state was an important component in a movement to liberate men from a social order defined by rank and privilege. The coming of age of Frankfurter and others of his generation marked the emergence of a new liberalism in which the state became an agent in the effort to restore competitive individualism to a society dominated by vast concentrations of private wealth and economic power. Throughout the stages of his political development—he was a "hot Hamiltonian"[5] during the years of Theodore Roosevelt's New Nationalism and later, under the influence of Brandeis, came to doubt the wisdom of centralizing power in Washington and sought a return to a market econ-

5. Quoted in Parrish, *Felix Frankfurter and His Times*, p. 210.

omy—he retained a faith that political power could be used to further common goals. In the hands of scientifically trained experts and great statesmen, the power of the state was not to be feared but to be used confidently to better conditions and ensure progress.

These political values led to a perception of the role of judges remarkably similar to his understanding of the role of the expert. Frankfurter's initial revolt against formalism found expression in the Progressive Movement's effort to free the scientifically trained expert from the constraints of the unverifiable dogma and "truths" which marked an earlier age. This freedom would permit the expert to pursue the experimentation that was inexorably linked to progress. The judge, in Frankfurter's political vision, could serve a similar function. Freed from absolutes and immutable first principles, the judge, through the disinterested exercise of judgment, could adapt principle to the changing needs of a progressive society. The rise of the expert, in his view, was democracy's inevitable response to a changing world; the judge, given the same freedom, would protect democracy from its own divisive forces.

Bull Moose Reformer

Felix Frankfurter's career during the first third of the twentieth century was extraordinary for the breadth and variety of his experiences and accomplishments. Arriving from Vienna in 1894 at the age of twelve and unable to speak a word of English, one of Frankfurter's earliest recollections was of a teacher in PS 25 in Manhattan who punished any of his schoolmates who spoke to him in German.[6] Perhaps not surprisingly, the image of public schools (and on a larger scale, education) as a means for achieving a homogeneous society was to remain with Frankfurter throughout his career. Frankfurter spent much time in his early years reading and, within two years of his arrival in the United States, was ready to attend high school. Although he

6. Harlan Phillips, ed., *Felix Frankfurter Reminisces* (New York: Reynal, 1960), pp. 4–5.

passed the entrance exams for a private school, his lack of funds
led him to City College.[7]

Upon graduation, he worked as a clerk in the newly established
Tenement Housing Department of the state of New York. It was
during this period that he first entertained the thought of a legal
career. The choice of Harvard Law School was an accident; he
had planned to attend Columbia University Law School, but he
became ill and a family doctor advised leaving New York City for
the country. To a young immigrant's son raised on the lower east
side of Manhattan, Cambridge, Massachusetts, was the "country."

The years as a student at Harvard were of the utmost significance in Frankfurter's development. For the first time he escaped
the confines of the lower east side; at Cambridge he was introduced to the world of the Boston Brahmin, and he would thereafter constantly seek acceptance in that world.[8] Cambridge was
the center of American intellectual life, and Frankfurter gloried
in it. During his final year at the law school, for example, he
roomed with Morris Raphael Cohen, a brilliant young philosophy
student. The friendship would last until Cohen's death many
years later. A decade after his graduation from the law school he
wrote Cohen reminding him that "in law school days I used to get
my jurisprudence from you."[9] Cohen became an important critic
of legal realism, and his criticisms often found a sympathetic
reader in Frankfurter.

Frankfurter excelled at Harvard, and he repaid it with "a quasi-
religious"[10] devotion. Two interesting themes in his thinking began to develop during the Harvard years. One was an awesome
respect for great teachers. He later described his teachers, among
them James Barr Ames and John Chipman Grey, in a tone ap-
proaching reverence: "Giants they were, and I revere their mem-
ory because they seem to me to represent the best products of

7. "In those days City College was an intensive course which crowded into
five years high school and college. . . . It was a fantastic thing really. For five days a
week, four hours a day, there was classroom work. . . . It was a great institution for
the acquisition of disciplined habits of work" (ibid., p. 11).

8. Hirsch, *Enigma of Felix Frankfurter*, p. 42.

9. FF to Cohen, 9/9/12, in Lenora Rosenfield, ed., *Portrait of a Philosopher:
Morris R. Cohen in Life and Letters* (New York: Harcourt, Brace and World 1962).

10. Phillips, ed., *Felix Frankfurter Reminisces*, p. 19.

civilization—dedication of lives of great powers to the pursuit of truth, and nothing else, complete indifference to all the shoddiness, pettiness and silliness that occupies the concern of most people who are deemed to be important or big."[11] Years later he would refer to statesmen such as both Roosevelts and Al Smith in the same tone and with the same reverence. Politics was a "process of popular education," and the image of the great statesman-educator was born in Frankfurter's early experience with the giants of the Harvard law faculty.

A similar respect was paid to the law school and the *Harvard Law Review*:

> What mattered was excellence in your profession to which your father or face was equally irrelevant. . . . The thing that mattered was what you did professionally. If a man was respected, it was because he was very good either because he showed up very well in the classroom or in private discussion, or, after the first year, the very good men were defined by the fact that they got on the *Harvard Law Review*. This was determined entirely on the basis of your work as a student by examinations at the end of the year. Election to the *Harvard Law Review* followed academic rank, an automatic affair.[12]

The *Law Review* as described by Frankfurter was hardly a democratic institution; it was, however, the quintessential liberal institution in which the advantages of birth and status were no guarantee of success. This confusion between meritocracy and democracy suggests much about Frankfurter who saw the individual success ethic as linked to the common good. There appears in his *Reminisces* and in several early letters to his friend Emory Buckner an almost petty preoccupation with grades.[13] An "A" man was better than a "C" man; the individual who received an

11. Ibid., p. 24.
12. Ibid., p. 27. A different view of the *Harvard Law Review* appears in Joel Seligman, *The High Citadel: The Influence of Harvard Law School* (Boston: Houghton Mifflin, 1978), p. 177: "It is difficult to imagine a reward system more demeaning, distorting of values or arbitrary."
13. Phillips, ed., *Felix Frankfurter Reminisces*, p. 28. Emory Buckner was a graduate of the law school and worked with Frankfurter under Stimson at the U.S. Attorney's Office. He later served as U.S. attorney and was a founder of the New York City law firm now known as Dewey, Ballantine, Busby, Palmer and Wood. Those early letters concerned placing Frankfurter's students with Buckner's firm.

"A" had a certain quality that one who received a "B" or "C" lacked. Frankfurter envisioned the "A" men as the disinterested, scientifically trained social engineers who would provide leadership for the modern democratic state.

Following graduation, Frankfurter joined the team of bright, young lawyers that Henry L. Stimson was assembling at the United States Attorney's Office in New York.[14] Like many of the men who were to play an important role in Frankfurter's life, Stimson was from a wealthy, prominent, WASP family. His dedication to public service was inbred; as an admiring biographer put it, Stimson was "born to govern."[15] A proponent of Theodore Roosevelt and Roosevelt progressivism, Stimson advocated a strong and efficient central government. Stimson accepted the position of U.S. Attorney on a fixed salary—previous U.S. Attorneys had amassed large fortunes through contingency fee cases and continuing private practice on the side—and hired as his assistants the best and the brightest from the finest law schools. Frankfurter found the opportunity to practice law without a client and in the public interest irresistible. Stimson proved that America's elite could dedicate their lives to public service, and he became, for Frankfurter, the symbol of the capacity of the Republican party to be the agent of liberal reform.[16] Stimson provided a role model for Frankfurter and introduced him to America's governing elite.[17]

Through Stimson, Frankfurter met Theodore Roosevelt. A hero to an age of Progressives, Roosevelt proclaimed the virtues of strong, centralized leadership, the regulation of business, civic responsibility, and a grudging acceptance of the growing labor

14. Frankfurter spent a few months in private practice in New York. Buckner described Frankfurter's private practice as "fifteen or twenty minutes in the Hornblower office" (quoted in Martin Mayer, *Emory Buckner* [New York: Harper & Row, 1968], p. 21).

15. Richard Current, *Secretary Stimson* (New Brunswick, NJ: Rutgers University Press, 1954), p. 54.

16. In a letter concerning Stimson's speech to be delivered before the Republican convention, Frankfurter wrote: "I assume that your large purpose is to identify the Republican Party in the public mind as the liberal party and thereby more immediately further the interests of the Administration as the exponent of liberalism" (FF to Stimson, 9/9/11, FFLC 164-2173).

17. See Hirsch, *Enigma of Felix Frankfurter*, pp. 24–31.

movement as a means of heading off more violent revolution. Characterized later as the "Conservative as Progressive," Roosevelt readily identified with the power of the state.[18] "He *is* genuinely stirred to the new social function of government, and *does* realize that it's the business of statesmanship to effect by policy what revolution effects by force," Frankfurter wrote of Roosevelt.[19] Young Progressives including Frankfurter and Walter Lippmann rallied to Roosevelt's call along with many civic-minded gentry such as Stimson. Not yet in his thirties, Frankfurter was already becoming an intimate and adviser to America's powerful few.

Roosevelt declined to run in 1908, paving the way for his protégé, William Howard Taft, to assume the presidency. In 1910, Stimson resigned his post to run for the governorship of New York with Frankfurter as his principal aide. Roosevelt agreed to campaign for Stimson and, as a result, Frankfurter was brought into closer contact with the champion of progressive thought. The campaign provided an important step in Frankfurter's political education. If Stimson was born to govern, it was in the capacity of administrator and not of politician; he was an ineffective campaigner. Frankfurter later remembered Roosevelt admonishing Stimson: "Harry, it's all very good. The stuff is all there. But you must remember, a political speech should be a poster and not an etching." That remark, Frankfurter recalled, "stuck with me."[20] Stimson lost; he was simply too austere and reserved to reach the people. Roosevelt and Stimson symbolized the distinction between the statesman-educator and the expert administrator. The two formed almost a symbiotic relationship, each necessary for the success of the other and both of critical importance to the fate of democracy in a twentieth-century world.

In 1911 Stimson joined Taft's cabinet as Secretary of War, and Frankfurter followed his mentor as chief assistant. As a "Stimson man" he had ready access to the great and powerful, and his contacts multiplied. He began keeping a diary because, as he noted in

18. Richard Hofstader, *The American Political Tradition* (New York: Vintage, 1974), chap. 9.

19. Quoted in Parrish, *Felix Frankfurter and His Times*, p. 24.

20. Phillips, ed., *Felix Frankfurter Reminisces*, p. 50.

the opening entry, "I am fortunate enough to meet men of rare spirit, vaulting vision and fine deeds."[21] He shared a house (dubbed the "House of Truth") with several young lawyers and intellectuals, including Lord Eustace Percy, Robert Valentine, and Winfred Dennison.[22] Important men of affairs were invited to the house to dine and discuss current events. Justice Holmes was a frequent visitor, as was Louis Brandeis, the famous "people's lawyer" from Boston. By the age of thirty, Frankfurter had established firsthand acquaintance with the progressive leaders of his day, which was to have an enormous impact on his view of the polity and, later, on his understanding of the role of judges. A faith in the capacity of men such as Stimson and Roosevelt to exercise the disinterested leadership necessary to make a democratic state functional in the modern world pervaded his political vision. He knew them personally and recognized their capacity for dynamic leadership. Later, his image of the judge was shaped by his friendship with Holmes, Brandeis, and Cardozo. Power in the hands of such men, he believed, would be power employed to further the common goals of a progressive society.

An important topic at the House of Truth was the growing split between the Taft and Roosevelt wings of the Republican party. By 1912, Frankfurter was an ardent Bull Mooser. He found in Roosevelt's third-party effort a recognition of government as the dominant force in reforming America. The need to reshape American life consistent with both modern realities and democratic principles was a lifelong task for Frankfurter. In 1909 Frankfurter had met Herbert Croly, and the impact of Croly's *The Promise of American Life*, coupled with Roosevelt's Bull Moose campaign, stirred the young progressives at the House of Truth.[23]

21. Joseph Lash, ed., *From the Diaries of Felix Frankfurter* (New York: Norton, 1975), p. 102.

22. Percy, the son of the duke of Northumberland, served with the British Embassy. Valentine, a member of a New England patrician family, studied with Fredrick Taylor and then became the commissioner of Indian affairs and later an industrial labor relations counselor in Boston. Dennison, an old friend of Frankfurter from his law school days and the U.S. Attorney's Office, later made the initial inquiry to the law school concerning a teaching position for Frankfurter.

23. The Taft-Roosevelt split further sharpened Frankfurter's image of the statesman. Taft "had no appreciation of his job, no directing zeal for or understanding of its potentialities." Roosevelt "realizes the affirmative demands of the

Much of the impact of Croly's book stemmed from its challenge of the traditional democratic faith in the common man. Democracy in a modern world required not greater participation but powerful leadership to direct the people in the public interest. The simple democratic belief in equal rights and free competition was naive. Large corporations were an economic fact of life; a simple faith in trust-busting must be replaced by national regulation of corporations in the national interest. *The Promise of American Life* called for powerful leadership directing a powerful, centralized state. For a generation of reformers attached to Jeffersonian ideals, Croly's book represented a disturbing and challenging dilemma.[24]

There was much in *Promise* that appealed to Frankfurter, and he found those elements operationalized in Roosevelt's campaign. Croly's and Roosevelt's emphasis on the national interest, dynamic and strong leadership, and the importance of experts coincided with much of Frankfurter's developing political vision. He was particularly offended by "[Woodrow] Wilson's sneer against government by experts. . . . We are singularly in need in this country of the deliberateness and truthfulness of really scientific expertise."[25] He was angered by Brandeis's support of Wilson, but, although Frankfurter believed in Roosevelt's New Nationalism, the gulf between Frankfurter and Brandeis was never great. "I

Presidency. He senses the problems of the day and his stirring sympathies strive to be translated into ameliorating action. . . . Of course, Roosevelt's main contribution is moral rather than intellectual" (FF to Buckner, 3/14/12, quoted in Mayer, *Emory Buckner*, p. 65).

24. Frankfurter later wrote of Croly: "To omit Croly's *Promise* from my list of half a dozen books in American politics since 1900 would be grotesque" (quoted in Archibald MacLeish and E. F. Prichard, Jr., eds., *Law and Politics: Occasional Papers of Felix Frankfurter, 1913–1938* [Gloucester, Mass.: Capricorn Books, 1939], p. 307). Croly in 1915 approved a *New Republic* editorial which described the choice confronting America: "We can put our ideals behind us and worship them or we can put them ahead of us and struggle toward them." The choice was between "old immutable idealism and new experimental idealism" (Charles Forcey, *The Crossroads of Liberalism: Croly, Weyl, Lippmann and the Progressive Era, 1900–1925* [New York: Oxford University Press, 1961], p. 21). Frankfurter concluded that Croly was "seeking illumination for the problems of politics from the slow accretions of insight into human behavior" (MacLeish and Prichard, eds., *Law and Politics*, p. 312).

25. Quoted in Parrish, *Felix Frankfurter and His Times*, p. 56.

should have little faith," Brandeis wrote Frankfurter in the year following the election,

> in a small group of men evolving a social system or important elements of such a system. We must rely upon all America (and the rest of the world) for our social inventions and discoveries; and the value of inventions and alleged discoveries can be best tested by current public discussion.
>
> On the other hand, it seems to me that a small group of able, disinterested, well equipped men, who could give their time to criticism and discussion of legislative proposals, discouraging those that appear to be unsound, would be of great assistance in the forward movement.

Frankfurter replied:

> I found your differentiation between the democratic factors necessary to secure social advance and the function of disinterested groups in bringing about such advance most illuminating. Of course, we can't hand the government over to a little group of experts because the kind of government we want must have a base as broad as all the people. But we do increasingly want men specially to concern themselves with the field of social invention, as you put it, and to combine the efforts of such laboratory men with the work of our public leaders.[26]

Frankfurter and Brandeis, as well as many of the Progressives, were both elitists and democrats. Liberalism's faith in the competitive race of life was reconciled with democratic principles through an enduring faith in the power of education and the ability of the masses to perceive the public interest. To Stimson Frankfurter wrote: "Any suggestion of the fixity of human nature always makes me purr. All too frequently 'against human nature' is the pseudo-scientific excuse for the standpatism of a Butler. To my mind the fundamental assumption of civilization is the conscious ability to modify and enlarge human nature."[27] Throughout his career, Frankfurter exhibited an almost Rousseauean belief in the capacity of the masses through great leadership to transcend narrow and selfish interests to further the common good. What was needed in the years ahead, he wrote his friend Buckner in 1914,

26. Brandeis to FF, 1/28/13; FF to Brandeis, 1/30/13, FFLC 30-517.
27. FF to Stimson, 4/19/13, FFLC 104-2174.

was education to provide "imaginative leadership in directing the thought of the country."[28]

Harvard Professor

The defeat of Taft and Roosevelt left Frankfurter a holdover in the Wilson administration. Stimson returned to New York City and private practice; Frankfurter had little desire to follow. His brief years in Washington had confirmed his belief in the need for expert administration in government. When the offer came to join the Harvard law faculty, Frankfurter pondered his next move. "I am not a scholar, qua scholar," he wrote to Stimson. "On the other hand, I do feel very deeply the need of organized scientific thinking in the modern state. . . . In other words, I am struck with the big public aspect of what should be done by our law schools."[29] The law school could be the "source of trained men for public life" so vital to his, as well as the Progressives', view of government.[30] Although Holmes warned that "academic life is but half-life" and Brandeis and Stimson counseled against accepting the position, in the summer of 1914 Frankfurter began what was to become a truly remarkable career at Harvard.

He remained at Harvard for the next twenty-five years. During World War I he was summoned to Washington as an assistant to Secretary of War Newton Baker. One of his first assignments was to accompany Henry Morgenthau to Turkey in an abortive attempt to settle the Palestine problem. On his return to the United States, Frankfurter was named secretary and general counsel to the new Mediation Commission created to deal with strikes in defense-related industries. Here he authored the Bisbee report[31] as

28. FF to Buckner, 11/7/14, FFLC 30-517.

29. FF to Stimson, 6/26/13, FFLC 103-2145. In 1932, when the governor of Massachusetts offered him a seat on the state's highest court, Frankfurter declined, explaining that he could be of greater service as a professor. Those who urged him to accept the position did not "understand what a teacher is, or what he is capable of being or doing" (Phillips, ed., *Felix Frankfurter Reminisces*, p. 232).

30. Quoted in Lash, ed., *From the Diaries of Felix Frankfurter*, p. 13.

31. The report documented the roundup of striking IWW workers in Bisbee, Arizona, by the local sheriff, aided by Jack Greenway, a former Rough Rider with Roosevelt. The workers were shipped to New Mexico, where they were abandoned without adequate food or water. The Bisbee incident, as well as the Mooney Report, described in the following note, are detailed in Parrish, *Felix Frankfurter and His Times*, chap. 5.

well as a report recommending clemency for labor leader Tom
Mooney.[32] At Harvard he continued his interest in scientific
management through his association with Frederick Taylor and
the Taylor Society, often speaking at the society's meetings and
contributing to its journal. When Willard and Dorothy Straight
agreed to give Herbert Croly financial aid to develop a journal
dedicated to "liberal ideas," Croly sought Frankfurter as an editor. He declined but was listed as a trustee for the *New Republic*
and supplied editorials and articles to the new journal.[33] He was
a founder of the American Civil Liberties Union, an adviser to the
NAACP, a crusader for Sacco and Vanzetti. He represented the
National Consumers League in important cases before the Supreme Court. A steady stream of correspondence issued from his
office in Cambridge to friends in the legal, political, and academic
communities of the United States and Europe. He traveled constantly between New York and Washington; his friend Buckner
called him the "human shuttle." His life at Harvard, in short, was
clearly not that of a cloistered academic.

But it was at Harvard that he began his real study of the Supreme Court and the role of courts and judges in the modern
state. His decision to come to Harvard had been influenced by the
opportunity to work with Roscoe Pound. "But, with Pound there,"
Frankfurter wrote Learned Hand of the Harvard offer, "I see this
as an opportunity for somebody to help fashion a jurisprudence
adequate to our industrial and economic needs."[34] Pound was

32. Mooney had been sentenced to death for planting a bomb that exploded
during a parade in San Francisco in 1916. The commission found that his conviction had been secured through perjured testimony, and Frankfurter prepared the
report urging Wilson to seek clemency from the governor of California. The governor, however, commuted the sentence to life imprisonment, thus precluding a
retrial, and Mooney remained imprisoned until 1939. Both the Bisbee and Mooney reports outraged many, including Roosevelt, who believed Frankfurter was
championing the cause of murderers and anarchists. Frankfurter, however, did
not accept the political ideology of Mooney, or for that matter, of Sacco and
Vanzetti; he was not a radical. He did believe in procedure, and his work on behalf of Mooney was founded on the belief that the authorities had
failed to adhere to fair procedure.

33. Ronald Steel, *Walter Lippmann and the American Century* (Boston: Little,
Brown, 1980), pp. 59–62, describes the birth of the *New Republic*.

34. FF to Hand, 6/28/13 quoted in Harry Wigdor, *Roscoe Pound: Philosopher of
the Law* (Westport, Conn.: Greenwood, 1974), p. 201.

considered even by 1913 one of the great legal scholars of his day; his "sociological jurisprudence"[35] appeared to operationalize Frankfurter's developing political vision. In 1910, Frankfurter and Buckner campaigned to have Pound brought to Harvard, and a few years later they sought to organize support for his appointment to the Supreme Court. They were successful only in the first endeavor, and Pound remained a member of the Harvard law faculty from 1910 through 1937, serving as dean from 1916 to 1936.

Pound was the first legal realist. His work reflects the influence of William James and Arthur Bentley, who were important figures in the rise of scientific naturalism.[36] Like James, Pound questioned the existence of ultimate truth and, like Bentley, he found the clash of diverse groups and interests to be at the core of politics. For Pound the task of the legal system was to accommodate as many demands as possible consistent with the need of society for stability and peace. The approach was founded upon "the adjustment of principles and doctrines to the human conditions they are to govern rather than to assumed first principles."[37] The governing principles used to decide cases were neither immutable nor assumed; they were derived from the social and economic values of the times. The goal was to inform judges of the effects of laws and whether legal decisions and rules were, in actuality, achieving their assumed purposes. Drawing upon the social sciences, the judge was to read "the spirit of the day," and the ultimate test of a legal rule or precedent was its social and economic consequences.

Gary Jacobsohn has characterized judges in Pound's view as "democratic fact-finders," and the description is apt.[38] The task of the judge was not to develop a fixed standard by which to mea-

---

35. The impact of Pound on legal realism is described in Wilfred E. Rumble, *American Legal Realism: Skepticism, Reform and the Judicial Process* (Ithaca, N.Y.: Cornell University Press, 1968), pp. 1–47.

36. Gary Jacobsohn, *Pragmatism, Statesmanship and the Supreme Court* (Ithaca, N.Y.: Cornell University Press, 1977), pp. 72, 90–91. Wigdor, *Roscoe Pound*, pp. 185–187, sees the same influences.

37. Roscoe Pound, "Mechanical Jurisprudence," 8 *Columbia Law Review* 605, 609 (1908).

38. Jacobsohn, *Pragmatism, Statesmanship and the Supreme Court*, p. 79.

sure claims but to satisfy as many claims as possible consistent with
the interests of society. Fundamental moral choices remained with
the members of the community, but the judge's duty was to ascertain these choices and attempt to accommodate the claims of litigants. There was much in this jurisprudence that appealed to
Frankfurter. In his political vision, ultimate power remained with
the people, but the trained expert was to make the day-to-day decisions to effectuate the popular will. The role envisioned by
Pound for the judge closely resembled Frankfurter's conception
of the role of experts. With Pound at Harvard, he believed the
law school would inevitably move toward sociological jurisprudence and thereby would further reform.[39]

Although by the end of his career at Harvard Frankfurter had
become a bitter critic of Pound,[40] Frankfurter's initial scholarly
writing reflected the liberating influence of Pound's jurisprudence. Frankfurter's first essays on the Supreme Court attacked
the mechanical, formalistic jurisprudence that dominated the era.
In the context of his developing political vision, this viewpoint was
hardly surprising. Frankfurter's faith in expert administration
had become well established: if the expert was to direct the progress of society, the immutable first principles of a mechanical jurisprudence had to be shattered. Absolutism was incompatible
with scientific administration and experimentation, and thus a
constant and repeated theme in Frankfurter's writing was to destroy "the mischievous assumption that our judges embody pure
reason, that they are set apart from the concerns of the community, regardless of time, place and circumstances, to become the
interpreters of self-determining words with fixed content, yield-
ing their meaning to a process of inexorable reasoning."[41] Frank-

39. Parrish, *Felix Frankfurter and His Times*, p. 59.

40. The dispute was not over scholarship but over Pound's administration of
the law school. Pound increasingly sought to expand the size of the school, de-
stroying the intimacy that Frankfurter cherished. In addition, Frankfurter believed Pound remiss for not challenging Harvard President A. Lawrence Lowell's
obvious anti-Semitism. Pound also accepted an honorary degree from the University of Berlin presented at Harvard by the German ambassador. Because he believed this act to be a legitimation of the Hilter regime, Frankfurter refused to attend. For his part, Pound believed Frankfurter's political activities as well as his
efforts on behalf of Sacco and Vanzetti were detracting from his teaching.

41. Many of Frankfurter's writings on the Court are collected in Philip Kurland, ed., *Felix Frankfurter on the Supreme Court* (Cambridge, Mass.: Belknap Press

furter would continually return to this point. Judges were human beings and must be understood as such, and the law was the product of human beings and also must be understood as such:

> Granted that the power of judicial review in this widest field of social policy is to be retained, its true nature should be frankly recognized. Since the nine Justices are molders of policy instead of impersonal vehicles of revealed truth, the security of the powers which they exercise demands that, in this realm of law, the most sensitive field of social policy and legal control, the judicial process should become a *conscious* process. The Justices will then recognize that the "Constitution" which they "interpret" is to a large measure the interpretation of *their own experiences*, their "judgment about practical matters," their "ideal picture of the social order."[42]

An oracular model of constitutional decision making assumed immutable first principles from which judges reasoned downward to reach results consistent with those principles. The Progressive mind of the early twentieth century challenged the existence of immutable principles in all areas of human endeavor. Because society was constantly in a state of flux, principles had to be measured against contemporary knowledge. A similar understanding powered Pound's sociological jurisprudence and Frankfurter's early realism.[43] For Frankfurter, to shatter the "myth of the robe" was to undercut the oracular model of judging and make choice an important element of constitutional law. Absolutism precluded choice and made the judge supreme over the expert. Frankfurter's use of realism, in effect, was to free the expert from judicial dominance. Nevertheless, as Karl Llewellyn (himself an important proponent of realism) later pointed out, realism was not a theory; it was simply a method.[44] Having used the realist technique to destroy the premises on which a formalistic oracular jurisprudence was based, Frankfurter was faced with the task of developing a new basis for constitutional decision making.

---

of Harvard University Press, 1970). The following references to that volume include the year the article appeared. The quotation is from p. 43 (1916).

42. Ibid., pp. 119–120 (1922) (footnotes omitted).

43. See G. Edward White, "From Sociological Jurisprudence to Realism: Jurisprudence and Social Change in Early Twentieth Century America," in White, *Patterns of American Legal Thought* (Indianapolis: Bobbs-Merrill, 1978).

44. Grant Gilmore, *The Ages of American Law* (New Haven: Yale University Press, 1977), p. 79, n. 26.

It was at this stage that contradictory themes appear in Frankfurter's early view of the Court. Pound's concept of the judge as
social engineer was predicated on the judge reflecting the common values of society through reference to the philosophical, political, and ethical ideas of the times.[45] Frankfurter at times appeared to embrace warmly this concept of the judicial role. The
decision in *Muller* v. *Oregon*[46] and the process at work in that case
appeared to confirm this faith. It was, he believed, an "epoch
making" case for the Court,

> not because of its decision, but because of the authoritative recog-
> nition by the Supreme Court that the way in which Mr. Brandeis
> presented the case—the support of legislation by an array of facts
> which established the reasonableness of the legislative action, how-
> ever it may be with its wisdom—laid down a new technique for
> counsel charged with the responsibility of arguing such constitu-
> tional questions, and an obligation on the court to insist upon such
> method of argument before deciding the issue.[47]

Muller changed the "method of approach to constitutional questions" because it placed the judge in the role of social engineer.
The facts must be presented to the judge so that he could evaluate modern conditions and fashion principles not responsive to
particularized interests or arguments but reflecting the commonly
held values of the community. *Lochner*, for example, was wrongly
decided because an immutable first principle was substituted for
facts in a matter "calling for essentially scientific determination."[48] The critical problem for a judge in questions of public
law was understanding the complex problems of an industrial
state. The burden upon lower courts and lawyers was to be certain that the relevant facts were adequately presented to the

45. Pound's concept of the judge as social engineer appears most clearly in his
"The Theory of Judicial Decision," 36 *Harvard Law Review* 641, 802, 940 (1923).
The image of the engineer is important because the engineer carries out the de-
sign of others. The judge, in Pound's view, does the same by determining the
moral choices of the community by reference to empirical data and the literature
of the social sciences and humanities. The faith that science, particularly the social
sciences, could make clear that which for centuries was unclear is perhaps another
example of the enormous impact scientific investigation had on the thinking of the
era.

46. 208 U.S. 412 (1908). See Chapter 1, n. 70.

47. Kurland, *Felix Frankfurter on the Supreme Court*, p. 13 (1916).

48. Ibid., pp. 14, 18.

Court. Without such a factual presentation, Frankfurter concluded, "there is a danger that Constitutional adjudication will be
determined by abstractions or jejune generalizations or obsolete
data."[49]

Although Frankfurter's progressivism found its jurisprudential
analog in Pound's sociological jurisprudence, his realism initially
led to questions of whether judges could be trusted to play such a
central role. In 1911 Frankfurter wrote Stimson:

> This necessity for careful ascertainment of the facts—testing theo-
> ries by the available light of experience called forth by demonstra-
> ble conditions—is particularly indispensable in this country where
> social legislation must meet the test of constitutionality. And, that
> legislation which comes properly accredited by sustaining proof of
> experience and examination and will be upheld by the Supreme
> Court, decisions like the [*Muller*] case . . . clearly demonstrate.[50]

Thirteen years later, he again wrote Stimson:

> "Due Process" is the rock on which most social legislation found-
> ers. Both because the questions at issue are really social and eco-
> nomic, and therefore not the kinds of things on which the Supreme
> Court should be involved, and because the Fourteenth Amend-
> ment is too powerful an instrument of undue centralization, I think
> the "due process" clauses ought to go.[51]

That same year a similar conclusion appeared in the *New Republic*:

> An informed study of the work of the Supreme Court of the
> United States will probably lead to the conclusion that no nine men

49. Ibid., pp. 200–201 (1928).
50. FF to Stimson, 9/9/11, FFLC 164-2173.
51. FF to Stimson, 6/10/24, FFLC 103-2152. In 1921 he wrote Learned Hand:
"Tomorrow they [the Court] might easily knock out the minimum wage law. And
so I say . . . the price we pay for this judicial service is too great, the advantages too
slim for the cost. A Court *dominantly* composed of Holmes and Brandeis and Learned Hand and Cardozo—that's one thing, but taking the judicial fish as they run,
we have no business to build our institutions on such problematic and unlikely
happenings." When two years later the Court did overturn a minimum wage law,
Frankfurter again wrote Hand: "And my own mind has about found lodgment
where yours has: namely, that the possible gain isn't worth the cost of having five
men without any reasonable probability that they are qualified for the task, determining the course of social policy for the state and the nation" (quoted in Hirsch,
Enigma of Felix Frankfurter, p. 132).

are wise enough and good enough to be entrusted with the power the unlimited provisions of the due process clauses confer. We have had fifty years of experiment with the Fourteenth Amendment, and the centralizing authority lodged with the Supreme Court over the domestic affairs of forty-eight widely different states is an authority which it simply cannot discharge with safety to either itself or the States. The due process clause ought to go.[52]

The transition in Frankfurter's thought from 1911 to 1924 was the result of a Court that continued to read the tenets of eighteenth-century liberalism into the Constitution of the twentieth century. At the center of his political vision was an expanding role for experts in government. Pound suggested that the judge could be treated as an expert, and Frankfurter enthusiastically responded to this view. By the mid-1920s, history and a social science increasingly focused on human behavior suggested that judges might be incapable of playing that role. Frankfurter's faith in experts remained unaltered, but to fulfill that faith appeared to require a judiciary stripped of its enormous power under the due process clause. Earlier Frankfurter had concluded an article about Holmes in the *Harvard Law Review* by quoting George Santayana to the effect that the word "absolute" was "the most false and the most odious of words."[53] Absolutes inhibited scientific investigation and, given Frankfurter's view of the polity, were incompatible with modern democracy. The judiciary remained a stronghold of absolutism, and if democracy was to survive, that stronghold had to be conquered.

Constitutional Law and the Problem of Value

By the 1930s, Frankfurter's view of the Court had again shifted. His scholarly and editorial writings no longer contained calls for the repeal of the due process clause. "Panaceas like the recall of judicial decisions or the requirement that more than a majority of the Court should declare legislation unconstitutional" were not the answer.[54] The justices had a posi-

52. Kurland, *Felix Frankfurter on the Supreme Court*, pp. 166–167 (1924).
53. Ibid., p. 42 (1916).
54. Ibid., p. 226 (1930).

tive role to play, and when they were educated to that role the Court would facilitate the general progress of society:

> The Justices of the Supreme Court are arbiters of social policy because their duties make them so. For the words of the Constitution which invoke the legal judgment are usually so unrestrained by their intrinsic meaning or by their history or by prior decisions that they leave the individual justice free, if indeed they do not compel him to gather meaning not from reading the Constitution but from reading life. Only an alert and self-critical process in these public controversies will avert the translation of discredited assumption or unconscious bias into national policy.[55]

The positive role for the Court was to guide and shape social change consistent with the goals and principles set forth in the Constitution. By the 1930s Frankfurter appeared to conclude that the Constitution did announce immutable principles but that social change could take place consistent with these principles. One aspect of his pre-Court writing which illustrated this position was Frankfurter's attempt to define "judicial statesmanship." The judicial statesman was "a participant in the effort to achieve political realization of constitutional principle."[56] As models for this role, Frankfurter often cited John Marshall and Oliver Wendell Holmes. Clearly Marshall conceived of the Court as an institution that would direct the progress of society consistent with the often vague principles set forth in the Constitution. Frankfurter appeared to find the same qualities in Holmes: "While fully aware of the clash of interests in society and of law's mediating function, Holmes had nothing in common with the crude notion according to which law is merely the verbalization of prevailing forces and appetites."[57]

Jacobsohn notes that this description of Holmes was probably incorrect and suggests that Frankfurter believed that immutable

---

55. Ibid., p. 290 (1933). See also Frankfurter's defense of the use of the due process clause in the *Scottsboro* case, ibid. p. 280.

56. Jacobsohn, *Pragmatism, Statesmanship and the Supreme Court,* pp. 123–132; quotation on p. 131.

57. Philip Elman, ed., *Of Law and Men: Papers and Addresses of Felix Frankfurter* (New York: Harcourt, Brace, 1956), p. 166.

principles existed by which "forces and appetites" could be evaluated.[58] By the twentieth century the means for judicial mediation of this "crude notion" was principally the due process clause, and thus judicial statesmanship appeared to involve the judge directly in determining the nature and quality of social change.

By the 1930s the split in the social sciences between those advocating a scientific examination of human behavior and those seeking a study of essential moral values had grown wider and the debate bitter. Jerome Frank's *Law and the Modern Mind*, which appeared in 1930, shifted the focus to legal scholarship. The publication of Frank's book coincided with the commencement of a controversy, primarily waged in various law reviews, over what has been termed American legal realism.[59] By the 1930s the realist movement had moved beyond Pound's sociological jurisprudence; at the center of the movement was the separation of the "is" from the "ought" in the study and teaching of law, a skepticism over the role played by precedent and rules in judicial decisions, and an acknowledgment of the rapidity of social change and hence the need for constant revision and updating of the law.[60] In *Law and the Modern Mind*, Frank presented the elements of legal realism in perhaps its most extreme form. Frank questioned the relevancy of precedent and legal doctrine; all that mattered was a particular judge's decision in a particular case at a particular time. Lawyers and judges, in Frank's view, had constructed a myth of certainty and rationality whereas in reality the legal system was founded upon irrationality and subjectivity. Each new set of facts came to the judge free from the restraints of legal precedent or doctrine. "Until a court has passed on these facts," he concluded, "no law on the subject is yet in existence."[61] Frank did not lament this lack of certainty. The problem was that a generation of scholars and lawyers sought certainty and principles within a legal system that was incapable of producing such results.

58. Jacobsohn, *Pragmatism, Statesmanship and the Supreme Court*, p. 130.

59. Rumble, *American Legal Realism*, presents an overview of this controversy.

60. It is difficult to describe a movement as diverse as legal realism, but the three elements are taken from Karl Llewellyn, *Jurisprudence: Realism in Theory and Practice* (Chicago: University of Chicago Press, 1962), pp. 53–57.

61. Jerome Frank, *Law and the Modern Mind* (New York: Brentano's, 1931), p. 50.

A recognition of the reality of the legal system and the psychological limitations of judges would permit a judicial system capable of flexibility and constant reevaluation of principles and beliefs.

The reaction to Frank and other "new" legal realists was swift. Frankfurter's old friend Morris Cohen chided the realists for sacrificing justice to prevailing opinion, for elevating the "is" over the "ought" in law. The failure to develop a standard "for what is good and what is harmful" was critical because, in Cohen's view, law, like science, was a self-correcting system of principles.[62] Another counterattack came from Roscoe Pound.[63] Although Pound's sociological jurisprudence was the necessary first step in the evolution of realism, judicial enforcement of values and principles remained a critical part of his jurisprudence. Moreover, Pound was firmly grounded in the common law tradition, and within the slow, ordered, incremental change that characterized this tradition, Pound sought the means to accommodate social change and order. His faith in what the realists saw as essentially a myth and his failure to take his initial insights into the judicial process to their relativistic extreme made Pound an anachronism to the behavior-oriented realists. Pound, in turn, charged the realists with stripping from the law any basis to criticize or repudiate the rise of totalitarian regimes. In the skepticism of the realists, Pound found the basis for political absolutism: "To the self-styled realist of today brutality seems to be the measure of actuality."[64]

Against the backdrop of world events as well as domestic eco-

62. Cohen's reaction is described in David Hollinger, *Morris R. Cohen and the Scientific Ideal* (Cambridge: Mass.: MIT Press, 1975). In 1937 Frankfurter wrote Cohen congratulating him on his review of Thurman Arnold's *The Symbols of Government*: "It was completely satisfying, not just to the fresh critical considerations in Arnold's book but also regardful of the profounder philosophic and logical factors that Thurman, and so many like him, blithely disregard. These are great days for throwing the baby out with the bath water" (FF to Cohen, 1/13/37, quoted in Rosenfield, ed., *Portrait of a Philosopher*, p. 282). Arnold's book, in the realism tradition, identified principles and rational thinking as obstacles to reform. Theory and principle too often stood in the way of scientific investigation. Cohen wrote of the book: "A study of biological facts may enable us to determine whether a diet of buttermilk will prolong life in the case of Bright's disease but it cannot settle whether we should wish to live on such a diet or prefer Bright's disease." The review appears in 31 *Illinois Law Review* 411 (1936).

63. The "sadly comic" tale of Pound's initial involvement appears in Gilmore, *Ages of American Law*, p. 78, n. 25.

64. Quoted in Purcell, *Crisis of Democratic Theory*, p. 162.

nomic collapse in the early 1930s, this debate, which in normal
times might have been confined to the halls of academia, took on
wider ramifications calling into question the very future of democratic government. If democracy was to survive, it clearly must
not only modernize but also stand for certain fundamental principles that would differentiate it from totalitarian regimes. Increasingly Frankfurter suggested that the Court could be the spokesman of those principles.

Frankfurter's initial reaction to *Law and the Modern Mind* was
positive although he feared a battle royal between the realists and
the Harvard faculty led by Pound.[65] Most of Frankfurter's early
letters to Frank were conciliatory in an attempt to diffuse what he
foresaw as an extended and acrimonious debate. In 1932, with
the battle lines sharply drawn, Frankfurter wrote Frank to sum-
marize what he believed *Law and the Modern Mind* represented:

> Suppose someone were to say:
> "Of course each case, even in law, cannot be decided as though it
> were a discrete instance. Not only would life in general and busi-
> ness in particular be impossible under such an electronic jurispru-
> dence, but there is in fact some system and order determining the
> adjudication of courts. How much, I know not. And it is the busi-
> ness of students of 'the law,' and particularly of law professors, to
> promote and create more order than there is by showing interrela-
> tions that judges in their *ad hoc* determinations do not see. In other
> words, if it isn't the business of universities to extend the area of or-
> der in the world, or at least to explain why, for the time, there can-
> not be more order than there is, then universities have really no
> *raison d'être*. So I neither wish to attack the need for order in life or
> law, nor to discourage the effort to wrest more order of the world's
> chaos.
> "But my business happens to be law-in-action. My job brings
> home to me very intimately the deflections and deceptions by
> which the ultimate law-makers, *i.e.*, the judges, make inroads upon
> the law-phrasers, *i.e.*, 'the law' as formulated in past decisions, in
> statutes and in the writings of law professors. And so I happen to
> be most aware of the anarchic and chaotic aspects of 'the law.' I
> think it is highly important that judges do not shelter themselves
> behind the thin screen of generalized formulas and doctrines in de-
> parting from the actual limitations upon such formulas and doc-

65. FF to Frank, 3/30/31, FFLC 55-1049.

trines. In other words, I think it is highly important to insist, with Holmes, that the work of judges becomes more civilized the more it becomes self-conscious.

"I deem it, therefore, my particular job to play the stream of criticism upon adjudications in which the generalized doctrine is offered to the reader but broken to the litigant. Thereby, not only will litigants and lawyers be better able to deal with actualities, but also, I believe, reason will be furthered—and I mean by reason the articulated awareness of what we are doing. Only when we know what we are really doing will we know the extent to which the general is embodied in the particular. Only thus will we really promote the empire of the coherent."

Would you object to the foregoing as a very, very summary statement of the moral of your *Law and the Modern Mind*?[66]

The Frankfurter files at the Library of Congress do not contain a reply from Frank. Nevertheless, a fair reading of *Law and the Modern Mind* strongly suggests that Frank did consider each case a discrete instance and that adjudications by courts did lack system and order.[67] Just as he appeared to misuse Holmes in his attempt to define judicial statesmanship, so Frankfurter appeared to misstate Frank's position in a manner consistent with his own use of legal realism to undercut the absolutism of a mechanical jurisprudence and replace it with a jurisprudence that permitted social change and experiment consistent with the enduring principles of the Constitution. Frankfurter found much that was attractive in the new legal realism, but he consistently refused to acknowledge the positivism of Holmes or accept the relativism of the legal realists. His reaction indeed mirrored the reaction of many in law and the social sciences, who, in light of current events, resisted the relativism of realism and behavioral studies. In his political vision, no group or institution had been charged with the task of harmonizing social change with fundamental values; neither the statesman-educator, the expert, nor the masses was spokesman for enduring principles. To a large degree, this situation was the product of an optimistic progressive faith at the turn of the century grounded

66. FF to Frank, 1/5/32, FFLC 55-1052.

67. Three years later, Frank wrote Frankfurter: "I am convinced that particular cases are won by appealing to the particular attitudes of the particular judges by whom those particular cases are determined" (Frank to FF 11/29/35, FFLC 55-1058).

on the natural existence of common goals and assumptions. World War I shattered this optimism, and the dark days of the 1930s appeared to cry out for an articulation of the fundamental principles of the American experience. The classic personification of this transition appears in the career of Frankfurter's friend, Robert Hutchins.

Hutchins, a former dean of the Yale Law School, was named president of the University of Chicago in 1929. During the 1920s the University of Chicago was a center of social science research and scientific naturalism.[68] During the 1930s a group of scholars with a Thomistic faith in the study of values joined the university, and Chicago exemplified the conflict that developed within the discipline. Hutchins symbolized this conflict. Receiving his legal education at Yale, Hutchins became a confirmed legal realist. As a proponent of realism, he was named dean a mere two years after his graduation. Upon his arrival at Chicago, a transformation began to take place in Hutchins's thought. Although tracing this transformation is difficult, several factors stand out. For Hutchins, the Depression coupled with the demise of several European democracies appeared to suggest the disintegration of American society for which empirically based studies provided no remedies or counteracting principles. Furthermore, American education appeared to be losing direction and purpose. Scientific naturalism exalted fact-finding over moral truths; the university became fragmented, with each department dedicated to particularized research and specialized training. Hutchins found the cause for this disintegration in his own faith in legal realism. By the 1930s, Hutchins had renounced his commitment to realism and sought to develop a priority of truths and principles to order knowledge and society.

A favorite topic for Hutchins was criticism of legal education. Why, he asked, have law schools if the study of law was simply the study of facts and the goal simply to have students predict what courts would do? Under those standards the best legal education would be constant daily work in law offices. The laboratory method of case-by-case analysis stripped the law of values and

68. Purcell, *Crisis of Democratic Theory*, chap. 8, details the role of the University of Chicago and Hutchins.

principles and left the student without any appreciation of the
moral and ethical role that law could serve. "The duty of the legal
scholar," he concluded, "is to develop the principles and rules
which constitute the law."[69] Law must serve to order society and
direct human conduct toward fulfillment of the highest principles
of ethics and politics.

Frankfurter found much to admire in Hutchins's transformation and responded enthusiastically to his critique of legal education. "I did not find," he wrote in 1937, "appreciable disparity between your prescription for legal education and my attempts at
the practice of it, even though I have never told my pupils that I
am trying to train them in casuistry, in the sense in which lawyers
don't use the term." Frankfurter added:

> How can one rationally teach the cases without considering how
> they march—what the law means in actual operation—and how
> can one appraise the law in actual operation without having a set of
> values, i.e., a philosophy? In other words, not only is jurisprudence,
> "the ordered relation of all these studies," but every course on any
> subject, unless it be merely a decorous chaos of discrete instances,
> must be a course in jurisprudence in your conception of ju-
> risprudence.[70]

Although Frankfurter's journey from the hard-hitting realism
of his early writings was by no means as drastic as that of Hutchins, his writings during the Harvard years do reflect many of the
tensions and cross-pressures that shaped the social sciences of that
period. Realism remained for Frankfurter a means of undercut-
ting the formalistic, mechanical jurisprudence that severely restricted reform during the first third of the twentieth century; his
realism was to focus on judges as men and political actors and not
as the expounders of a fixed body of truth.[71] Nevertheless, he

69. Quoted in ibid., p. 147.
70. FF to Hutchins, 1/29/37, FFLC 69-1349. In the same file are several letters
from Hutchins attempting to convince Frankfurter to leave Harvard for Chicago.
71. "The inclination of a single justice, the buoyancy of his hopes, the intensity
of his fears, may determine the opportunity of a much needed social experiment
to survive, or may frustrate for a long time intelligent attempts to deal with a social
evil" (quoted in Alexander Bickel, "Applied Politics and the Science of Law: Writings of the Harvard Period," in Wallace Mendelson, ed., *Felix Frankfurter: A Tribute*
[New York: Reynal, 1964], p. 171).

was unwilling to follow this realism through to the relativism of Jerome Frank. By the late 1920s, there appeared in Frankfurter's writings an acknowledgment that although the Court could not be the arbiter of all social policies, there were certain immutable principles by which the Court was to guide social progress. For Frankfurter, the action of the Court in the first third of the twentieth century in striking down socioeconomic legislation regulating, for example, the length of the work day, was not based upon principles that warranted the characterization of "immutable."[72] The question of which principles did warrant such a characterization, however, was to prove very difficult.[73]

The Public and Its Government

"All of Hoover's achievements were at times of war, famine, and flood—where he had unlimited sentiments on his side," wrote Frankfurter to Zechariah Chafee in 1928. "That's a very different thing from composing the needs of contending groups in a democracy."[74] Herbert Hoover was the expert cast in the role of the statesman-educator, and the result was near disaster. Democracy, in Frankfurter's mind, required a clear division of labor; he enthusiastically supported Al Smith during the 1928 campaign because Smith's record as governor proved that no other "man in public life today so deeply relies upon the expert for achieving reform." Smith was the "master of politics" because he was a "successful political educator" able "to waken popular interest in his aims and to enlist popular understanding of the technical means by which alone social policies can be realized."[75]

In 1930 Frankfurter was invited to deliver the Dodge Lectures on the responsibility of citizenship at Yale University. The invitation was testimony to Frankfurter's stature, for the lectures had

72. Bickel expands on this point, ibid.

73. There is a suggestion in some of Frankfurter's writings that the protection of the Bill of Rights might serve as the indicator of immutable principles. See ibid., pp. 182–189. As Bickel indicates, however, Frankfurter's discussion of civil liberties was purely speculative; during this period his primary concern was economic and social policy.

74. Quoted in Parrish, *Felix Frankfurter and His Times*, p. 203.

75. Frankfurter, "Why I Am for Smith," reprinted in MacLeish and Prichard, eds., *Law and Politics*, p. 324.

consistently attracted men prominent in both academic and world affairs, including Charles Evans Hughes, Graham Wallas, and William Howard Taft. Frankfurter's lectures, later published under the title *The Public and Its Government*, constitute one of the most complete statements of his idealized political vision.

The primary theme of his lectures was the need for public regulation of utilities, but in addressing this theme Frankfurter developed several others which were at the heart of his political and social thought. At the outset, he warned the members of his audience that they must sweep away the "vague and uncritical assumptions" they might hold about American democracy. The belief that government was simple, that all that good government required was to "abolish autocratic rule, remove tyranny, and the innate goodness of man will prevail," could no longer serve as the foundation for a modern democratic state. The vast problems of an industrial, democratic state and the extraordinary technical skills needed to attempt to solve those problems were beyond the grasp of even the most sophisticated voter. The fate of the modern state lay in the development and training of a group of disinterested experts to guide the progress of the state. Governing is art, said Frankfurter, "and that is why the art of governing has been achieved best by men to whom governing itself is a profession."[76]

Throughout his lectures, Frankfurter repeated a secondary theme: "Government means experimentation."[77] Scientific management in government required experimentation, and experimentation required laboratories. Frankfurter's dedication to the principles of federalism and the states as laboratories for social reform was one element separating him from the Croly Progressive faith in the centralization of powers.[78] At the same time,

76. Felix Frankfurter, *The Public and Its Government* (New Haven: Yale University Press, 1930), pp. 6, 15, 160. "The promotion of public service as permanent career for the nation's best abilities in a way has been my predominant interest in the school here" (FF to FDR, 1/18/37, quoted in Hirsch, *Enigma of Felix Frankfurter*, p. 198).
77. Frankfurter, *The Public and Its Government*, p. 49.
78. In 1923 Frankfurter and Croly disagreed over the appropriate forum for the control of child labor. "I don't give a damn as you know about 'States' rights' but I do about states' responsibilities," he wrote Croly. "And I am not so much worried about 'centralization' as I care for the gain through the educative process

Frankfurter was aware that during the twentieth century the Supreme Court, using the due process clause of the Fourteenth Amendment, had severely restricted the states' police power and hence the states' functions as social laboratories. By the date of his Dodge Lectures he made no call for the abolition of the due process clause but rather expressed a need for judicial statesmanship: "In simple truth, the difficulties that government encounters from law do not inhere in the Constitution. They are due to the judges that interpret it. . . . That document has ample resources for imaginative statesmanship, if judges have imagination for statesmanship." The demands of modern civilization precluded the doctrinaire interpretation of the Constitution. Great justices, men such as Marshall and Holmes, understood constitutional adjudication as an exercise in statecraft and the Constitution itself "not as a text for interpretation but the means of ordering the life of a progressive people."[79] The Constitution did not obstruct government, and the path to reform did not lie in radical amendments but in educating the judiciary to its statesmanlike task. The same year in which he gave the Dodge Lectures, Frankfurter wrote Owen Roberts on the day following Roberts's nomination to succeed Justice Sanford:

> As one whose chief preoccupation is the work of the Supreme Court and whose devotion to it is exceeded by none, perhaps I may add a word before you take the veil, without being guilty of even constructive contempt. There is a good deal of loose talk about "conservative" and "liberal." The characterizations hardly describe anybody since we are all a compound of both. What divides men much more decisively is the extent to which they are free—free from a dogmatic outlook on life, free from fears. And that is what cheers me so about your appointment. For you have, I believe, no skeletons in the closet of your mind, and are a servant neither of blind traditionalism nor of blind indifference to historic wisdom. Yours, I believe, is the spirit of Maitland, who defined the function of history "as that of explaining, and therefore lightening the pressure that the past must exercise upon the present and the present upon the future."[80]

---

of having the people in each state secure social conditions which are within the social compass" (FF to Croly, 1/8/23, FFLC 50-925; this letter appears in draft form in the Frankfurter file; it is unclear whether an original was actually sent).

79. Frankfurter, *The Public and Its Government*, pp 79–80, 76.

80. FF to Roberts, 5/10/30, FF HLSL 171-1.

The words "disinterested," "public-spirited," and "unselfish" appear throughout the Dodge Lectures. An often implicit theme was a fear and distrust of private groups and particularized interests. "In a democracy, politics is a process of popular education," Frankfurter concluded,

> the task of adjusting the conflicting interests of diverse groups in the community, and bending the hostility and suspicion and ignorance engendered by group interests toward a comprehension of mutual understanding. For these ends *expertise* is indispensable. But politicians must enlist popular support for the technical means by which alone social policies can be realized.[81]

The weakness of faith in the spoils system was not simply that government was too complex for the average citizen but that, without more, the average citizen was incapable of governing in a disinterested manner. Only the expert, with an intellect and temper of mind molded by the scientific method, was, in the first instance, capable of proceeding in the public interest. The job of the statesman-educator was to educate the masses to the public interest through leadership and example. This point was critical in Frankfurter's political vision. Drawing upon his faith in the flexibility of human nature Frankfurter believed that, given dynamic leadership, the masses could transcend self-interest. To Walter Lipmann, whose faith in the wisdom of the people had all but disappeared by the 1930s, Frankfurter wrote:

> Yes I know the old Adam is in all of us, and the poor are greedy and the veterans are selfish and the farmers want pap. But I really think you underestimate the extent to which decency and fairness and live-and-let-live can be won from the great masses so long as they don't feel they are the victims of great inequalities. Compare for instance the immediate occasion that produced the Pullman Strike in '94 with the lack of strike in this depression. And since writing you last . . . Buxton, the hard-boiled editor of the Republican Boston Herald was telling me that Legion people in his composing room have been saying to him they are quite ready to forego "theirs" if they are sure the big fellows are not getting theirs.[82]

81. Frankfurter, *The Public and Its Government*, p. 161.
82. FF to Lippmann, 3/11/33, FFLC 278-1576.

The impact of education and the power of the statesman and other elites to mold public opinion and generate popular support for sacrifice and reform in the name of the public good were fundamental to his vision of the new democratic state. Indeed, it was this assumption that held his democratic faith together. Thus Frankfurter placed special responsibility upon newspapers, for they were the primary means by which the elite spoke to the masses. In his Dodge Lectures he decried "the opportunities for arousing passions, confusing judgment, and regimenting opinion, that are furnished by chain newspapers, cheap magazines, the movies and radio." He did not see the press as simply a means by which conflicting views were presented; he was reluctant to accept a "marketplace" view of the press. The duty of the press was "to promote more responsible and informed understanding" on the part of the public.[83] He later defined this responsibility as a care as to "what news is presented and how the news is presented." As a guiding rule for the press, Frankfurter offered a quote from Holmes: "The answer for most of our problems is to grow more civilized."[84]

For Frankfurter, "to grow more civilized" was to act in a manner consistent with the larger public interest. The particularized interests and groups that appeared to dominate American politics were not, contrary to the view of the pluralist theorists who played an important role in the scientific naturalism movement in political science, a virtue of the system. Indeed, the power and influence of groups represented a failure of leadership. Properly operating, the modern democratic process would mold disparate groups into a homogeneous whole. Thus when Lippmann, in the early days of the New Deal, called for greater centralized power in the executive to avoid the delay inherent in a group-dominated institution like Congress, Frankfurter, although a strong supporter of Roosevelt, demurred. He wrote Lippmann in 1933:

> My conviction is that executive leadership that knows which way it wants to go, and can educate the nation to that way through the fa-

83. Frankfurter, *The Public and Its Government*, pp. 128, 34.
84. Frankfurter, "The Big City Press and Democracy," reprinted in Elman, ed., *Of Law and Men*, p. 242.

cilities so readily open to the President, will prevail also with Congress. . . . And to my way of thinking, in Al's [Smith] phrase, the surest way of subduing and keeping subdued the unreasonable appetites of minorities is the process of successfully educating the electorate and the Congress to the common and transcending national interest by the methods of education appropriate to particular situations.[85]

So great was Frankfurter's faith in education and the "transcending" national interest, that Congress was seen not as furthering particularized interests and their influence but as a means of securing consent and bending various groups into the larger whole. The wisdom of acts furthering the public good would dissolve dissent and opposition. A few days later he wrote Lippmann:

> Precisely because I want great success for Roosevelt—and all that it implies for the country and the world—I want not abdication of Congress but true collaboration. I call the debate on the Economy Bill all to the good. That the hardened feelings of hundreds of thousands of our people, who in their nature are no more grafters than you or I should be considerably dissolved instead of steamrolled into sullen discontent, is to me the kind of national good which, in multitudinous other instances, it will be important to secure.[86]

The Public and Its Government illustrates how far removed from the traditional liberal fear of the state Frankfurter was in the 1930s. The entire focus of the address was on the need to expand the boundaries of government action and the role of experts within those boundaries. Power was not to be feared but to be applied to the problems of the day. Although Frankfurter was quick to assert that he was not calling for "a new type oligarchy, namely, government by experts," he spent little time detailing the safeguards against administrative abuse. Ultimately that protection rested on procedure and "on our respect for one another and the common good."[87] Frankfurter's primary fear, however, was not the abuse of power but a failure to appreciate its uses. The Frank-

85. FF to Lippmann, 3/6/33, FFLC 278-1576.
86. FF to Lippmann, 3/15/33, FFLC 278-1576.
87. Frankfurter, *The Public and Its Government*, pp. 157, 159.

furter of the 1930s did not, for example, fear judicial power but
rather sought to instill in judges an appreciation of their statesmanlike task. Judges were the quintessential experts, and within
that role they could work to order "the life of a progressive
people."

"The most influential single individual in the United States"

In 1936, *Fortune* magazine described Frankfurter as
"the most influential single individual in the United States."[88] His
former students, the "A" men, were spread throughout the New
Deal agencies, and they formed an important network of influence and information. For years he had provided law clerks for
Justices Holmes and Brandeis, and upon Holmes's retirement he
did the same for Justice Cardozo. So great was Frankfurter's apparent influence that those who opposed the New Deal philosophy saw him as a Svengalilike figure. The mistaken philosophy of
the New Deal was the fault of Frankfurter, Westbrook Pegler
wrote, "through his contamination of mischievous cub lawyers."[89]
Even his friend Lippmann warned in 1936 against members of
university faculties involving themselves in the ambitions and purposes of politicians. Lippmann's article, obviously directed at
Frankfurter, coupled with his equivocal stand with respect to Nazi
Germany, was to separate the two forever.[90]

Frankfurter first met Franklin Roosevelt during his early Washington days. He warmly greeted Roosevelt's victory in the 1928
New York gubernatorial campaign and during the period
1928–1932 he wrote frequent letters offering advice on Roosevelt's attempts to reform the New York public utilities commission.[91] Although Frankfurter originally supported Al Smith for
the nomination in 1932 and expressed reservations about Roose-

88. *Fortune*, January 1936, reprinted in Max Freedman, ed., *Roosevelt and
Frankfurter: Their Correspondence* (Boston: Little, Brown, 1967), pp. 303–310.

89. Quoted in Lash, ed., *From the Diaries of Felix Frankfurter*, p. 53.

90. Ibid., pp. 48–49; Steel, *Walter Lippmann and the American Century*, pp.
320–321.

91. Freedman, ed., *Roosevelt and Frankfurter*, pp. 35–96.

velt,[92] after Roosevelt secured the nomination Frankfurter was important in bringing the Smith and Roosevelt forces together. Soon after Roosevelt's election, Frankfurter began supplying men to staff the new administration. The task was not without conflict; Roosevelt's closest advisers—Rexford Tugwell, Adolph Berle, and Raymond Moley—all sought to establish a planned, centralized economy while Frankfurter remained a spokesman for Brandeisian liberalism seeking to establish the decentralized market economy of the nineteenth century. As H. N. Hirsch notes, at this early stage the factions that separated the first and second New Deals were developing.[93]

Nevertheless, throughout the first New Deal, Frankfurter remained loyal to Roosevelt; as a spokesman for Brandeis he continually urged Roosevelt to move away from a government-business coalition but nonetheless supported the administration's measures.[94] On May 27, 1935 ("Black Monday"), in three sweeping, unanimous decisions the Supreme Court invalidated key portions of the first New Deal, including the National Industrial Recovery Act. (NIRA).[95]For Frankfurter this action presented both an opportunity and a problem. The Court's decisions mandated a change in policy, and Frankfurter's constant urgings to Roosevelt to abandon a business-government alliance began to take hold. The second hundred days saw new legislation such as the Wagner Act and a restriction on holding companies, which had been con-

92. "Despite all, I should vote for Roosevelt. I know his limitations. Most of them derive, I believe, from lack of an incisive intellect and a kind of optimism which sometimes makes him timid, as well as an ambition that leads to compromises with which we were familiar in Theodore Roosevelt and Wilson. But on the whole he has been a very good governor" (FF to Lippmann, 12/23/30, quoted in Hirsch, *Enigma of Felix Frankfurter*, p. 182). The letter was written at the conclusion of FDR's first term as governor.

93. Ibid., pp. 185–186.

94. Bruce Allan Murphy, *The Brandeis/Frankfurter Connection: The Secret Political Activities of Two Supreme Court Justices* (New York: Oxford University Press, 1982), details Frankfurter's efforts on behalf of Brandeis.

95. *ALA Schechter Poultry Corp.* v. *United States*, 295 U.S. 553 (holding NIRA unconstitutional); *Louisville Joint Stock Land Bank* v. *Radford*, 295 U.S. 555 (holding Frazier-Lemke Mortgage Act invalid); *Humphrey's Executor* v. *United States*, 295 U.S. 602 (holding the president was not free to remove members of independent regulatory agencies at will).

sidered before Black Monday but were now pushed by Roosevelt.[96] By the summer and fall of 1935, Frankfurter believed he had won the ideological battle for Roosevelt's sympathies.[97]

But Black Monday posed a problem for it appeared to require a reexamination of the role of the Court in American society. Frankfurter's claim that the Constitution was flexible enough to permit social change if the Court had access to all the facts and the wisdom to follow them appeared inadequate to several of his friends, including Morris Cohen. Following Black Monday Cohen wrote to Frankfurter:

> I should be lacking in candor if I did not say frankly that the fundamental weakness of your position in this matter is due to your thinking in terms of personalities and neglecting ultimate issues. You think in terms of Holmes, Brandeis and Cardozo, and you think more men of that type would make the Supreme Court a good institution. In this you ignore the fact that it is only accident that men of that type can get on the Supreme Court. . . . But more important than that is the fact that the whole system is fundamentally dishonest in its pretensions (pretending to say what the Constitution lays down when in fact they are deciding what is good for the country).[98]

Nevertheless, by 1935 (and in part because of the influence of Cohen) Frankfurter envisioned an important role for the Court in directing the progress of society. Any measures to reform the Court must be carefully considered in light of the Court's higher purpose. "I have written predominantly against the Court's confusion between the majority's notion of policy and the requirements of the Constitution," he reminded Cohen, adding, "But that is not the whole story of the Court's function and performance."[99] Frankfurter's advice to Roosevelt was to secure passage of measures that marked the second New Deal, and if the Court were to strike them down, Roosevelt would have the popular

96. William Leuchtenburg, *Franklin D. Roosevelt and the New Deal* (New York: Harper & Row, 1963), pp. 149ff. describes Frankfurter's influence. See also Murphy, *Brandeis/Frankfurter Connection*.

97. Hirsch, *Enigma of Felix Frankfurter*, p. 216.

98. Quoted in Lash, ed., *From the Diaries of Felix Frankfurter*, p. 56.

99. Ibid.

mandate to secure a constitutional amendment giving the national government power to deal with economic emergencies. That approach, Frankfurter urged, was wiser than an attack on "the Supreme Court's vague general powers," which would be "unlimited in the changes it *may* cause."[100]

Frankfurter's involvement with the Court-packing plan of 1937 has been discussed at length in various works.[101] It is clear that Frankfurter did not approve of the plan and that Roosevelt's decision to proceed with it was made without consultation with Frankfurter. Nevertheless, Frankfurter was loyal to Roosevelt and accepted the decision. Soon he was sending Roosevelt material documenting the Court's abuse of its power and advising on tactics. Publicly Frankfurter remained silent, and to his friends who criticized him for his silence he remained resolute. Frankfurter's loyalty to Roosevelt was soon rewarded; eighteen months later he was named to fill the seat on the Court once held by Oliver Wendell Holmes and Benjamin Cardozo.

The American Dream

Felix Frankfurter lived the American Dream and he knew it. In return he expressed a love for America that was so "unabashed" it was "almost childlike."[102] "I can express with limited adequacy," he said in 1938, "the passionate devotion to this land that possesses millions of our people, born like myself under other skies, for the privilege this country has bestowed in allowing them to partake of its fellowship."[103] Frankfurter was anything but a dispassionate observer of the American scene; his was not a political picture developed out of detached analysis and study. Like Socrates, who sought the elements of the good state in a detailed study of the good citizen, Frankfurter found in his own life the critical components for his vision of the modern democratic state. His unrelenting faith in education, expertise, and elites was

100. FF to FDR, 5/29/35 in Freedman, ed., *Roosevelt and Frankfurter*, p. 272.

101. See, e.g., Lash, ed., *From the Diaries of Felix Frankfurter*; Parrish, *Felix Frankfurter and His Times*; Hirsch, *Enigma of Felix Frankfurter*; Murphy, *Brandeis/Frankfurter Connection*.

102. Paul Freund quoted in Sanford Levinson, "The Democratic Faith of Felix Frankfurter," 25 *Stanford Law Review* 430 (1973).

103. Mendelson, ed., *Felix Frankfurter*, p. 221.

not the product of abstract study but part of his own identifica-
tion with America. Although Frankfurter often envisioned himself as the outsider—the "Jew-alien"[104]—his career and success
confirmed his faith in America and the wisdom of his political
vision.

Holmes's expression, "we live by symbols," was one of Frankfurter's favorites. In a liberal, democratic state freed from a he-
reditary hierarchy or state religion, symbols structured and gave
meaning to life. The flag, the presidency, the public schools all acquired almost mystical importance for Frankfurter. These and
other symbols served to reify ethereal concepts such as the public
interest which were critical to his political picture. From his experience with the great teachers of Harvard through his apprentice-
ship under Stimson and his friendship with Holmes, Brandeis,
and Roosevelt, his models were not distant historical figures but
men of his generation. As his friend Morris Cohen suggested,
Frankfurter's remedy for the ills of America, at its simplest, was a
government staffed by his friends and like-minded men.

Thus by the eve of his appointment to the Court, Frankfurter
had a clearly established, idealized political picture of American
democracy. Firm in his belief that politics was a continual process
of education, he refused to justify the state as merely a referee
presiding over the clash of partisan interests and groups; rather,
it was a harmonious machine, powered by a faith in education
and the public interest, slowly progressing toward commonly held
goals. At the very center of his democratic faith was a confidence
in the average citizen's ability, given the right leadership, to for-
sake individual interests and to sanction, through the democratic
process, action in furtherance of the public interest.

Frankfurter envisioned an important role for the Supreme
Court in his personal vision of democracy. Although his early
brand of realism would shatter the myth of the robe and focus on
the law not as eternal truth proclaimed by judges but as the product of judicial personality and politics, by the mid-1930s he saw
the Court as the means by which certain immutable principles,
fundamental to American democracy, could be protected. For

104. FF to Burlingame, 3/16/37, FFLC 34-579.

Frankfurter this altered view did not constitute a retreat from Thayer's rule of restraint; so great was his faith in the harmonious operation of the democratic state under leadership such as Roosevelt's that rarely would the great power of judicial review be necessary to protect those immutable principles. In the turmoil that confronted both the Court and the country in the ensuing years, that faith would be sorely tested.

3 Hugo Black:
Politics as Conflict

What difference does it make to whom you give too
much power? Too much power is dangerous, whether
it be vested in a government or a group of specially
privileged plutocrats, in a religious group, or any other
group. The real liberal, who has come down through
the ages holding aloft the torch of human liberty, has
not stood for concentrations of power in a centralized
government or in the hands of any particular group.

Hugo L. Black, 1932

The Few and the Many

Like many of his contemporaries who came of age
during the Progressive era, Hugo Black had a powerful belief in
progress, a faith that the present was better than the past and that
the future would be better than the present. Several years after
his appointment to the Court, when his son Sterling expressed
skepticism about government, Black wrote him: "I have long since
decided that it works about as well as anybody could expect, despite the petty political mistakes which crop up in the activities in
the public service. Furthermore, I think we have a much better
government today than we had in 1789 and will have still a better
one in 1989."[1] This faith in progress was tempered and shaped
by his reading of history and his understanding of human nature

---

1. HLB to Sterling Black, 4/11/44, HLBLC 6.

and politics. The reality of the American experience, as Hugo Black saw it, was the enduring conflict between the rich and the poor, the few and the many, the followers of Hamilton and the followers of Jefferson. To Black the historian, this conflict explained the past; to Black the politician, it described contemporaneous events; to Black the judge, it shaped his understanding of the role of the Supreme Court. The victory of the many was the ultimate goal of the progressive state. Until that victory was assured, however, conflict would shape American politics, and an understanding and appreciation of the nature of this conflict is critical to an understanding of Black's view of the polity.

Interests rather than ideas powered Black's understanding of the workings of society. Because human nature was essentially unchanging and greed and self-interest were at the core of human behavior, trust in an elite, regardless of its training or detachment, was naive and dangerous. Absent in Black was any faith in experts as the agents of progress in the modern state. Government had to be sufficiently powerful to ensure that private concentrations of wealth and power did not prevent control by the many, but government also had to be subject to sharply drawn limitations for fear it would serve narrow and powerful interests.[2] This ambivalence concerning power was at the heart of Black's understanding of the polity. In a 1932 debate over the LaFollette-Costigan relief bill, he asserted: "If it be liberalism to favor centering more power in the Government bureaus of Washington, then I confess I trust that the party to which I pledged assistance may never adopt any such reform of liberalism. It is based upon the Hamiltonian theory that the people cannot be trusted." Moments

2. Black believed despotism impossible in a society marked by the free exchange of ideas. Early in his career, he viewed the protections of the First Amendment as necessary to ensure that majority interests were protected from powerful minorities. For example, in a debate over an amendment to the Smoot-Hawley Tariff banning the importation of seditious and salacious publications, Senator Black opposed the measure because of the power it vested in customs officials. He was against any plan to ban the distribution of literature "so long as the juries in the state, where public sentiment is made, have it within their power to condemn the distribution of that literature as being deleterious to the morals of their people" (72 *Congressional Record* 418 [1929]). Thus although Black feared the control of literature by an agency of the state, a similar fear was not present when the same power was exercised by juries in the name of the people.

later in the same speech he declared: "What difference does it make to whom you give too much power? Too much power is dangerous, whether it be vested in a government or a group of specially privileged plutocrats, in a religious group, or any other group. The real liberal, who has come down through the ages holding aloft the torch of human liberty, has not stood for concentrations of power in a centralized government or in the hands of any particular group."[3]

Black was, of course, correct; the classical liberal did fear power. The liberalism of Hobbes and Locke was a reaction against a hierarchical social order in which individuals were born to social rank. Liberalism served to free men from an aristocratic social order to enter one in which individuals were defined by their own accomplishments. As such, the liberal feared the power of the state as a constraint upon both free thought and the free market. By the late nineteenth and early twentieth centuries, however, the liberal was confronted by a social order in which unregulated accumulations of wealth appeared to inhibit individual freedom in much the same way as an imposed moral and social order had done generations earlier. A basic fear of power was met by a realization that the power of the state was necessary to ensure the conditions in which competitive individualism could flourish. Hugo Black reflected this ambiguity for he was basically a Jeffersonian confronted by the reality—and necessity—of the New Deal.

Thus Black did not envision the state as merely the umpire presiding over the activities of atomistic individuals. The polity was split between the weak and the powerful, and the task of government was to protect the weak and ensure the dominance of the many. To achieve this end required the exercise of power and, although Black warmly endorsed the goal, he was often ambivalent about the means to achieve it. The "iron law of oligarchy" was a basic truth, and his ambivalence concerning power coupled with his dualistic view of the polity was at once the source of his radicalism and a major constraint upon it.[4]

3. 75 *Congressional Record* 3516 (1932). The measure provided for a federal emergency relief board to distribute millions of dollars to needy Americans.
4. Black's son recounted that his father once told him that his study of Marcus

Agrarian Radicalism

One key to understanding Hugo Black lies in the state of his origin, Alabama. Black's perception of America was drawn from the political life of his home state. At the turn of the century there were, in effect, two Alabamas.[5] The northern hill country less suited to farming and plantation economics was the home of the small white farmer. The area contained few black people and, with its strong Jacksonian tradition, resisted secession and later became a stronghold of the agrarian movement of the late nineteenth and early twentieth centuries. Dominated by no single interest or machine, it was an area where traditional southern myths appeared to exercise limited influence and where tenant farms and the crop-lien system defined the world for black and white alike.[6]

Cutting across the southern portion of the state was a wide swath of fertile land known as the Black Belt, an area of former plantations, where blacks outnumbered whites and Bourbon Democratic rule prevailed. A land of basic Whig sympathies, the Black Belt's wealth and traditions stood in stark contrast to the poverty of the northern part of the state. Since the days of Reconstruction, the aristocratic families of the Black Belt had controlled

Aurelius subverted his faith in democracy because "this fella decrees good without debate. . . . But look at his successors, then you know why we've got to have democracy" Hugo Black, Jr., *My Father: A Remembrance* (New York: Random House, 1975), p. 3. Black continually feared the exercise of power by individuals. For example, his copy of Lord Acton's *Essays on Freedom and Power* was heavily marked and indexed. See the section, "I have done more reading," below.

5. See V. O. Key, *Southern Politics* (New York: Random House, 1947), chap. 3; Neal R. Pierce, *The Deep South States of America* (New York: Norton, 1974).

6. Lawrence Goodwyn, *The Populist Moment* (New York: Oxford University Press, 1980), pp. 20–25, describes the crop-lien system. In brief, the system was the means by which a merchant would provide the farmer with supplies during the year and in return receive a lien on the fall's crops. The merchant operated on a two-price system: a cash price and a higher price for credit customers. On top of the higher price was the interest charged for the credit. The result was that credit customers often paid a 100 percent increase over the cash price. Needless to say, if cotton prices declined, few farmers were able to pay the outstanding balance. The merchant would then take a note secured by an interest in the land. After several years, the note might be foreclosed and the farmer would become a landless tenant. Of some importance is the fact that Black's father was the most successful merchant in Ashland, Alabama.

Democratic politics in Alabama. Although shifting and fluid coalitions often appeared to dominate, an enduring feature of Alabama politics was the cleavage between the Bourbon Black Belt and the poorer remaining areas of the state.

Hugo Black was born in 1886 in Harlan, Alabama, the youngest of the eight children of William and Martha Black. Harlan is in Clay County in the scrub-pine region of the hill country of Alabama. Within a few years of Black's birth, the family moved a few miles to Ashland, where William became a successful merchant and better educational facilities existed for the children.

The year of Black's birth is of some significance. To the west in Texas, the same economic forces and the crop-lien system which imprisoned the small farmers of Alabama had led to the stirrings of an agrarian protest movement that would soon sweep the farmlands of America. By 1886, the cooperative movement of the Farmers' Alliance began to take hold in Texas. Soon Alliance lecturers were dispatched eastward to spread the gospel of farmers' cooperatives and the evils of the money trusts, the gold standard, and a national private banking system.

Clay County was receptive to this voice of agrarian radicalism. By 1890, the lien system, hard money, and deflated cotton prices were a vicious cycle that proved ruinous to the Clay County farmer. Not surprisingly, Clay became the center of agrarian radicalism in Alabama. In 1892, Joseph Manning founded the People's party of Alabama in Clay County as a third-party challenge to the rule of the Bourbon Democrats. One indication of the depth of the dissatisfaction of Clay's farmers was their apparent willingness to desert the "party of their fathers." A measure of the agrarian movement throughout the South was the extent to which small farmers would perceive the inadequacy of the political culture imposed by the two-party system.[7] To convince the southern farmer in the 1890s to abandon the traditional Democratic party

7. Ibid. Goodwyn's thesis is that political tranquillity is ensured when all political activity takes place within the confines of the established political order. Protest is tolerated because it will not disturb existing power and privilege. To succeed, the Populist movement thus had to confront the two-party system directly; without such a confrontation, the movement would be co-opted by either or both of the two parties.

was a difficult undertaking. Nevertheless, when Reuben Kolb, Alabama's foremost reform spokesman, preached loyalty to the Democratic party, he was met with "dead silence" by the farmers of Clay County.[8] The intensity of Clay County's attachment to the agrarian movement forced Kolb into a third-party insurgent campaign for governor. Although Kolb narrowly lost the 1892 gubernatorial election—principally as the result of Bourbon vote fraud and manipulation of the black vote—the new party won several local posts in Clay County. In 1894, Manning was successful in his campaign to represent Clay in the Alabama House of Representatives. Manning and his regular Democratic opponent scheduled fifteen debates throughout the county with the finale on a Saturday night in Black's home town of Ashland.

These debates were Black's earliest exposure to politics. He later remembered attending every one of the political debates in Clay County and traced his early economic views to the influence of the Populist speeches.[9] Although the Black family, with its relatively elevated economic status for Ashland, was not part of the Populist constituency, it was impossible to remain unaffected by the political turmoil that shook Clay County in the 1890s. The rhetoric of the Populists—proclaiming the evils of centralized wealth tied to corporate power and the ideal of the people using political power to improve their lives—moved the young Black in ways that would profoundly affect his later career.

In Ashland, William Black became the county's most successful merchant. Hugo Black's relationship with his father was strained. Although the Black family lived according to a strict moral code—coffee, alcohol, and tobacco were not permitted in the house—this code was honored more in the breach than the observance by the elder Black. Black's attitude toward his father was "cold indifference": he could respect his father as a businessman but not as a human being.[10] Black came to see his father even in his role as a businessman as a vital cog in the hated crop-lien system. "I am afraid my father, if living," Black wrote a friend in

8. Ibid., p. 225.
9. HLB to Dillard, 7/13/62, HLBLC 25; HLB to Frank, 1/20/48, HLBLC 460.
10. Black, *My Father*, pp. 4–5.

1962, "would rather strenuously object to being classified as a Populist. He was, in fact, about as far from that as anyone I knew in Clay County."[11]

Black held his mother in highest esteem, and although it is tempting to picture Black as a self-educated man, this image is not entirely accurate. Martha Black was an avid reader and instilled in her young son love of books. He attended and excelled at Ashland College, a combination high school and junior college.[12] At the urging of his brother, Orlando, Black spent a year at the Birmingham Medical School. Concluding that law and not medicine was his future, he journeyed to Tuscaloosa and the University of Alabama. Anxious to complete his undergraduate education, Black applied for admission to the liberal arts college as a sophomore. When he found he would have to matriculate as a freshman, he crossed the street and entered the two-year program at the law school.

For all its beauty and charm, Tuscaloosa was not Cambridge, and the University of Alabama Law School was not Harvard. With an entering class of forty and a faculty of two, it bore little resemblance to the more prestigious law schools of the North.[13] Black excelled at law school, but his years at Tuscaloosa had nothing of the impact of the Cambridge years on the young Frankfurter. Frankfurter's student days at the Harvard Law School emancipated him from the immigrant's world of the lower east side and placed him with America's elite. Hugo Black's experience was entirely different. Years later, commenting on Black's nomination to the Court, the *Nation* wrote that unlike many who sat on the Court, Black "did not have in his blood and at his command the tradition of intellectual enlightenment" because "he had no one like Emerson near him to discuss Plato as Holmes did, no expen-

---

11. HLB to Dillard, 7/13/62, HLBLC 25.

12. Black never received a degree. When his sister, who also attended the school, was disciplined by a male teacher, Black rose to her defense and was expelled (Black, *My Father*, p. 15).

13. Black, in private, could be realistic about the limitations of his law school education. In an exchange of letters with Jerome Frank in 1948 concerning legal education, Black wrote that when he attended the University of Alabama law school it "did not have—and was not entitled to have—a very high rating in comparison with the modern law school" (HLB to Frank, 1/21/48, HLBLC 29).

sive Harvard training as Brandeis did."[14] The years at Tuscaloosa did not remove Black from the life and politics of Clay
County.[15] Although he fondly remembered his two professors at
the law school teaching him that legislators and not judges made
law and although he was one of seven to graduate with honors,
his success did not guarantee status and entry into America's elite.

Moreover, although the Black family had been well off by Clay
County standards, the line between poverty and affluence was
narrow in Clay; Black knew poverty face to face. It was perhaps
another indication of the limited impact of his Tuscaloosa years
that following graduation he returned to Ashland to practice law.
He invested the estate of his parents, both of whom had recently
died, in a library and set up his practice. Clay, however, could
barely support the one experienced lawyer it had; the lack of clients and a disastrous fire that destroyed his library led Black to
seek his fortune in Birmingham.

The First Judgeship

The Birmingham to which Black traveled in 1907
typified the beginnings of a new industrial South. That same year
the United States Steel Corporation acquired the properties of the
Tennessee Coal, Iron and Railroad Company, established offices
in Birmingham, and became the largest owner of coal and iron
properties in central Alabama. The Alabama Power Company was
also organized in 1907 with its offices in Birmingham and within
a few years would come to symbolize for Hugo Black the evils of
corporate control of America. Lacking the genteel nature of older
southern cities, Birmingham became a city of contrasts. Corporate

14. *Nation*, October 10, 1937.
15. By 1904, the year he entered law school, the agrarian movement in the
South was in disarray. The nomination of William Jennings Bryan in 1896 first as
the Democratic presidential candidate and then as that of the People's party undercut the independence of the movement. In Alabama, the regular Democrats
had succeeded in blunting and absorbing much of the Populist impulse. In 1901,
through a constitutional amendment, many poor whites and blacks were disen-
franchised, and this "cleansing" resulted in Bourbon control. See Sheldon Hackney, *Populism to Progressivism in Alabama* (Princeton: Princeton University Press,
1969), chap. 8. Although Populism had ceased to be a significant, organized political movement in Alabama, the economic conditions that led to the movement were
still present, particularly in Clay County.

wealth was juxtaposed with a population of poorly paid miners and mill workers, and a reform business ethic coexisted with a crime rate among the highest in the nation. "Hard times comes first and stays longest" was an old saying about Birmingham. And it was here that Hugo Black was to make his mark as one of Alabama's finest trial lawyers.

The beginning was inauspicious. Black shared an office with four lawyers and proceeded to seek clients. He investigated applicants for a mail order insurance company and received fifty cents per applicant. He became a constant joiner. During his years in Birmingham he joined every fraternal and civic organization open to him; the American Legion, the Knights of Pythias, the Civitans, the Odd Fellows, the Pretorians, and the local Moose Lodge counted Black among their members. Such an effort was understandable for a lawyer seeking clients, particularly a lawyer with possible political ambitions. Groups were a fact of life in the South, and they became a fact of life for Hugo Black.[16] In his larger vision of the polity, the task of uniting disparate groups in the continuing conflict of the many against the few was a critical step to progress and freedom.

His first real client was a young black convict named Morton. Alabama had developed the convict leasing system under which convicts were removed from prison and leased as laborers to private companies. Morton had been leased to a steel company, which had held him fifteen days longer than his sentence. Black sued for damages, and the judgment of $150 was split $75 to Morton, $37.50 to Black, and $37.50 to the lawyer who had referred the case to him. The case's importance extended beyond the fee; the trial judge was so impressed with Black that he remembered him when an opening developed on the police court. The case also identified Black as an opponent of the leasing system, and soon the fledgling labor unions of Birmingham were among his clients. But even more significant, this first case set the tone for Black's future practice. In 1907 he had little choice of cli-

16. "Those tinpot fraternal orders which afford an opportunity to strut in uniform or costume or to posture as the champion of heroic causes have nowhere flourished more than in the southern cotton mill towns and villages" W. J. Cash, *Mind of the South* (New York: Knopf, 1946), p. 243.

ents, but even when he was one of Birmingham's most successful lawyers, contingent fee cases arising out of personal injuries would dominate his practice. He was, in lawyer's terms, a "plaintiff's lawyer," bringing actions on behalf of individuals against corporate and business interests.[17] The contingent fee was a product of the great concentrations of wealth which marked the Gilded Age; it was often virtually the only means by which indigent victims could secure counsel and pursue claims against corporate wrongdoers. For the lawyer it was a high-risk undertaking, requiring stamina in handling a heavy caseload and skill in presenting cases to juries. It appealed to Black because it was a means of making a living while retaining independence. With few exceptions, during his career as a practicing attorney, the only organized interests to which he was on retainer were labor unions.[18]

In 1911 Black was appointed a police court judge. The appointment was not particularly prestigious, and Black continued in his private practice. The caseload in the police court underscored the seamy side of Birmingham life with vagrancy, simple assault, and prohibition cases predominating.[19] Just as Black was introduced to politics in the agrarian revolt of the 1890s and his early legal practice was the representation of victims in negligence cases, his first judgeship placed him face to face with the realities of urban industrialization. His early career experiences thus differed from those of lawyers who traditionally rise to the pinnacle of their profession.[20] His formal education was not shaped by elite institu-

17. Contingent fee lawyers have been scorned by their "elite" colleagues as "higglers" who commercialize the law and lower the status of a professional elite (Jerold S. Auerbach, *Unequal Justice* [New York: Oxford University Press, 1972], pp. 45–46).

18. See HLB to Dillard, 7/13/62, HLBLC 25.

19. As a result of the melodramatic reporting of the *Birmingham Age Herald*, Black became a bit of a local folk hero while serving as police judge. See Virginia Hamilton, *Hugo Black: The Alabama Years* (Baton Rouge: Louisiana State University Press, 1972), pp. 41–45, for examples of this reporting. By all accounts, given the times, Black was a fair judge, particularly in dealing with black defendants. After Black acquitted a black man, one reporter, somewhat taken aback, wrote: "When a nigger succeeds in convincing Judge Black of his innocence despite the testimony of arresting police officers, he is going some" (ibid., p. 43).

20. For example, John R. Schmidhauser concludes his collective portrait of Supreme Court justices by saying: "If it is in this sense that the Supreme Court is the keeper of the American conscience, it is essentially the conscience of the American upper-middle class, sharpened by the imperative of individual social responsibility

tions, his legal practice was not the representation of the rich and powerful, and his first judicial appointment was at the lowest level of the judicial system. In short, Black's entry into the legal and judicial profession was not, an entry into the aristocracy; indeed, it did little to shake the Populist foundations of his political thought.

In 1914 Black entered his first political campaign for the solicitorship of Jefferson County. For a politically ambitious young attorney, the decision to run for the post was natural. The Birmingham business reform interests backed another candidate, who was supported by several newspapers and corporate interests. In a campaign strategy that he would employ repeatedly in the future, Black linked the "reform" candidate with entrenched interests while asserting that he, Black, was supported by simple folks and not "capitalists" or a "ring of politicians."[21] The campaign was based on face-to-face contact with voters; he made a particular effort to campaign in the most rural areas of Jefferson County. In the primary, Black easily defeated the incumbent and the establishment candidate; years later a similar campaign would bring him to the United States Senate.

The job as solicitor did not represent a significnt break with his Populist past. Although his primary task was to bring up to date an overloaded docket of serious and petty criminal cases, he found time to prosecute several coal companies for short-weighting their employees, and he refused to aid insurance companies claiming abuses on the part of "ambulance-chasing" attorneys. When he became curious about the extraordinary number of confessions secured in the town of Bessemer's jail, he instigated a grand jury investigation and prepared the report that disclosed confessions secured by torture and beatings. Although the Bessemer jail investigation placed Black's name in the headlines, the newspaper reports were hardly sympathetic and there was little political profit in the undertaking.[22] Indeed, the investigation

---

and political activism, and conditioned by the conservative impact of legal training and professional legal attitudes and associations" (*Judges and Justices* [Boston: Little, Brown, 1979], p. 99).

21. Quoted in Hamilton, *Hugo Black*, p. 52.

22. One newspaper wrote: "There was some criticism of Solicitor Black and the manner in which he conducted the investigation, during which Alderman W. S. Suratt stated that he did not blame Black for asking questions as that was his job.

galvanized many of Black's opponents, who by 1917 had gained sufficient strength to undercut his power and independence. Black resigned and, with the country at war, enlisted. Although anxious for overseas duty, he served out the war in training camps in California and Oklahoma.

The years following the war were important ones for Black. He married and started a family. His law practice flourished as he continued to represent injured plaintiffs and labor unions. His reputation grew, and he remained in the public eye as a result of the substantial verdicts he often won. He continued to eschew corporate clients although his income increased rapidly; by 1925 he was making almost $40,000 a year. He lived in a fashionable section of Birmingham and even joined the Birmingham Country Club. To all appearances, the roots of Clay County Populism were receding quickly into the past.

"said they needed good people in the Klan"

In 1923, Black joined the Ku Klux Klan. By the mid-1920s Birmingham had become the center of Klan power; of its thirty-two thousand voters, the Klan was said to control almost eighteen thousand.[23] Bourbon interests, having weathered the third-party insurgency movement decades before, ruled the regular Democratic party. Given Black's roots in agrarian radicalism, the decision to join the Klan was hardly surprising. Nevertheless, in an interview with the *New York Times* published after his death, Black gave several reasons for his decision.

> In fact it was a Jew, my closest friend, Herman Beck, who asked me to join, said they needed good people in the Klan.
> Any way, the only reason I didn't join before I did was I was too busy with other organizations. . . . But before I finally agreed to join, on the night I was supposed to join, I got up first and told 'em I was against hate, I liked Negroes, I liked Jews, I liked Catholics and if I saw any illegality going on . . . I'd turn them in to the grand jury. . . . You want to know the main reason I joined the

'There are ways, though, to ask a white man questions,' interrupted Alderman Moss Crotwell, 'and I never talked to a negro working for me in the manner Black spoke to me'" (see HLBLC 17).

23. David M. Chalmers, *Hooded Americanism* (New York: Doubleday, 1965), p. 79.

Klan? I was trying a lot of cases against corporations, jury cases, and I found out that all the corporation lawyers were in the Klan. A lot of jurors were too, so I figured I'd better be even up.[24]

Earlier in his career he had asserted that "an old law partner got me to join."[25] In retrospect, for a man whose typical responses to interview questions were terse and direct, Black's expressed reasons for joining the Klan appear startingly disjointed and confused.[26] Although it is clear that Black was hardly a racist in the worst tradition of southern politicians, he nevertheless did not rebel against the racism of the society in which he lived.[27] Black found it easy to use racially charged phrases such as "Anglo-Saxon patriots" and consciously and unashamedly distrusted the Catholic church. He felt little constraint in playing upon the racial fears of juries and refused to question the action of an Alabama jury in convicting "negro rapers" in the famous Scottsboro case. Indeed, he could relate tales of a "nigger in a woodpile" on the floor of the Senate.[28] Thus for every indication of fairness to

24. *New York Times*, 9/16/71.
25. Quoted in Gerald T. Dunne, *Hugo Black and the Judicial Revolution* (New York: Simon and Schuster, 1977), p. 113.
26. Daniel M. Berman, who interviewed Black in 1957, asserted that he spoke easily and without hypersensitivity about the issue ("The Political Philosophy of Hugo L. Black" [Ph.D. dissertation, Rutgers University, 1957]).
27. Charles Houston of the NAACP, who knew Black as a senator, asserted that "he never descended to the villainy and cheap abuse certain southerners heap upon negroes" ("Proceedings of the Southern Conference for Human Welfare," 4/3/45, HLBLC 478).
28. The phrase "Anglo-Saxon patriots" appears in a speech he gave during a Klan gathering in 1926 (see Hamilton, *Hugo Black*, p. 136). His distrust of Catholicism rested on a fear of the concentration of power in the hands of the pope and bishops (see Black, *My Father*, p. 104). During the summer of 1921, Father James E. Coyle, leader of Birmingham's Catholics, was shot by a Methodist pastor, Edwin Stephenson. Black represented Stephenson in a sensational murder trial. His defense was that his client was emotionally distraught over his daughter's plan to convert to Catholicism and marry one Pedro Gussman. Black played upon Gussman's Latin background, pulling the shades in the courtroom to emphasize his dark complexion and dwelling upon his ancestry in the summation to the jury. Stephenson was acquitted, and the newspapers devoted substantial space to the story. The phrase "negro rapers" appears in a letter from Black to a constituent thanking the constituent for commending his support of Alabama juries during the *Scottsboro* case (HLB to Hatley, 4/30/32, HLBLC 158). The "nigger in the woodpile" phrase is quoted in Berman, "Political Philosophy of Hugo L. Black," p. 214, n. 34.

blacks, there is in his early career more than a suggestion of un-conscious or unreflective racism in his actions. Regardless of sub-sequent explanations, membership in the Klan was a politically wise move, which did not seriously compromise his racial views. Black was not a violent man, and the floggings and terrorism of the Klan were out of character for him; nonetheless, the Klan of-ten spoke the language of populism, invoking the image of the common man against centralized wealth and power. This ideal appealed to Black as well as to his constituency, and the fact that racism was a significant element of that appeal did not seriously trouble him.[29]

His membership in the Klan, however, must also be considered in light of his career as a police judge and solicitor, his reputation for fairness, and his support of the quintessential Wall Street law-yer, John W. Davis, in the 1924 presidential election.[30] Black was a man of extraordinary contrasts generated by his dualistic view of the polity. The ultimate failure of the agrarian revolt was its in-ability to break the restraints established by the two-party system; the failure to develop a coherent third party resulted in eventual co-option by the traditional parties. A similar fate befell Black's radicalism. What is most striking about Hugo Black is his almost fanatical loyalty to the Democratic party, given its checkered his-tory of reform in Alabama.[31] Although for many of his contem-poraries this loyalty was the product of racial fears and memories of Reconstruction, for Black it rested on firmer ground.

When he returned from World War I in 1919, Black began a reading program that was to blossom when he became a United

29. Perhaps the kindest interpretation was suggested by Max Lerner, who noted that the Klan "combined a spurious radicalism with terrorism. Those who leaned toward the first were able to shut their eyes to the second" (quoted in Berman, "The Political Philosophy of Hugo L. Black," p. 17, n. 58).

30. Clifford Durr, Black's brother-in-law, recalled that his wife's family referred to Black as that "young Bolshevik" ("Mr. Justice Black: A Personal Appraisal," 6 *Georgia Law Review* 1 [1971]). "Black made a few speeches for John W. Davis in 1924, remaining a good Democrat in face of the lure of the LaFollette-Wheeler Progressive Ticket" (John Frank, *Mr. Justice Black: The Man and His Opinions* [New York: Knopf, 1949], p. 32).

31. The Black files are filled with letters proclaiming the virtues of the Demo-cratic party. See, e.g., 1/17/30 letter to McCain, HLBLC 104: "The Democratic Party means too much to Alabama, the people of the South and to the people of the Nation" for it to be split by conflicting ambition.

States senator in 1926.[32] From this early reading came the first evidence of the conflict theory that was to dominate his view of the polity. The conflict theory also fit neatly within his understanding of Alabama politics. While a U.S. Senator, he wrote a constituent describing his understanding of the basic elements of Alabama politics:

> In the days before the War between the States, the "Black Belt" of Alabama was a Whig stronghold. This was on account of the fact that the land was divided up among a few large plantation owners, who constituted what was then called "Alabama Aristocracy."
>
> Our section of the state and that further north was the home of Jacksonian Democracy. Our people owned few slaves. They owned small tracts of ground and cultivated it themselves. For this reason, they never failed to support the great champion of the common people, and when these Jacksonian votes rolled down into the Black Belt, it was a common saying that the Whigs of the Black Belt had been submerged under "the Avalanche."
>
> The political philosophy of these two sections has not changed with the arrival of new generations. While there is at present an artificial coalition called the Democratic Party, the Black Belt is not at heart sympathetic with the rights and privileges of the average citizen, nor have they ever joined with Governor Comer or any other man who sought to stem the rising tide of plutocracy.[33]

The political differences that separated the Black Belt from the remainder of Alabama served as a model for politics on a national level. The idea of a conflict between the few and the many, the rich and the poor, powered Black's view of the American polity and at the same time severely limited his political options. Although he might speak of the Democratic party as an artificial coalition, throughout his political career he would do nothing to disturb that coalition. In Black's mind, the Democratic party was the means by which the many confronted the few. In 1930 he wrote the chairman of the state Campaign Committee: "It is my belief that the Republican party is operated and manipulated by a small number of men who favor government by Plutocracy. Never be-

32. HLB to Frank, 1/20/43, HLBLC 460. These readings are discussed in the section "I have done more reading," below.
33. HLB to McCain, 12/20/29, HLBLC 104.

fore has this country been so completely under the domination of avaricious and predatory beneficiaries of special privilege. The average man has been forgotten. The farmer, the mechanic, clerk and laborer have no possibility of an effective champion unless the Democratic party remains true to its slogan of 'equal justice to all, special privilege to none.'"[34] To break with the Democratic party was to ensure the dominance of the few over the many. In Black's view of the polity, reform could be generated only by the Democratic party; the "greatest evil" was rule by the organized wealth of the Republican party. Given this highly static, dualistic view of the political universe, a third-party movement was unthinkable.[35]

The result was a personality that at once could inveigh against concentrated wealth and yet campaign for John W. Davis as his party's presidential candidate. Membership in the Klan was symptomatic of the same impulses. Even if Black had had serious objections to joining, his dualistic view of the polity gave him little choice. The Klan represented the many; to take an anti-Klan position was to split the ranks of the many and assure the ascendancy of the few. A belief in conflict which generated much of his reform impulse also curtailed his options.

Sometime in 1925 Black decided to run for the Senate seat held by Oscar Underwood. Espousing a free silver position in 1896, Underwood had gradually moved to the right, reflecting the decline of the Populist impact on Alabama politics. In an unsuccessful drive for the Democratic nomination for president in 1924, Underwood had denounced the Klan. When the Klan subsequently met for its own convention in Kansas City, the call was to retire Underwood in 1926. Underwood, educated at the Univer-

34. HLB to Fuller, 9/5/30, HLBLC 195. In another letter he wrote: "It is my honest opinion that Louis fourteenth never looked with more dogged indifference upon the poverty, want and misery of the common people, than do the bosses who control the Republican Party today" (HLB to Ellis, 8/28/30, HLBLC-195).

35. See HLB to Moore, 6/28/30, HLBLC 104. When an independent movement led by his Klan constituency did take place (see the section "principles are bigger than men," below) he opposed the movement, contending that the Republican party was the enemy of the common man, and "the only party to give it battle today is the Democratic party." If the friends of the common man "abandon the Democratic party, what hope of assistance is there for the masses of our people?" (HLB to Ellis, 9/28/30, HLBLC 195).

sity of Virginia and son-in-law of one of Birmingham's leading in-
dustrialists, had risen steadily through the House of Representatives and the United States Senate while representing Alabama's
growing business and industrial interests. His failure to secure the
1924 Democratic presidential nomination was attributable to a significant degree to Klan opposition, as was his decision to retire
from the Senate in 1926. Although the race to succeed him appeared wide open, Hugo Black, whose only previous elected office was as solicitor of Jefferson County, was truly a long shot.

His first step was to resign from the Klan. It was a politically astute move.[36] The Klan was at the peak of its power, and by qui-
etly resigning Black gained all the benefits of membership (he was
still considered the Klan's candidate) without any of the liabilities.
Immediately following his resignation he announced his candidacy and gave his keynote address, fittingly enough, in Ashland,
his childhood home and the birthplace of the Alabama People's
party. The speech was in the finest Populist tradition.[37] He defined the enemy as concentrated wealth and power, constantly reminding the crowd that he had never been a railroad, corporation, or power company attorney. This argument for Black was
more than mere campaign rhetoric; already emerging was a static
and inflexible view of human nature. What a man might become
in the future was dictated by his past; past associations were useful in predicting future associations. Black's skill as an orator was
reflected in the fact that as a well-paid attorney, living in a fine
Birmingham suburb, he was still capable of articulating the fears
and hopes of his constituency. His candidacy, he proclaimed,
challenged the Bourbon belief that "only the rich and powerful
sons of the great can serve the state." The son of Clay County had
come far but not so far as to forget his roots—at least that was his
message.

With five candidates in the field and the traditional fluidity of
Alabama politics at work, personalities soon became the crucial issue, and Black was expert at linking his opponents with powerful,
established interests. The result was the frequently heard com-
plaint that Black set interest against interest and group against

36. Dunne, *Hugo Black and the Judicial Revolution*, p. 117.
37. A copy appears in HLBLC 476.

group.[38] He spent little on advertising, preferring the face-to-face contacts that had distinguished his previous campaign.[39] It was a successful technique; almost an unknown at the beginning of his campaign, Black received sufficient first and second place votes under a new Alabama election law to give him the nomination.

> ## "I have done more reading since I came to Washington than ever before"

Like many freshman senators, Black spent his initial months in the Senate in respectful silence. He found this a good time to continue his reading program. He began with Adam Smith's *Wealth of Nations*, and throughout the remainder of his adult life he would proceed through several hundred volumes.[40] He read the works of Plato, Aristotle, Herodotus, Livy, Aquinas, Rousseau, Shakespeare, Hamilton, Jefferson, Franklin, John Adams, and many others. The histories of Greece, Rome, and England were of special interest to him as were the writings of Charles Beard and Vernon L. Parrington on American history. It was an extraordinary undertaking, made all the more remarkable by Black's careful indexing and underlining in each text.[41]

As John Frank, a friend and former law clerk, pointed out, although Black had a passing interest in many of the social sciences, his primary interest was history.[42] His favorite historians—Beard, Parrington, and Frederick Jackson Turner—were scholars who saw the development of American history in terms of economic and social conflict.[43] Economic interests were at the core of American political and social history, as was evidenced by a continual tension between elite and popular interests. Beard

38. Hazel Black Davis, *Uncle Hugo* (Privately published, 1965), p. 19.

39. Black, *My Father*, pp. 58–62.

40. On 1/20/48 Black provided John Frank with a rough list of his reading material from 1926 to 1937. See HLBLC 460.

41. For an informative essay on Black's reading material as well as an index of his library see Daniel Meador, *Mr. Justice Black and His Books* (Charlottesville; University Press of Virginia, 1974).

42. Frank, *Mr. Justice Black*, p. 47.

43. Richard Hofstader, *The Progressive Historians: Turner, Beard and Parrington* (New York: Vintage, 1970); Samuel P. Huntington, "Paradigms of American Politics: Beyond the One, the Two and the Many," 89 *Political Science Quarterly* (1974).

and Parrington (and indeed Black) were clear in their preferences. As Parrington wrote:

> From the first we have been divided into two main parties. Names and battle cries and strategies have often changed repeatedly, but the broad party division has remained. On one side has been the party of the current aristocracy—of church, of gentry, of slaveholder, of manufacturer—and on the other the party of commonality—of farmer, villager, small tradesman, mechanic, proletariat. The one has persistently sought to check and limit the popular power, to keep the control of the government in the hands of the few in order to serve special interests, whereas the other has sought to augment the popular power, to make government more responsive to the will of the majority, to further the democratic rather than the republican ideal—let one discover this and new light is shed on our cultural tendencies.[44]

Black often recommended Parrington's *Main Currents in American Thought* because it reflected the struggle between the "plain people" and those who "exploit" them, a struggle that had been going on since the beginning of history.[45] Black's political education was shaped by the division in Alabama life between the Whig interests of the Black Belt and the yeoman farmer of the north. Books that viewed history as a continuing class conflict took on special meaning for him. Another favorite was Claude Bowers's *Jefferson and Hamilton: The Struggle for Democracy in America*, which personified this conflict by contrasting Jefferson and Hamilton. Black's disdain for Hamilton was readily apparent. He always described the Republican party as the party of Hamilton and never tired of reminding his audience that Hamilton believed the people to be "beasts."[46] A constant theme of his speeches was the critical difference between Jefferson as the spokesman of the many and Hamilton as the idol of the wealthy and how these differences continued to be reflected in the Democratic and Republican parties of his day.[47] Black's library contained almost every

44. Parrington quoted in Hofstader, *Progressive Historians*, p. 438.
45. Black, *My Father*, p. 159.
46. 75 *Congressional Record* 3516 (1932).
47. Ibid. See also speech given in Montgomery, Alabama, in 1930, a copy of which appears in HLBLC 176.

piece of writing by Jefferson, and each piece is carefully marked and indexed. Black took particular care to note each instance Jefferson spoke of the wisdom of the people and his faith in democratic rule. In the back cover of his edition of the *Memoirs of Jefferson*, volume 1, Black quoted Jefferson: "It is an axiom in my mind that our liberty can never be safe but in the hands of the people themselves, and that too, of the people with a certain degree of instruction. This is the business of the state to effect."

Black read and disputed those who challenged his understanding of the polity. Not surprisingly, in his edition of Tocqueville's *Democracy in America* he frequently wrote "not true" and "wrong" in the margins. Like many liberals, Black feared the power of the state and began with little appreciation of the capacity of civil society to inflict tyranny. Tocqueville was acutely aware that a passion for equality and democracy could lead to despotism. This was an insight alien to Black's understanding of the polity. In his copy of *Democracy in America* appears the following:

> In America the majority raises very formidable barriers to the liberty of opinion [here Black noted a "?"]: *within these barriers an author may write whatever he pleases, but he will repent it if he ever steps beyond them* [Black's underlinings] . . . but no sooner has he declared them [these opinions] openly than he is loudly censured by his overbearing opponents [here Black noted "Why not?"], whilst those who think without having the courage to speak like him, abandon him in silence. He yields . . . as if tormented by remorse for having spoken the truth.[48]

Tyranny of the few was Black's primary fear; at this stage in his development he gave little thought to the despotism of the many. A democratic and not a republican vision powered his thought. In volume 1 the following exchange takes place between Black and Tocqueville:

> *Tocqueville*: It frequently happens that the electors, who choose a delegate, point out a certain number of positive obligations which he is pledged to fulfill.
>
> *Black*: [in margin] Why not?

48. Black's copy of Tocqueville, *Democracy in America*, vol. 1, p. 268.

Tocqueville: [underlined by Black] *With the exception of the tumult, this comes to the same thing as if the majority of the populace held its deliberations in the market place.*[49]

The notion of a delegate simply carrying out the wishes of a majority of his constituency did not offend the populist Black in the manner it did the aristocratic Tocqueville.

English history was another favorite topic, and Black brought to these studies his understanding of class conflict. In his copy of Hallam's *Constitutional History of England* the material on Thomas Cromwell's efforts to promote the Reformation received special attention. When Cromwell advised the king to partition abbey lands to avoid possible return to papal control, Hallam wrote that the land was given to old, established families who supported liberal hospitality, promotion of industry, and the cultivation of English society. The advantages of such a disposition were twofold: to ensure the loyalty of the aristocracy and to promote cultural development, which, in Hallam's view, was dependent on the aristocracy. Although disdainful of papal power, Black had no sympathy with this hierarchical, preliberal concept of social relations. In the margin he wrote: "But would it not have been still better if land had been distributed to small homeowners?"[50]

Black's understanding of human nature also developed from his readings and the conflict theory of history. Greed and a thirst for power and control were at the heart of human nature. In his copy of John Stuart Mill's *Principles of Political Economy*, Black indexed and made special note of Mill's statement: "It is never safe to assume that a class or body of men will act in opposition to their immediate pecuniary interest."[51] In another note in Hallam on Cromwell's efforts to vest the property of the church in private landowners to ensure their loyalty to the crown, Black wrote: "Private interest [illegible, perhaps "bestowal"] to secure support for private action," and in the inside cover he noted that the general laws of nature result in people being more willing to accept actions that ensure their own personal estates.

49. Ibid., p. 259.
50. Black's copy of Hallam, *A Constitutional History of England*, vol. I, p. 108.
51. Black's copy of John Stuart Mill, *Principles of Political Economy*, p. 398.

The desire for wealth and power were constant themes in the histories. Black read little fiction except the Greek and Roman classics because they were "instructive, sound examples of unchanging human nature."[52] One of his favorite books during his Court years was *The Greek Way* by Edith Hamilton, and he carefully noted her description of Thucydides: "He reasoned that since the nature of the human mind does not change any more than the human body, circumstances swayed by human nature are bound to repeat themselves, and in the same situation men are bound to act in the same way unless it is shown to them that such a course in other days ended disastrously."[53]

Human nature was unchanging, and this understanding produced in Black a fear of power.[54] History provided Black with little evidence that men were capable of rising above self-interest and proceeding in a disinterested fashion. Power would always be used to further self-interest, and ultimately power would be used to the advantage of the few against the many.[55] The result was a basic distrust of the state and of powerful men who might use the state to their advantage. It was a vision of human nature born of the English tradition of John Locke rather than a romantic tradition which conceived of the perfectibility of human nature. Nevertheless, by the twentieth century, government could not be a neutral observer. Like many liberals in the New Deal era, Black found himself on the horns of a theoretical dilemma. The problem of balancing a distrust of the state with the necessity of its use to combat the evils of industrial civil society required a political theory that cut between the Jefferson-Hamilton division in American thought.[56] Black's allegiance to the conflict theory and his

52. Black, *My Father*, p. 158.
53. Black's copy of Hamilton, *The Greek Way*, p. 184.
54. The only notation in Black's copy of Francis Hackett, *What Mein Kampf Means to America*, was the underlining of the following sentence in the Preface: "The forces he [Hitler] has gathered until their directed velocity has become uniquely destructive are forces that have always been latent in human nature."
55. In *Main Currents of American Thought*, Parrington quotes Robert Wallace to the effect that the lust for power always sets man against his neighbor to the ultimate benefit of the rich. In his copy, Black wrote in the margin: "Is this confirmed by labor leaders dispute" (p. 820).
56. Otis Graham, Jr., *Encore for Reform: The Old Progressives and the New Deal* (New York: Oxford University Press, 1967), pp. 166–186.

preference for his understanding of Jefferson were great, but by 1926 he was obviously aware that reform and the application of government power were inextricably linked.

In 1926 he began reading Adam Smith. Although Black shared Smith's disdain for an unproductive aristocratic order, he took issue with Smith's contention that government inevitably upsets the workings of the marketplace. When Smith wrote, "All the different parts of its price will rise to their natural rate and the whole price to its natural price," Black noted in the margin: "Asserted as a law but it clearly does not work."[57] When Smith wrote that all that was needed to put industry in motion were materials, tools, and wages, Black saracastically noted: "omits something else necessary to put industry to work—we now have materials to work with—tools and wages but industry is not at *work*." At another point, Black commented: "All this seems based on naive assumption that customers are automatically supplied and all that is needed is more capital to sell more goods." When Smith wrote of the law of supply and demand, Black added: "This *theory* does not always work, witness farmers in particular."[58]

Thus by the late 1920s, Black was forced to take issue with the classical liberal vision of society in which the unseen hand of the market directs progress and economic development. Over the ensuing years Black struggled to fit the necessity of state-directed reform into a vision of the polity which rested on a basic and fundamental distrust of power. The liberalism of Adam Smith appeared to sanction a status quo that served only the rich and powerful. Black fervently believed that government existed to serve the many. How to achieve this end in a world of extraordinary technical advance was a question for which neither Jefferson nor Black provided a ready answer.

"principles are bigger than men"

The principal issue that concerned Black during his early years in the Senate was the impending nomination of Al

---

57. Black's copy of Adam Smith, *The Wealth of Nations*, was in the *Harvard Classics*. This notation appears on p. 61.

58. Ibid., p. 244, 247, 61.

Smith by the Democratic party in the 1928 presidential race.[59]
The nomination of Smith presented the difficult choice of supporting a wet, big city Catholic or bolting the Democratic party. In
a letter to Senator Pat Harrison, a member of the Democratic National Committee, Black explained the problem:

> If you will remember in the several conversations which we had
> with reference to Alabama before the Convention, I stated to you
> that the nomination of Governor Smith would bring consternation
> to Democracy in this state. It has done so. Thousands of Democrats
> will not vote for Governor Smith. . . . The general opinion is that
> Governor Smith has, by the injection of the Prohibition issue, the
> immigration issue, and the appointment of his campaign manager,
> given the Democrats of this state a very heavy load to carry. This
> doubtless was good politics in the East, but brought consternation
> and confusion to Alabama.[60]

Almost immediately Alabama's senior senator, Thomas "Tom-
tom" Heflin, announced his support of Hoover. Heflin, known

59. In his initial years in the Senate, Black's primary legislative concern was the
development of Muscle Shoals, built on the Tennessee River during World War I
as a munitions plant. After the war there was substantial disagreement over its future use. Senator George Norris of Nebraska favored government operation to
provide power for the Tennessee Valley, while Black supported a lease agreement
with private operators (in this case Henry Ford) to produce nitrates for fertilizer.
Farmers, Black declared, "are asking for the bread of nitrate and they get the
stone of power. . . . We care nothing for power" (70 *Congressional Record* 4189,
4190 [1927]). A third option was outright sale to power companies, and Black and
Norris found common ground in opposition to this proposal. Norris soon ex-
panded his plan to include nitrate production, and Black became his strongest
supporter. When the Norris Bill was passed over strong power company opposition, President Coolidge pocket-vetoed the measure. The development of Muscle
Shoals was to remain a continuing controversy through the New Deal. See Preston
J. Hubbard, *Origins of the TVA* (Nashville: Vanderbilt University Press, 1961).

60. HLB to Harrison, 2/19/38, HLBLC 72. Black supported Prohibition and opposed increased immigration on the ground that it provided cheap labor at the expense of native-born Americans. Smith's appointment of Jacob Raskob as campaign manager presented further difficulties because of his links to business and
the machine politics of the North. A letter written by FDR in 1928 explained the
thinking behind the Raskob appointment: "The appointment was a bold stroke to
try to end the 99% of business (big and little) preference for the Republican party.
I told Smith quite plainly that it would make the whole situation more difficult for
the Democracy of the South; but Smith felt that we should take our chances on
this, as we would lose anyway if we did not carry the big industrial states" (quoted
in Frank Freidel, *FDR and the South* [Baton Rouge: Louisiana State University
Press, 1965], pp. 25–26).

for his racist and anti-Catholic outbursts, was a continuing source of embarrassment and anger to the Bourbon elements of the Democratic party. Heflin and Black shared a similar constituency, and Helfin's support of Hoover placed Black in a difficult position. Black had worked hard to prevent Smith's nomination; bolting from the Democratic party, however, was never a viable alternative. The Democratic party represented the many in the battle with the few; to split the party was to ensure the ascendancy of the few. Publicly Black remained silent, save for a statement to the *Montgomery Advertiser* disassociating himself from Smith's wet and pro-immigration policies while commending his position on public power as a "clarion call to Progressive Democracy."[61] To friends and constituents he professed support for the ticket. Nonetheless, he refused to take an active role in one of the ugliest campaigns in Alabama history in which both those remaining loyal to the Democratic party and those supporting Hoover played upon racial fears to secure support.[62] Black's expressed reason for refusing to take part in the campaign was that he was needed to reunite the party after the campaign. To Harry Ayers, a personal friend and editor of the *Anniston Star*, he wrote:

> There are of course many like yourself, who are vigorously opposed to Governor Smith's Prohibition Program, who are supporting the Party by reason of their loyalty to it. After this fight is concluded, it will take the best efforts that you, myself, and others can

61. A copy of Black's telegram is in HLBLC 72. Privately Black urged Smith to come to Alabama to speak on Muscle Shoals. See HLB to Harrison, 9/28/28, HLBLC 72.

62. HLBLC 72 and 73 contain copies of numerous letters written by Black urging friends and constituents to support the ticket. A typical letter reads in part: "I have considered for some time becoming actively engaged on the stump in the interests of the party. Outside of the two views of Governor Smith on Prohibition and Immigration, I think his political principles are thoroughly Democratic. Much reflection has convinced me, however, that it is not in the best interests of the Party for me to engage in a speaking campaign" (HLB to Striplin, 10/4/28, HLBLC 72). In another letter a constituent asked whether Black believed the country would be in danger with a Catholic in the White House. Black replied that the religion of a candidate was a proper factor for a voter to consider. Black noted, for example, that Catholics favored increased immigration and "those who favored the restriction on immigration might naturally be permitted to assume that a person belonging in this faith would most nearly carry out those convictions. . . . Lest you do not understand exactly, I will state that a person in America has a

give, in order to reunite the forces standing for the Progressive Principles which we have championed. The present chasm in our ranks is broad, and deep, and it is my best judgment that if I should take an active speaking part, it would aid in making it more nearly impassable in the future. . . . The principles for which you and I have fought for many years are in serious jeopardy by reason of the present schism. Their permanent supremacy in my judgment depends upon our efforts and ability to bring about a reunion of the present split forces *after the election*. This fight is now so bitter and vituperation so general, that speaking is largely ineffectual at the present time.[63]

Hence Black remained silent, attempting to satisfy the demands of the regular party without alienating his natural constituency. In the end, Smith carried the state by the unusually small margin of seven thousand votes.

The reaction of the regular Democrats to the defection of Heflin was swift. In future elections, those who sought the Democratic nomination had to take an oath that the candidate had supported Smith in 1928. The loyalty oath was designed, in part, by the regular Democrats to rid the party of Heflin—who was up for reelection in 1930—and shift control of the party to the Bourbon interests. Once again Black was placed in a different position. To his sister-in-law in California, Black explained his predicament:

A small majority of Democratic Executive Committee has ruled that no one of the 60,000 or more voters who voted for Hoover can run for office on the Democratic ticket. . . . It places me in a most embarrassing situation. If I remain in the Party, it will be with my political enemies. If I shall go out with my friends, I shall likewise be *read out* before the next election. While I have protested vigorously against the action of the Committee, I have not made any definite statement concerning my future action.[64]

Even in 1929 Black identified the Heflin forces as his friends and the regular Democrats as enemies. Not surprisingly, Black

---

right to belong to any church in any state he sees fit. There are times, however, when a man's alignment necessarily shows to some extent the bent of his views, and when such is true, it is not improper to consider them" (HLB to Nixon, 2/23/28, HLBLC 73).

63. HLB to Ayers, 10/16/28, HLBLC 72.

64. HLB to Blossom Black, 1/31/29, HLBLC 1.

opposed the exclusion of Democrats who had bolted in 1928; he argued that if one could vote in the party's primary—and the party could ill afford to exclude voters who had failed to support Smith—one could run on the ticket. And though Black may have feared that the exclusion rule would come to haunt him for his lukewarm support of Smith in 1928, he also viewed the issue in terms of the dualistic construct which dominated his thought. To a supporter he wrote:

> The void and illegal Resolution passed by the Democratic Committee was, in my judgment, the result of wet-corporate-Advertiser [*Montgomery Advertiser*] influence. What the Black Belt political philosophers could not do with the votes of the average man, they have attempted to accomplish by political skullduggery and manipulation. They are not after Senator Heflin very much. . . . What this small clique wants is control of Alabama for and by the clique, and in the interest of special privilege and plunder.
>
>   Their political judgment is good, in so far as the desire to get party control is concerned. They have deliberately planned to rule or ruin. Which will result only time can tell. What is the duty of a plain, ordinary man who is seeking to represent the best interests of the common people of Alabama, I have not yet decided. I am waiting to see if there is any chance of recision. I do not feel I am bound by a void and illegal resolution. . . . If I reach the definite conclusion, however, that it is a fight to the finish between this wet-corporate-Advertiser crowd, and the good progressive Democrats of Alabama, I shall take my place on the firing line.[65]

The fight apparently never went to the finish for Black never found the need to take his place on the firing line. Heflin sought an injunction to prevent the holding of the Democratic primary. When the Supreme Court of Alabama denied relief, Heflin ran as an independent "Jeffersonian" Democrat in the general election. John Bankhead, a member of a wealthy and influential Bourbon family, was the Democratic candidate for Heflin's seat. Again Black was on the horns of a dilemma. To support the Bankhead candidacy was to alienate the Klan and small farmer constituency that had been so important to his electoral success; to continue to fight the regular Democrats might result in an irreparable split of

65. HLB to McCain, 12/30/29, HLBLC 104.

the party. Once again, the fear of this eventuality dominated Black's actions, and when Bankhead easily defeated the insurgent "Jeffersonian" Democrats, it symbolized the decline of the dry, labor, and Klan coalition that had been so vital to Black's electoral success. When old friends and supporters angrily protested that he had led them to believe that he supported Heflin but had done nothing to aid Heflin's campaign, Black's only defense was his dualistic view of politics. He asserted that he had never urged anyone to desert the party; the principles of the Democratic party were more important than any personality. Any independent movement "splits the forces whose union is essential to the success of the principals which brought it about. The election of three independent candidates would not solidify these forces. It was only by following a course by which all voters entered the Primary that a solid front could have been presented. It is my belief that principles are bigger than men. Some now take the view point that loyalty to men is to be the criterion of loyalty to principle."[66] The fact was, however, that Black's political enemies now controlled the Democratic party, and although the party remained supreme in Alabama it was a different party than the one that had elected Black in 1926. The fear of rule by a Republican party of the few led Black to accept a Democratic party controlled by those far removed from his constituency. Indeed, when Heflin continued his battle on the floor of the United States Senate, leading the opposition, in the name of the Democratic party of Alabama, was Hugo Black.

Although Black's support of Bankhead may be viewed as a political move to the right, Black saw a significant "difference in opposing a rule *within a group* and leaving a group by reason of it."[67] Clifford Durr, Black's brother-in-law, has described Black as a dissenter rather than a rebel.[68] His vision of the polity precluded rebellion; on the other hand, it required dissent. The balance between liberty and order, individualism and economic progress was difficult to maintain and, from Black's perspective, reform could easily become an abuse of power and any break with

66. HLB to Ellis, 8/28/30, HLBLC 195.
67. Ibid.
68. Durr, "Mr. Justice Black."

the coalition that formed the Democratic party a step toward rule by the privileged few.[69]

Senator Black

In the years following the Heflin-Bankhead dispute Black's political vision took on broader perspectives. When an interviewer from Alabama suggested he was becoming too preoccupied with national affairs, Black responded: "Haven't you thought your way beyond state boundaries? Haven't you learned that all that there is wrong here in Alabama can never be righted, if we try to right it in Alabama alone?"[70]

Black's initial political vision had been born out of the economic hardship that produced the Populist movement. In times of prosperity that vision had little relevance to those who enjoyed the benefits of increased industrialization and organization. With the Crash of 1929 and the ensuing Depression, however, Americans were often quick to focus on the apparent distance between the ideal and the reality of the American Dream, and their reactions were often contradictory. A critique of the growth of economic organizations and the destruction of the liberal market system was often met by a belief that unrestrained competition had prevented the marketplace from organizing to ensure efficiency. Such ambivalence marked much of the New Deal.[71] Within this setting, Black, though a supporter of the New Deal, often served as a spokesman for those who feared increased organization and efficiency. In Black's mind, efficiency and organization often led inexorably to unemployment and a caste system: "Now we have the argument to consolidate all the railroads, all of it in the name of 'efficiency'; and when we get the most efficient government the world has ever had we are going to have a government where

69. Strikingly absent from the records of Black's public as well as private discussions is any critical thought concerning whether rule by the many was possible within the structure of the Democratic party.

70. *Birmingham News Herald* 1/31/37.

71. Ellis W. Hawley, *The New Deal and the Problem of Monopoly* (Princeton: Princeton University Press, 1974), suggests that although from a policy perspective, the New Deal may appear confused and ambivalent, this course actually served a political purpose because many voters reflected a similar ambiguity and confusion.

practically all of the dollars and the power is in the hands of a very few men."[72]

More than many in the Senate, Black was aware of the suffering caused by the Depression.[73] Nevertheless, he fought reform measures that served to centralize power. The LaFollette-Costigan relief bill proposed a federal emergency relief bureau to allocate millions of dollars to needy Americans; Black fought the measure for several years, contending that "bureaus are immortal" and warning against the centralization of power: "Do we trust our government to the people who make it up or to certain specially favored bureaus in the Capital of the Nation. . . ? The proposal to centralize power in Washington was Hamiltonian and not Jeffersonian."[74] His overriding fear was always concentration of power in the state or in private parties. As the New Deal appeared to vacillate between a planned corporatist state and a market economy, Black battled the former and yet was dubious of the latter. As his notes on Adam Smith make clear, he had little faith in the natural laws of the marketplace establishing a just and prosperous society. Increasingly he came to believe that the economic ills of the day were caused not by a lack of production but by a lack of consumption. Efficiency had reduced the number of jobs and hence the power to consume had failed to keep pace with the power to produce; to redress this balance required not the invisible hand of the market but the guiding hand of government. This guiding hand could not be that of a few experts in the public or

72. 71 *Congressional Record* 9547, 9551 (1930).

73. Many of his letters to his sister-in-law Blossom in California reflect his appreciation of conditions in Alabama. For example, "Conditions in Alabama have gotten steadily worse. Real estate has practically ceased to have any value. It is my understanding that between fifty and sixty thousand people are being fed by charitable organizations in Birmingham. This will give you an idea of the terrible conditions" (12/13/32, HLBLC 1).

74. 75 *Congressional Record* 3516 (1932). Another reason suggested for his opposition was racial; if administered by the federal government, aid would cut across racial lines. Nevertheless, even in his private correspondence, Black consistently emphasized his fear of the state: "You, perhaps, read the speech I made against the LaFollette-Costigan Bill and the creation of a new bureau. If you did, you will remember that I said *bureaus are immortal*, and that they were always greedy for more power and more money. It is exceedingly difficult to reduce them in any way" (HLB to Beeland, 6/21/32, HLBLC 223).

private sphere; if government was to act, Congress had to be the agent of that action.

In the final days of the Hoover administration, Black offered the most important piece of legislation he would introduce during his years in the Senate. From his reading of Adam Smith as well as G.D.H. Cole and Stuart Chase, Black concluded that a limitation on the hours of weekly employment would result in greater employment and redress the balance between production and consumption.[75] His thirty-hour work week bill prohibited the shipment in interstate commerce of goods produced by manufacturers whose employees worked more than thirty hours a week. To those who believed the measure unconstitutional, Black asserted that although the Constitution might announce principles, the "application of principles change with conditions. They are not inflexible. They are not unalterable."[76]

With no support from a lame duck administration, Black's proposal failed to reach the floor. Although facing reelection, Black spent much of 1932 campaigning for Roosevelt. In March 1933, when Roosevelt took office, Black urged him to include the thirty-hour-week proposal in his program. Roosevelt, however, opposed the measure, believing that it would retard recovery as well as

75. Black described the genesis of the idea in a letter to John Frank: "My interest in wages and hours legislation came from a number of different reasons. During the intensive reading I undertook after being elected to the Senate, many of the books I read had to do with unemployment. If you will go back and look at the history of that period you will find that there were quite a multitude of publications on that subject, including much written by Stuart Chase and people who called themselves technocrats. I probably read everything that was written on the subject at the time. I favored shorter hours for several reasons. One was that I thought it would help more people to get jobs and that even though they worked at shorter hours it would be impossible for industry to reduce their wages in anything like the proportion of the reduced number of hours. I became convinced as I still am convinced that this country can produce as much under our present system with a number of working hours much lower than we have yet achieved. I studied the social legislation laws that had been adopted on various countries of Europe. My information did ñot come from discussions with people in the unions. As a matter of fact, so far as I know no member of any union anywhere knew that I intended to offer such a bill at the time my 30-hr. week measure was put into the hopper. My aim at that time was a 40-hr. week bill sometime in the future" (HLB to Frank, 1/20/48, HLBLC 460).

76. 77 *Congressional Record* 1125 (1935).

being inflexible and probably unconstitutional.[77] Black reintro-
duced the measure without administration support. It quickly
passed through committee and surprisingly was enacted by a
53–30 margin in the Senate.

While the Black measure was being debated in the House, the
administration was forced to work quickly to develop a recovery
measure, and the NIRA was the result.[78] When the administration's bill reached the Senate, Black joined Senators William
Borah and Burton Wheeler to oppose the antitrust exemptions
and the rulemaking power of private industry. The NIRA's fatal
flaw in Black's view was that it removed from Congress the power
to control industry and placed it in private hands. "This bill . . .
will transfer the lawmaking power of this nation, insofar as control of industry is concerned, from Congress to the trade associations. This is exactly what happened in Italy."[79] With administration efforts focused on the recovery act, Black's bill was forgotten.

When in 1935 the Supreme Court held unconstitutional portions of the NIRA in the *Schechter* case, Black resumed his battle
for the thirty-hour week. In 1937 he introduced the Black-Con-
nery Bill. The new measure, promoted and supported by the administration, differed from Black's earlier proposal in that it provided for a fair labor standards board to administer a program of
wages and hours. With Black presiding, a joint House-Senate labor committee severely circumscribed the discretion and power of

77. William Leuchtenberg, *Franklin D. Roosevelt and the New Deal* (New York:
Harper & Row, 1963), and Hawley, *The New Deal and the Problem of Monopoly*, agree
that FDR opposed the plan. Black, however, disagreed. Years later he wrote Irving
Dillard: "President Roosevelt was for the bill and it was at the President's tele-
phone call that our Leader, Senator Joseph Robinson, brought up the bill for consideration in the Senate. . . . When the bill came to the House an amendment was
tacked on which would have provided a practical embargo against all goods
shipped from any country in the world produced in whole or in part by workers
who worked more than thirty hours in any one week. The President was against
that amendment as was I. It was under these circumstances that the President
came out for the National Industrial Recovery Act which I spoke out against in the
Senate. Not only did I speak out against the bill but I refused to offer the measure
for consideration" (HLB to Dillard, 1/13/62, HLBLC 25).

78. Hawley, *The New Deal and the Problem of Monopoly*, describes the administration's reaction to the Black bill's Senate victory and the events leading to the
NIRA.

79. HLB quoted in Dunne, *Hugo Black and the Judicial Revolution*, p. 150.

the board. Although many industries were exempted, the bill as reported to the Senate set the maximum hours per week at forty. Black defended the compromise measure throughout the summer of 1937. Many of the attacks on the bill came from the South, reflecting a fear that the traditional regional cost differences would be destroyed, thus eroding the increasing industrialization of the South.[80] The Black files are filled with letters from Alabama protesting the limitation on hours.[81] Black, long the consummate politician, was undeterred; throughout the long debate on the bill, he continually asserted that he spoke for a larger constituency, the little men and women of both "Alabama and the Nation."[82]

His support of wages and hours bills was but one example of his continual move from regional to national concerns. His famous service on several Senate investigatory committees not only brought him national publicity but also alienated him from the Bankhead wing of the party.[83] But the final step in Black's eman-

80. For example, see "Wage and Hour Bill Survives Southern Oratory on Uses of Poverty," *Newsweek*, August 7, 1937.

81. HLBLC 160.

82. Frank, *Mr. Justice Black*, p. 94.

83. When Senator Norris investigated the efforts of power company lobbyists during the Muscle Shoals controversy, he invited Black to sit with the committee. The findings from Black's initial exposure to Senate investigations were an important step in his political education. Black had supported plans to lease the facilities to private companies to produce nitrates; the investigation revealed secret plans by these companies to sell power to private power companies. In a note to himself, Black later wrote: "The combined power of organized wealth and its organized propaganda never ceases to fight every honest effort to save us from the terrible abuses incident to the exploitation of the many by the powerful few" (Black, *My Father*, p. 147). His subsequent investigations into the awarding of air mail contracts and lobbying efforts on behalf of entrenched interests confirmed a view of the polity torn between the interests of the few and the many. For example, the Senate version of the Wheeler-Rayburn Act of 1935 provided for the dismantling of every public utility holding company that could not justify its existence. This "death penalty" provision stirred great controversy and an intense lobbying effort which resulted in a milder House bill. The administration's strategy was to keep the measure in a joint conference committee while Black investigated the activities of pressure groups. The hope was that Black's findings would result in a surge of public support for the Senate measure. The investigations made Black a national celebrity, revealing that power companies had spent vast sums sending phony letters and telegrams to congressmen. Black's investigatory techniques resulted in the ACLU warning that heavy-handed use of subpoenas and questioning of witnesses could be used to combat as well as support progressive measures. For Black the issue was not the First Amendment or protection against unreasonable searches and

cipation from a provincial to national view was his enthusiastic support for Roosevelt's Court-packing plan.

Throughout his career Black had been suspicious of the power of courts. His early political education in the Populist movement had suggested and his reading program appeared to confirm this distrust. Much of the Populist rhetoric and anger of the 1890s had been directed at the Supreme Court and the federal judicial system. The Court served as a convenient symbol of the control of government by centralized wealth, and many of its decisions striking down legislative attempts to control railroad rates, hours of labor, and the like were serious setbacks to the Populist movement.[84]

Parrington had emphasized the use made by Federalist judges of natural law doctrines to impose judicial will on the populace, and in Black's copy of the *Memoirs of Jefferson* (particularly volume 3) there are numerous notations of Jefferson's faith in juries as the voice of reason and his distrust of judges. During his Senate years, Black was a constant and vocal critic of the judiciary. With grave doubts concerning the power of judicial review exercised by judges appointed for life, he called for the popular election of judges. "I believe in a democracy," he said, "and I believe in the election of judges by the people themselves. . . . Whose government is this?"[85] During Roosevelt's first term, when many New Deal measures were severely handicapped by injunctions issued by lower federal court judges, Black cosponsored a measure to expedite such appeals to the Supreme Court. The Black-Sumners Bill was designed both to circumvent the delays inherent in intermediate review and to undercut the Supreme Court's control of its docket.[86] During his investigations into lobbyist activities, sev-

---

seizures but deception. Every citizen had the right to air his views but not under the guise of overwhelming public support; such a deception represented the ultimate threat of the few against the many. For a further articulation of his views see the text of a radio address given by Black on 8/8/35 in defense of his investigations (HLBLC 182). Ultimately the "death penalty" provision was defeated. Hamilton, *Hugo Black*, chaps. 10 and 11, reviews Black's Senate investigations at length.

84. See Alan F. Westin, "The Supreme Court, the Populist Movement and the Campaign of 1896," 15 *Journal of Politics* 1 (1953).

85. 79 *Congressional Record* 6629 (1935).

86. Chief Justice Hughes as well as Brandeis and Van Devanter testified against the measure. Frankfurter also opposed the bill.

eral objects of the investigation sought judicial relief from Black's use of the subpoena *duces tecum*, prompting Black to threaten on the floor of the Senate to seek legislation removing from the federal courts the jurisdiction to restrain congressional committees.

As a senator, Black found little that was sacred in the judiciary and the Supreme Court. The federal judiciary symbolized control by the few, and it is not surprising that Black viewed congressional-court relations as an expression of the conflict between the few and the many.[87] When sit-down strikes broke out after the Court struck down minimum wage legislation and local attempts to establish economic control, Black contended that workers were left only with "the bayonet and the gun."[88] Thus when Roosevelt announced his Court reorganization plan, Black solidly backed the proposal.

Black defended the Roosevelt plan in several radio addresses. To attack the plan was to attack the wisdom of the founders of the republic; he constantly reminded his audience that the Constitution vested control of the size and jurisdiction of the Court in Congress and the president. The Roosevelt plan was a constitutionally valid means of popular control of the Court, and Black urged the populace to remember that both Jefferson and Jackson were charged with packing the Court. Moreover, from his reading of history he concluded that it was always the special and privileged interests which defended the Court.[89]

The move to reshape the Court easily fit within Black's political vision. Throughout history, courts had always been associated with special interests and those who feared the power of the popular will. Following the Court's opinion in *United States* v. *Butler*, overturning the Agricultural Adjustment Act, Black announced: "This means that 120 million people are ruled by five men."[90] In the South, however, growing frustration with the New Deal found expression in attacks on the Roosevelt Court plan. Black, in turn, was bitterly attacked for his support of Roosevelt. The *Alabama*

87. HLB to Sterling Black, 3/26/36, HLBLC 6.
88. Quoted in Dunne, *Hugo Black and the Judicial Revolution*, p. 165.
89. HLBLC 478.
90. 297 U.S. 1 (1936); quoted in Dunne, *Hugo Black and the Judicial Revolution*, p. 163.

Magazine labeled him a "radical administrationist," contending that his support for the plan was based on a desire for a Court that would uphold a thirty-hour week as well as "the political embrace of John Lewis."[91] Black's support of Roosevelt thus further estranged the senator from a constituency that looked with disfavor upon his efforts for a limited work week, his support of labor, and his senatorial investigations. When later that year Justice Van Devanter tendered his resignation, it is, in retrospect, hardly surprising that Roosevelt turned to the senator from Alabama whose political views had moved far beyond those of his constituency at home.[92]

Liberals and Reform

The reform movements in America during the late nineteenth and early twentieth centuries faced both a common enemy and a common theoretical problem. Both Populists and Progressives sought a means to control the private concentrations of wealth and power that marked the Gilded Age. By the turn of the century, it was readily apparent that corporate power could be controlled only by the application of greater public power. A simple Jeffersonian faith in limited government could no longer serve as the basis for American reform. To develop from that Jeffersonian tradition a theory of the use of power to combat private power was the dilemma common to American reformers at the turn of the twentieth century.

For Felix Frankfurter, this power was to be found in the modern administrative state. His faith in experts, scientific management, and the development of a civil service were all important steps in the emergence of an independent, powerful state in American life. The goal was progress; party affiliation or group loyalty was an impediment to progress. Society could be governed through disinterested, public-spirited scientific management. Power was neither to be feared nor distrusted but to be used con-

91. *Alabama Magazine*, March 1 and 22, 1937.
92. The controversy surrounding Black's appointment is described at length in Dunne, *Hugo Black and the Judicial Revolution*, and Charlotte Williams, *Hugo Black: A Study in the Judicial Process* (Baltimore: Johns Hopkins University Press, 1950).

fidently by the social engineers of a generation. The check on that power was a faith that through education and training a disinterested use of power was possible.

Before his appointment to the Court, Black, unlike Frankfurter, never developed a coherent theory to justify the use of public power as a means of reform. The Populist movement sought in increased participation in the democratic process the means by which government—and not necessarily small government—would serve the reform impulse. Although the Populist rhetoric was the source of many of Black's political truths, his understanding of the polity precluded·action outside of the Democratic party. Confined by a political understanding that would not permit a third-party movement, Black's reform instincts were limited by the realities of the Democratic party.

Although Black increasingly viewed Congress as the means by which political power could be employed on behalf of the many, he had a consistent distrust of the use of power that Frankfurter lacked. Frankfurter fashioned a political theory that appeared to satisfy his democratic faith and the realities of the political world. Although Black had a clearly developed understanding of the polity, before his appointment to the Court he was unable to formulate a coherent political theory based upon that political vision. Black's ideal state—strong enough to control private concentrations of power but not strong enough to destroy personal freedom—reflects his ambiguity about power. Ultimately Black feared both private power and the growth of public power. It was this continuing, unresolved ambiguity concerning private and public power that was to mark his initial years on the bench.

4 Due Process and the Fourteenth Amendment: The Limits of Judicial Decision Making

Adoption of one or the other conflicting views as to
what is "decent," what is right, and what is best
for the people is generally recognized as a legislative function.

> Hugh Black, unpublished concurring
> opinion in *Louisiana ex rel Francis* v.
> *Resweber*, 1946

This could only be on the assumption that we cannot
trust five members of the highest court of the land
to exercise a judgment of whether or not a thing
does offend fundamental decency because forsooth
they would vest too much discretionary power in a
majority of the Court, who one would suppose are
disciplined by the responsibility of their office
and the great tradition of the history of this Court.

> Felix Frankfurter, conference statement
> *Buchalter* v. *New York*, 1943

Felix Frankfurter and Hugo Black came to the Supreme Court as the products of the progressive reform tradition
that flourished in America at the turn of the century. As such,

they shared a deep antipathy for a constitutional jurisprudence which, through the "vague contours" of the Fifth and Fourteenth Amendments, found certain immutable principles which both men believed severely restricted progress in America. In addition, they shared a deep respect for the progressive power of education and a strong preference for legislative solutions to social ills. United in their distaste for established, vested interests, both warmly embraced Franklin Roosevelt and the New Deal. Despite many shared beliefs and goals, however, American liberal thought has never been unitary; within broad agreement over goals has existed vast differences over means. Thus although both Frankfurter and Black were regarded as "liberals" upon their appointment to the Court, this categorization masked significant differences in their political thought which would emerge during their careers on the Court.

Central to the liberalism of Felix Frankfurter was an enduring belief in the power of education, the flexibility of human nature, and the wisdom of the application of scientific methods by trained experts as a means for ordering the modern state. Absolutes and immutable principles were anathema to progress and change; a core of common beliefs and goals shared by a homogeneous population served to unite the nation in its progressive development. His model of constitutional decision making was based upon similar assumptions. He sought to control the judicial subjectivity and lawmaking of an earlier era while at the same time avoiding inflexible, absolute standards designed to control that same subjectivity. To accomplish this task, he built his role conception of the Supreme Court justice around his image of the scientific expert—capable, through training and an understanding of American traditions, history, and goals, of exercising power and judgment in a disinterested and public-spirited manner. His understanding of progress rested upon freeing experts from unexamined dogma which prevented experimentation and change; similarly, his model of constitutional decision making sought to free judges from inflexible standards that would restrict judicial judgment. The jurisprudence of Felix Frankfurter did not seek to prevent judicial enforcement of principle; it did, however, seek to make the choice of principle as well as the means and extent of enforcement a matter of enlightened judicial judgment. The er-

ror of Justice Field and his intellectual heirs was not in their attempt to enforce principle but in their failure to temper that enforcement with disinterested, scientific judgment.

Frankfurter's jurisprudence thus rested upon a contradiction
that would remain throughout his judicial career. For much of his
pre-Court life, he had been one of the first legal realists, persua-
sively arguing against the oracular theory of judging and urging a
more human understanding of the Supreme Court. The Court,
he asserted, was the history of the personalities of the justices;
therefore, the background, beliefs, and understandings of individual justices were critical to the evolution of American constitutional law.[1] As his constitutional jurisprudence evolved, however,
Frankfurter steadfastly resisted the imposition of an external
standard to restrict the play of these individual attributes, relying
instead upon the ability of judges, molded by tradition, wisdom,
and professional education, to exercise the great power of judicial
review in a disinterested manner. To reconcile this apparent contradiction was an impossible task. Judicial choice and judgment
were not merely inescapable but would soon become critical elements in his understanding of the judicial role.[2]

Judicial choice was anathema to Hugo Black. The era of Field-

1. See, e.g., Alexander Bickel, "Applied Politics and the Science of Law: Writings of the Harvard Period," in Wallace Mendelson, ed., *Felix Frankfurter: A Tribute*
(New York: Reynal, 1964).

2. This view is reflected in Frankfurter's devotion to James Bradley Thayer,
whose rule of administration (see Chapter 1) assumed that judges were capable of
exercising the power of judicial review in a disinterested manner and, as a result,
judges could be entrusted with the enforcement of principle. Frankfurter accepted both these assumptions despite the insights of his early writings and his antipathy for the dominant constitutional jurisprudence of the late nineteenth and
early twentieth centuries. He wrote to Charles Wyzanski in 1944: "But there is no
reason I should not recall a talk between Ezra Thayer and myself nearly thirty
years ago. . . . Dean Thayer asked me how long our system of judicial review could
survive. I replied: 'As long as the people have confidence that they can depend on
the more or less continuous presence on the Supreme Court of at least five men
endowed with and capable of practicing real disinterestedness of judgment'" (FF
to Wyzanski, 2/19/44, FFLC 113-2376). Frankfurter added that Dean Thayer expressed some surprise at Frankfurter's reply because Thayer's father (James Bradley Thayer) had given the same answer years before. Noteworthy is Frankfurter's
use of the word "disinterested." It is the same word he constantly used to describe
the critical quality of the scientifically trained expert. Judicial statesmanship was
the disinterested application of principle to new situations as well as the disinterested accommodation of conflicting principles. See Gary Jacobsohn, *Pragmatism,
Statesmanship and the Supreme Court* (Ithaca, N.Y.: Cornell University Press, 1977).

ian jurisprudence and its impact on the Populist movement confirmed Black's fear of judicial power. The Court remained the symbol of the Hamiltonian few controlling the density of the Jeffersonian many. Absent in Black was any faith in the wisdom of experts or the possibility of the disinterested use of power. Black's democratic vision rested upon a government responsive to majority will, and the Court was symbolic of an elite minority's distrust of that will. Nevertheless, to ensure that government was responsive to majority will required that government be subject to specific and definite limitations; without these limitations—particularly those found in the First Amendment—the opportunity for government to serve the powerful few at the expense of the many dramatically increased. From this basic democratic understanding came both a distrust of judicial power and a recognition of its use. Black's concept of the role of the Court appeared to welcome absolutes and restraints upon judicial judgment as protection against the abuses of an earlier era. The paradox of Black's jurisprudence was that in finding in the Constitution absolutes that severely narrowed the scope of judicial judgment, the Court became the primary guarantor of the values contained in those absolutes. Black's vision of the Court and Constitution, born of a fear of judicial power, thus produced the anomaly of vastly increasing the impact of the Court in modern American life.

The remainder of this study is an attempt to understand and examine the jurisprudence of Felix Frankfurter and Hugo Black in the light of the respective political visions that powered it. The subject of this chapter is the impact of the Fourteenth Amendment upon state criminal procedures, with particular emphasis on the period from Black's appointment to the Court through the 1946 term. For both men, these cases raised problems that extended well beyond the issues posed by the litigants; although both would call upon history and precedent to support their respective positions, the debate between Frankfurter and Black was not simply over particular results in particular cases but in a larger sense over the role of courts and judges in the American democratic system.[3]

    3. The debate over the "nationalization" of the Bill of Rights, a major controversy in the 1950s and 1960s, had its roots in the 1940s. Frankfurter and Black

Due Process and the Fourteenth Amendment

From the date of the passage of the Fourteenth Amendment through the era of Black and Frankfurter, the judicial task of giving content to the procedural guarantees of the Fourteenth Amendment can be viewed as a constant tension between the desire to achieve a fixed meaning and confine judicial subjectivity and the need to maintain flexibility.[4] Although the primary concern of the Court in the period following the passage of the Fourteenth Amendment was the impact of that amendment upon the states' use of police power to govern economic activity within their borders, the response to the occasional case posing the issue of the amendment's limitations upon state criminal procedures was well within the flexibility versus fixed meaning pattern. In the typical case,[5] the petitioner contended that the state had failed to adhere to the procedural limitations contained in the Bill of Rights, that the Fourteenth Amendment made the provisions of the Bill of Rights binding on the states and, as a result, the petitioner's conviction in the state courts should be overturned by the Supreme Court. In each case this claim for a fixed content to procedural due process based upon the provisions of the Bill of Rights was rejected by a majority of the Court. Rather, the approach employed by the majority required a decision in each case as to whether the procedures of the state had denied the petitioner a "fundamental principle of liberty and justice which inheres in the very idea of free government."[6]

To answer this question required the Court to attempt to discern the basic moral choices of the community. Unwilling to concede to the subjective nature of such an inquiry, this view of due process rested on two fundamental assumptions: first, that the

---

were the major protagonists in this early debate, and the cases described in this chapter, particularly the early confession cases, illustrate the issues in the debate as well as the process of decision making developed by Black and Frankfurter.

4. Sanford Kadish, "Methodology and Criteria in Due Process Adjudication: A Survey and Criticism," 66 *Yale Law Review* 319 (1957).

5. See, e.g., *Hurtado* v. *California*, 110 U.S. 516 (1884); *Maxwell* v. *Dow*, 176 U.S. 581 (1900); *Twining* v. *New Jersey*, 211 U.S. 78 (1908).

6. *Twining* v. *New Jersey*, 211 U.S. 78, 106 (1908). In the cases cited in n. 5 Justice Harlan dissented on the grounds that the Fourteenth Amendment did serve to incorporate the Bill of Rights.

original determination of the state court or legislature must be given great deference, and second, that there existed objective criteria for determining the basic moral choices of the community.[7] One possible source of these objective guidelines was the Constitution, and the flexible approach did not preclude looking to specific provisions in the Bill of Rights for aid in determining the content of procedural due process in the Fourteenth Amendment. But the source of the limitation upon state procedure was not the specific provision of the Bill of Rights but the more flexible standard of the Fourteenth Amendment. The Sixth Amendment and the famous case of *Powell* v. *Alabama*[8] provides an example. The Sixth Amendment calls for the assistance of counsel in all criminal cases. In *Powell* the Court held that the Fourteenth Amendment guaranteed against state infringement the effective assistance of counsel in all capital cases. By carefully identifying the source of the right as the Fourteenth Amendment (but using the Sixth Amendment as an indication of the standards of the community), the Court was free to limit its holding to the assistance of counsel in capital cases. Furthermore, by considering the Fourteenth Amendment independent of the Bill of Rights, the Court could, in appropriate circumstances, find in the Fourteenth Amendment principles that were not included in the Bill of Rights.[9]

Thus by 1937, the year of Hugo Black's appointment to the Court, there appeared to be a long, if not voluminous, line of authority which called for a flexible, nondoctrinaire application of the Fourteenth Amendment to the criminal procedures of the various states. In his first term on the Court, Black joined Justice Cardozo's famous opinion in *Palko* v. *Connecticut*,[10] which constituted Cardozo's attempt to articulate the practical, as well as the theoretical, underpinnings of the flexible due process approach. Refusing to tie the meaning of the Fourteenth Amendment to the fixed principles of the Bill of Rights, Cardozo reviewed the past procedural due process decisions of the Court in an attempt to

7. Kadish, "Methodology and Criteria in Due Process Adjudication," p. 327.
8. 287 U.S. 45 (1932).
9. See, e.g., *Mooney* v. *Holohan*, 294 U.S. 103 (1935), in which the Court held that the knowing use of perjured testimony by the state violated due process.
10. 302 U.S. 319 (1937).

find unifying principles. From his review of these cases, Cardozo concluded:

> There emerges the perception of the rationalizing principle which gives to discrete instances a proper order and coherence. The right to trial by jury and the immunity from prosecution except as the result of indictment may have value and importance. Even so, they are not of the very essence of a scheme of ordered liberty. . . . We reach a different plane of social and moral values when we pass to the privileges and immunities that have been taken over from the earlier Bill of Rights and brought within the 14th Amendment by a process of absorption. If the 14th Amendment has absorbed them the process of absorption has had its source in the belief that neither liberty nor justice would exist if they were sacrificed.[11]

Despite Cardozo's attempt to identify the unifying principles at work in the procedural due process cases and his attempt to catalog certain rights, his theory of the Fourteenth Amendment ultimately rested upon the exercise of sound judicial judgment because the result in each case called for a determination of whether fundamental principles inherent in the concept of ordered liberty were at issue. It was a theory of due process that was inescapably subjective and general; it placed upon the states the primary responsibility of determining fair criminal procedure while reserving for the Supreme Court the task of measuring these procedures against what the Court determined to be the fundamental moral choices of the community.

Justice Black's decision to join in Cardozo's opinion is more than a little surprising; he later contended that he had had serious doubts and joined the opinion out of enormous respect for Cardozo.[12] Even in his initial term on the Court, Black was not reluctant to dissent, particularly when the case appeared to touch upon his deeply held political convictions.[13] Moreover, the same year in which he joined Cardozo in *Palko*, Black explicitly with-

11. 302 U.S. at 321.

12. Jerome A. Cooper, "Mr. Justice Hugo L. Black: Footnote to a Great Case," 24 *Alabama Law Review* 1 (1972).

13. See, e.g., *Connecticut General Life Ins. Co.* v. *California*, 303 U.S. 77 (1938), in which Black argued in dissent that a corporation was not a person for purposes of the Fourteenth Amendment. Black's willingness to dissent troubled his new colleagues, particularly Justice Stone. See Alpheus Mason, *Harlan Fiske Stone: Pillar of the Law* (New York: Viking, 1956), p. 469.

held his approval from Justice Stone's equally famous footnote 4 in the *Carolene Products* case,[14] and this action was perhaps more indicative of his emerging judicial philosophy.

Stone's effort in that note constituted a preliminary attempt to solve a dilemma that would plague the Court in the ensuing years: to require judicial deference to legislative judgments in the realm of social and economic affairs while at the same time justifying judicial activism in the area of personal and political rights.[15] The first paragraph of the note as published came at the suggestion of Chief Justice Hughes and reflects Cardozo's opinion in *Palko*: certain provisions of the Constitution (unidentified in the note) were absorbed into the Fourteenth Amendment, and when legislation on its face appeared to contravene these provisions the Court owed little deference to the legislative judgment. Thus paragraph one of the note rested on the text of the Constitution. But paragraphs two and three, written by Stone and his law clerk, Louis Lusky, rested not on the constitutional text but upon a broadly conceived role of the Court as the protector of insular minorities and the democratic process. In a letter to Hughes, Stone explained his thinking behind these paragraphs:

> You are quite right in saying that the specific prohibitions of the first ten amendments and the same prohibitions when adopted by

14. *United States* v. *Carolene Products Co.*, 304 U.S. 144 (1938). Writing for the Court, Justice Stone upheld a federal statute excluding "filled" milk from interstate commerce. In footnote 4 he wrote: "There may be a narrower scope for operation of the presumption of constitutionality when legislation appears on its face to be within a specific prohibition of the Constitution, such as those of the first ten amendments which are deemed equally specific when held to be embraced within the Fourteenth. . . .

"It is unnecessary to consider now whether legislation which restricts those political processes which can ordinarily be expected to bring about repeal of undesirable legislation, is to be subjected to more exacting judicial scrutiny under the general prohibitions of the Fourteenth Amendment than are most other types of legislation. . . .

Nor need we inquire whether similar considerations enter into the review of statutes directed at particular religious . . . or national . . . or racial minorities . . . whether prejudice against discrete and insular minorities may be a special condition, which tends seriously to curtail the operation of those political processes ordinarily to be relied upon to protect minorities, and which may call for a correspondingly more searching judicial inquiry,"

15. The background to the note is set out in Mason, *Harlan Fiske Stone*, p. 516.

the Fourteenth Amendment leave no opportunity for presumption of constitutionality where statutes on their face violate the prohibition. There are, however, possible restraints on liberty and political rights which do not fall within these specific prohibitions and are forbidden only by the general words of the due process clause of the Fourteenth Amendment. I wish to avoid the possibility of having what I have written in the body of the opinion about the presumption of constitutionality in the ordinary run of due process cases applied as a matter of course to these other more exceptional cases.[16]

Although Black did not explain his refusal to join in Stone's note it is likely that the extraconstitutional nature of paragraphs two and three were among the reasons.[17] The notion that due process extended beyond constitutional provisions, while perhaps implicit in *Palko*, was made explicit in *Carolene Products*.[18] Black, early in his judicial career, was certainly not averse to a priority of rights based upon constitutional standards. In *Avery* v. *Alabama*,[19] Black wrote in his draft opinion: "The power of the states to regulate property must be distinguished from constitutional procedural rights protecting human life and liberty."[20] In *Avery*, Black was moved by concerns similar to those that prompted Stone's efforts in *Carolene Products*—to justify greater judicial scrutiny in cases involving personal freedom. Unlike Stone, however, Black appeared to tie his priority of rights to the constitutional text. Nevertheless, after his draft opinion was circulated, several members of the Court questioned the wisdom of

16. Stone to Hughes, 4/19/38, Stone LC 63.

17. Black concurred in the result and opinion in *Carolene Products* save for the section containing footnote 4. He may have refused to join in this section because of Stone's conclusion that economic legislation would be upheld unless it lacked any "rational basis."

18. One could read *Palko* to the effect that the "concepts of ordered liberty" test was to be used to determine which provisions of the Bill of Rights were to be applied to the states. It appears clear, however, that Cardozo did not intend for the Fourteenth Amendment to be limited by the provisions of the Bill of Rights. See Henry Abraham, *Freedom and the Court* (New York: Oxford University Press, 1977), pp. 67–69.

19. 308 U.S. 444 (1940). In a capital case, the petitioner in *Avery* contended that he had been denied the effective assistance of counsel because the trial judge had denied a motion for continuance to permit his attorney additional time to prepare his defense. Writing for a unanimous Court, Black affirmed the conviction.

20. A copy of the draft is in HLBLC 256.

such a statement.[21] Hughes acknowledged Black's "excellent opinion" but expressed reservations about the inclusion of a statement so "highly controversial in nature." "Of course, I agree that we must be careful to preserve constitutional procedure in protecting human life and liberty. But the due process clause is not limited to life and liberty, but extends to 'life, liberty and property.' . . . The primary procedural rights demand notice and the opportunity to be heard whether the case relates to property or life or liberty."[22] Black immediately withdrew the offending sentence.

Black's refusal to join with Stone in the *Carolene* note coupled with his draft in *Avery* suggests a good deal about Black's early view of the Court and procedural due process. Notwithstanding Hughes's objection, Black did see a distinction between property and personal rights; the defense of property had been used by the Court to thwart the reform movements of the recent past. In linking increased judicial scrutiny to the provisions of the Constitution, Black, in effect, had made the Court the prime agent in enforcing these limitations upon government. At the same time, again by tying judicial scrutiny to the text of the Constitution, Black had presumably limited the judicial subjectivity he had long feared. Given Black's distrust of human nature and unrestricted power, to acquiesce in Stone's formulation was to invite the Court to become the agent of the few at the expense of the many. Like Stone, Black could envision the court as a protector of the democratic process; unlike Stone, however, his primary fear was not tyranny of the majority but tyranny of a powerful few.[23]

Chambers v. *Florida*: The Initial Black Approach

From the time of his nomination to the Court, the liberal community had been skeptical of Black because of his past association with the Ku Klux Klan. Hughes, aware of his predicament, made a conscious effort to assign Black opinions that would rehabilitate him in the view of the liberal community. One such

21. See circulation returns from Justices Roberts and Reed in HLBLC 256.
22. Hughes to HLB, 12/29/39, HLBLC 256.
23. For the opposite conclusion concerning the impact of Stone's note on judicial review, see Louis Lucky, *By What Right?* (Charlottesville, Va.: Michie, 1975).

case was *Chambers* v. *Florida*.[24] In *Chambers*, four Negro tenant
farmers had been held in the Dade County Courthouse for five
days without access to counsel and friends until a confession to
the murder of an elderly white man had been secured. A Florida
jury found that the confessions had been voluntary and that physical brutality had not been used to secure the confessions. Although Black's opinion for a unanimous Court reversing the convictions would stand as one of his most eloquent statements in
defense of human liberty, the case did present serious problems.[25] Given Black's healthy respect for jury verdicts as the voice
of the community, the jury's finding that the confessions were voluntary presented a formidable obstacle. But even if the Court
might review a jury's findings of facts, the constitutional basis on
which to ground the reversal presented an even more difficult
problem.

Although closely related to self-incrimination, for years the rule
against the admissibility of coerced confessions had existed inde-
pendently of the Fifth Amendment privilege against self-incrimination. Indeed, the rule against admission in federal courts had
developed as a rule of evidence with no reference to the Fifth
Amendment.[26] In its first review of a state confession case, the
Court in *Brown* v. *Mississippi*,[27] through Chief Justice Hughes,
emphasized that the privilege against self-incrimination was not at
issue; rather, the action of the state of Mississippi in physically
beating a confession from three Negroes offended "a principle of
justice so rooted in the traditions and conscience of our people as
to be ranked fundamental."[28] *Brown* was well within the flexible,

24. 309 U.S. 227 (1940). Black, for example, was assigned the opinion in *Pierre*
v. *Louisiana*, 306 U.S. 354 (1939), reversing the murder conviction of a black man
because of the systematic exclusion of blacks from the jury rolls. On the back of his
circulation, Stone wrote Black: "I am glad you wrote this" (HLBLC 257).

25. Justice Douglas's docket book shows that Black originally voted to deny
certiorari in *Chambers* (Douglas LC 230). Black's reluctance to hear the case may
well have been caused by the difficulties it presented, given his view of the role of
the Court.

26. *McNabb* v. *United States*, 318 U.S. 332 (1943). The only departure from this
trend was *Bram* v. *United States*, 168 U.S. 532 (1897). In general, see Otis Stephens,
Jr., *The Supreme Court and Confessions of Guilt* (Knoxville: University of Tennessee
Press, 1973).

27. 297 U.S. 278 (1936).

28. 297 U.S. at 285 quoting from *Snyder* v. *Massachusetts*, 291 U.S. 97, 105
(1934).

fair trial approach to due process; the Court had merely held that under the circumstances of the case, the use of the coerced confessions violated due process of law.[29]

The problem of coerced confessions appeared to confirm the wisdom of the flexible approach to due process as well as Stone's concern in his letter to Hughes. The use of such confessions constituted a serious deprivation of liberty not governed by a specific provision in the Bill of Rights. In light of Black's refusal to join the *Carolene Products* note as well as his preliminary attempt to tie judicial scrutiny to the text of the Constitution illustrated in *Avery*, the issue of coerced confessions posed a difficult problem for him. The difficulty was further evidenced by a note Frankfurter sent Black eight days after the Court voted to hear *Chambers*:

> Dear Hugo: Perhaps you will let me say quite simply and without any ulterior thought what I mean to say, and all I mean to say, regarding your position on the "Fourteenth Amendment" as an entirety.
>
> (1) I *can* understand that the Bill of Rights . . . applies to state action and not merely to U.S. action and that Barron v. Baltimore was wrong. I think it rightly decided.
>
> (2) What I am unable to appreciate is what are the criteria of selection as to the nine Amendments—which applies and which does not apply.[30]

This note from Frankfurter in 1939 is the first concrete evidence of Black's movement toward the incorporation theory he would later champion. But it also illustrates the difficulty posed by *Chambers*; if Black was to find in the constitutional text the standards for restricting the discretion inherent in the flexible, fair trial approach, the petitioners in *Chambers* would face execution.

Black's initial draft opinion in *Chambers* thus contained little that suggests outright dissatisfaction with the fair trial concept. Acknowledging that "some have thought, contrary to the prevailing judgment of this Court however, that all the privileges and immunities protected from federal invasion by the Bill of Rights were

29. In *Brown* the brutality used to secure the confession was admitted.
30. FF to HLB 10/31/39. Although the context of this letter is unknown, J. Woodford Howard connects it to *Chambers* (*Mr. Justice Murphy* [Princeton: Princeton University Press, 1968], p. 428).

also protected against state invasion by the Fourteenth Amendment," Black found that "implicit in the concept of ordered liberty which the Fourteenth Amendment assures as the uniform law of the land is the need to give protection against torture, physical or mental [citing *Palko*]. That Amendment was intended to shield an accused with procedural safeguards essential to a fair trial."[31] There was little to distinguish Black's analysis from the prevalent due process approach. Black, however, was unhappy with his initial treatment of the Fourteenth Amendment issue. He handwrote several pages to be included in the due process section.

Many judicial and extra judicial controversies . . . have revolved around the interpretation of the 14th Amendment's true meaning, it scope and limitations imposed by it. [Here Black adds a footnote to the effect that although there has been a strong current of opinion that the 14th Amendment incorporated the Bill of Rights it had never been accepted by the Court.] Few have ever doubted, however, that the "due process of law" provision was intended to provide a shield of procedural safeguard sufficient to guarantee that all criminal trials must be conducted in a way that a state does not deprive an accused of his "life, liberty or property" in a proceeding which is a fair, open and impartial trial in form but not in fact. That procedural safeguards in criminal trials were thought to be of paramount importance in the formative period of our nation was made manifest both in the Declaration of Independence and the Constitution with the bill of rights amendments. Among the charges listed as justifying the abandonment of "all allegiance to the British Crown" were depriving Americans of trial by jury, transporting them "beyond the Seas to be tried for pretended offenses; while at the same time making judges in America dependent on his will alone" and protecting his armed troops "by a mock trial, from punishment for any murders which they should commit on the inhabitants of these states." And in spite of the jealous regard of the Constitution's Framers for preserving the rights of the states, two of the few express constitutional provisions, prohibiting state action were that no state should "pass any Bill of Attainder or ex post facto law." The Constitution also prohibited Congress from passing Bills of Attainder and ex post facto laws, prohibited suspension of habeas corpus except when in cases of rebellion or invasion the public safety required it; provided for "trial of all crimes except in

31. A copy appears in HLBLC 256.

cases of impeachment, shall be by jury . . . in the state where said crime shall be committed"; gave a limited definition of treason and prohibited the conviction of any person for treason unless on the testimony of two witnesses to the same overt act or in confession in open court. Thus did those who wrote the Constitution indicate their purpose to create a government in which punishment for crime should only follow a judicial trial in which the rights of the accused must be fully and fairly protected. But these safeguards did not satisfy the people—they demanded more. As a result the first Congress submitted to the people and the states promptly approved ten amendments; the first eight being usually referred to as the Bill of Rights. Amendments 5, 6, and 8 provided yet more detailed procedural safeguards to protect those accused of crime. . . . [Black here describes the particular procedural safeguards outlined in the Bill of Rights.]

This Court has decided in previous cases that some but not all of the rights made secure against federal action by the Bill of Rights are made secure against state action by the Fourteenth Amendment [citing *Palko*]. In determining what procedural prerequisites measure up to that due process guaranteed by that amendment . . . we cannot wholly ignore the constitutional background and history of that same clause in the Fifth Amendment together with its context. This convinces us that formal notice and hearing are not the only necessary procedural prerequisites to conviction for crime. The state cannot consistent with due process use its greater power to place an accused in such a helpless condition that his hearing amounts to no more than a mere formal recondition of a verdict of guilty made inevitable by confessions induced by physical or mental torture.

These notes suggest a good deal about Black's early view of Court and Constitution. *Chambers* was a different case than *Brown* because in *Chambers* the torture was psychological and not physical. Thus to find for the petitioners in *Chambers* required Black to move beyond *Brown*, and he could do so in one of two ways. One was to focus on the defendants, stressing their youth, inexperience, and general susceptibility to psychological pressure. The second was to find in the Constitution standards by which police behavior could be measured without regard to individual defendants. Black's notes reveal a marked preference for the latter. The entire thrust of these notes is a search of the text and context of the Constitution to determine the evils intended to be outlawed.

The fact that no specific constitutional command controlled the case was not dispositive; in Black's view an understanding of history gave flesh to the contours of the Constitution. It was, however, a use of history keyed not to understanding the evolving moral standards of the community but to fix in time the meaning of due process consistent with the intent of the framers.

Thus for Hugo Black in 1939 due process was not limited by a literal reading of the Bill of Rights. It was, however, not so subjective as to permit a case-by-case analysis of a defendant's psychological strength. By linking the meaning of due process in the Fourteenth Amendment to the same words in the Fifth Amendment, Black was ensuring a degree, albeit modest, of judicial discretion in the enforcement of the due process clause. In *Chambers* he construed that clause in the Fourteenth Amendment as independent of the guarantees of the Bill of Rights; the discretion inherent in such a construction of due process was restricted by a historical understanding of the term. From the outset, as his draft in *Chambers* illustrated, Black rebelled against a changing definition of due process keyed to judicial understanding of the evolving moral decisions of the community.

Because of his deep-seated distrust of judicial power, Black was unwilling to accept the open invitation to judicial judgment of Stone in *Carolene Products* and Cardozo in *Palko*. Nevertheless, his understanding of due process did not totally eliminate such judgment. Even the most flexible approach to due process acknowledged that notice, jurisdiction, and the opportunity to be heard were indisputably part of due process. For Black, however, these historically validated elements of due process served as guideposts for judges in giving to due process a meaning fixed by history. For other members of the Court, particularly Frankfurter, they served as a starting point by which judges strove to enforce their understanding of the evolving moral standards of the community.

The final draft of *Chambers* omitted much of the handwritten material. Acknowledging that the scope and operation of the Fourteenth Amendment "have been fruitful sources of controversy in our constitutional history," Black nevertheless found that the history and setting of the due process clause in the Fifth and Fourteenth Amendments removed any "doubt that it was intended to guarantee procedural standards adequate and appropriate, then and thereafter, to protect at all times, people charged with or suspected of crime by those holding positions of power and authority."[32] Relying on Hughes's opinion in *Brown*, Black held that the Fourteenth Amendment made operative against the states the requirement of conforming to fundamental standards of procedure in criminal trials. By emphasizing the general "helplessness" of the defendants, the opinion obscured Black's conviction that due process contained standards by which police behavior could be measured without regard to the effect on the individual.

As circulated, Black's opinion was almost unanimously endorsed.[33] Frankfurter noted "really fine" on his copy of the circulation.[34] Moreover, *Chambers* was a resounding public success.[35] The omission of his handwritten material and his emphasis on the status of the defendants placed his opinion easily within the flexible tradition. It certainly gave no hint of his incorporation position; in his opinion in *Chambers*, Black found it unnecessary even to discuss the privilege against self-incrimination contained in the Fifth Amendment.

The Frankfurter Approach

Later in 1939, while Black was at work on *Chambers*, Frankfurter sent him a friendly note remarking that he considered Black a Benthamite seeking to rid the law of the abuses of judges. Admitting that he, too, disliked legislating by judges, Frankfurter accepted it as a fact of life. The issue was not whether judges make law but "when and how and how much."

> I used to say to my students that legislatures make law wholesale, judges retail. In other words they cannot decide things by invoking

32. 309 U.S. at 236.

33. McReynolds noted his disagreement but chose not to dissent (HLBLC 256).

34. HLBLC 256.

35. At a news conference, President Roosevelt suggested that the press owed Justice Black an apology for its bitter condemnation of Black following the disclosure of his Klan membership at the time of his appointment to the Court. See Gerald T. Dunne, *Hugo Black and the Judicial Revolution* (New York: Simon and Schuster, 1977), p. 203.

a new major premise out of whole cloth; they must make the law they do make out of the existing materials and with due deference to the presuppositions of the legal system of which they have been made a part. Of course I know these are not mechanical devices, and therefore not susceptible of producing automatic results. But they sufficiently indicate the limits within which judges are to move.[36]

Thus whereas Black began with a deep fundamental distrust of judicial review and judges, Frankfurter, despite public professions to the contrary, easily accepted both. Both Frankfurter and Black were symbolic of the rebellion against the Fieldian jurisprudence of the turn of the century. But Black's reaction, even evidenced in his drafts of *Chambers*, was to narrow the scope of judicial subjectivity while Frankfurter sought to control its exercise through disinterested statesmanship. Thus Frankfurter's understanding of judicial restraint was not founded upon prophylactic rules to control judicial discretion but upon the internalized discipline and understanding that characterized judicial statesmanship.[37]

No case better illustrates Frankfurter's approach to judicial statesmanship than his opinion for the Court in *Minersville School District* v. *Gobitis*.[38] Since his earliest days in the Progressive movement, Frankfurter had rebelled against absolutes and rigid dogma; his political understanding stressed the value of dynamic leaders, trained experts, experimentation, and management. His view of judges and the judiciary reflected that ideal. Statesmanship required the exercise of judgment; it demanded that judges

36. FF to HLB, 12/15/39, FF HLSL 169–2.

37. Although Frankfurter often used the phrase "judicial statesmanship," a precise definition is difficult. Gary Jacobsohn provides a useful description by noting the attempts to "accommodate and apply timeless principles of constitutional government to contemporary realities in order to guide the future consistent with the view of justice prescribed in the principles of the Constitution" (*Pragmatism, Statesmanship and the Supreme Court*, p. 122). The critical word is "accommodate." Judges, as trained experts, bore responsibility for the development of a progressive society. To accommodate principle to progress was a task of judgment. Rigid application of principle precluded progress in the same way that faith in unverified dogma precluded scientific advance.

38. 310 U.S. 586 (1940). In *Gobitis* the children of a family of Jehovah's Witnesses were expelled from school for failure to salute the flag. The Court, with Stone dissenting, upheld the constitutionality of the expulsion.

come to cases with a historical appreciation of the past, a political understanding of the present, and a vision of the future. Deference to the other branches of government was a critical component of this jurisprudence. In Frankfurter's view, a properly functioning democratic state achieved progress through experimentation. Fundamental principles, however, could not be sacrificed to the scientific method, and when the state appeared to deviate from important, commonly held precepts it was the task of the judiciary to bring it back on course. Flexibility was thus critical in permitting a general judicial deference while retaining the power, when necessary, for judicial review. In Frankfurter's jurisprudence, Thayer-like judicial deference to legislative will was not inconsistent with judicial enforcement of fundamental principles.

In *Gobitis*, Frankfurter's judicial role orientation controlled his personal, civil libertarian values. At the conference following oral argument, both Stone and Black passed, and the remainder of the Court unanimously affirmed the judgment below.[39] Black eventually joined Frankfurter's majority opinion, no doubt in part because of his respect for Hughes and Frankfurter.[40] Stone, however, never at ease with the majority position, ultimately chose to dissent. Because the opinion was so important to Frankfurter, he wrote Stone in an attempt to convince him to join the majority:

> But no one has more clearly in his mind than you, that even when it comes to these ultimate civil liberties, insofar as they are protected by the Constitution, we are not in the domain of absolutes. . . . But there is for me and I know also for you, a great makeweight for dealing with this problem, namely, that we are not the primary resolvers of the clash. We are not exercising an independent judgment; we are sitting in judgment upon the judgment of the legislature. I am aware of the important distinction which you so skillfully adumbrated in your footnote 4 (particularly the second paragraph of it) in the *Carolene Products Co.* case. I agree with that distinction; I regard it as basic. I have taken over that distinction in

39. Douglas docket book, 1939 Term, LC.

40. Hughes made an impassioned speech at conference reminding the Court that "we have no jurisdiction as to the wisdom of this" (Howard, *Mr. Justice Murphy*, p. 286). William O. Douglas recalled, "In those days, Felix Frankfurter was our [Black, Murphy, and Douglas] hero" *The Court Years* [New York: Random House, 1980], p. 44).

its central aspect, however inadequately in the present opinion by insisting on the importance of keeping all those channels of free expression by which undesirable legislation may be removed, and keeping unobstructed all forms of protest against what are deemed invasions of conscience, however much the invasion may be justified on the score of the deepest interests of national well-being.[41]

Stone, of course, was not relying upon paragraph two in his view of *Gobitis* but upon paragraphs one and three. Whatever significance Frankfurter attached to Stone's note, however, was based on paragraph two.[42] Frankfurter never considered the judiciary the primary protector of civil liberties in the United States; such a view would severely restrict the Court's flexibility. Immediately before his appointment to the Court, Frankfurter wrote Osmond Fraenkel, who had requested comments on an article he was preparing on the Court and civil liberties.

> You should stress more than you do and more concretely the very limited area of civil liberties which the Court could protect in behalf of minorities were it to be as liberal as you please in construing the bill of rights. They [Frankfurter's suggestions] are important not merely in securing a just estimate of the meagre record of the Supreme Court in safeguarding civil liberties but also in making abundantly clear that stout reliance for the maintenance and enlargement of civil liberties in this country must be looked to quite elsewhere and otherwise than in the protection of the Courts.[43]

This theme resounds through Frankfurter's correspondence as well as his public writings both before and after he came to the

41. FF to Stone, 5/27/40, FFLC 165-2197.

42. During oral argument, Frankfurter wrote to Murphy, "Is it at all probable that the framers . . . would have thought that a requirement to salute the flag violates the protection of 'the free exercise of religion'" (Howard, *Mr. Justice Murphy*, p. 250). Thus Frankfurter clearly questioned whether *Gobitis* raised an issue cognizable under paragraph one of the Stone note.

43. FF to Fraenkel, 4/2/37, FFLC 55-1046. Here I differ from Hirsch's position. Hirsch posits that although Frankfurter had a strong commitment to civil liberties during his pre-Court years, while on the Court, for essentially psychological reasons, he was moved to assume a position of deference regarding the Court and civil liberties. My position is that Frankfurter never had a strong commitment to *judicial* protection of civil liberties. Given Frankfurter's understanding of the polity, it was not contradictory to be both a civil libertarian and an advocate of judicial restraint (H. N. Hirsch, *The Enigma of Felix Frankfurter* [New York: Basic Books, 1981]).

Court.[44] Frankfurter was at once a civil libertarian and a firm be-
liever in judicial restraint. If the Court was to assume the primary
responsibility for protecting civil liberties in the United States, the
ability to weigh and balance, critical elements of judicial statesmanship would be lost. Although Frankfurter would later publicly
repudiate the *Carolene Products* note,[45] his statement to Stone regarding the note was not duplicitous. To the extent that the Stone
note merely called for heightened judicial sensitivity in reviewing
civil liberty claims, it was consistent with Frankfurter's jurisprudence. When, however, the emerging theory of "preferred freedoms" appeared to deny judicial flexibility and statesmanship in
personal freedom cases, it ran afoul of Frankfurter's most basic
understanding of the role of the Court.[46]

Frankfurter concluded his letter to Stone with a telling paragraph:

> For please bear in mind how very little this case authorizes and how
> wholly free it leaves us for the future. This is not a case where con-
> finement either of children or of parents is the consequence of
> nonconformity. It is not a case where conformity is exacted for
> something that you and I regard as foolish—namely, a gesture of
> respect for the symbol of our national being—even though we
> deem it foolish to exact it from Jehovah's Witnesses. It is not a case,
> for instance, of compelling children to partake in a school dance or
> other scholastic exercise that may run counter to this or that faith.
> And, above all, it is not a case where the slightest restriction is in-
> volved against the fullest opportunity to disavow—either on the
> part of the children or their parents—the meaning that ordinary
> people attach to the gesture of respect. The duty of compulsion be-

44. In 1950, for example, Frankfurter wrote Zechariah Chafee: "As for the
guardianship of 'the liberties of the people' the truth of the matter is that sometimes the odd man on this Court is more 'liberal' than Congress and sometimes less.
You are quite right in believing I am quite impenitent regarding my central philosophy on this subject. . . . Had you my experience on this Court I am not so sure
you would feel very differently from the way Mr. Jefferson or Holmes felt about
relying on the courts for our liberties. About one thing I could not be more clear,
namely, that reliance on the courts against the timidities and evasions of Congress
is not the way to further habits of responsibility or to bring home to the people
their own responsibility for a decent democratic society" (FF to Chafee, 6/19/50,
FFLC 42–750).

45. *Kovacs* v. *Cooper*, 336 U.S. 77 (1949) (dissenting opinion).

46. Frankfurter's view of the doctrine of preferred freedoms is discussed in
Chapter 5.

ing as minimal as it is for an act, the normal legislative authoriza-
tion of which cannot certainly be denied, and all channels of affirmative free expression being open to both children and parents, I
cannot resist the conviction that we ought to let the legislative judgment stand and put the responsibility for its exercise where it
belongs.[47]

If the judge was to be a statesman and more than merely the po-
liceman of the Constitution, such considerations became critical
elements of judicial review. The disinterested evaluation of these
and similar considerations, with due regard to American traditions and goals, was ultimately what separated Frankfurter in his
own mind from the Fieldian jurisprudence of an earlier age.
From this perspective, Frankfurter's opinion in *Gobitis* stands as
an important measure of his jurisprudence in action.[48] The
themes developed in *Gobitis*—the overriding significance of national unity as well as deference to elected branches of government—were, of course, critical components in his political vision.
As he acknowledged in his opinion, "no mere textual reading or
logical talisman"[49] could be the basis for deciding a case such as
Gobitis. To the judiciary fell the task of weighing and balancing
the competing values.

At the same time, *Gobitis* illustrated the impossible burden
assumed by Frankfurter. To avoid the apparent positivism of
Black's emerging philosophy while at the same time escaping the
pitfalls of the Fieldian era was Frankfurter's dilemma. Despite
constant reference to disinterested judgment, the Anglo-Ameri-

47. FF to Stone, 5/27/40, FFLC 165–2197.
48. Hirsch concludes that had Stone not been the protagonist and had the issue not been so starkly relevant to Frankfurter, "it is at least conceivable that
Frankfurter could have gone the other way" (*Enigma of Felix Frankfurter*, p.
151). Hirsch's point is that in *Gobitis* Frankfurter began to lock himself into a narrow theory of judicial review. Although it is, of course, "conceivable" that Frankfurter might have reached a different result, my point is that Frankfurter's role
conception was to maintain for judges maximum flexibility in decision making to
permit a careful balancing and consideration of the circumstances of each case.
The fact that *Gobitis* struck him in a particularly relevant way was not contrary to
the essence of his jurisprudence, particularly when he was voting to uphold the
decision of another branch of government. Neither the facts of *Gobitis* nor his relations with his brethren pushed Frankfurter any further than his view of the polity
and the role of judges had already taken him.
49. 310 U.S. at 596.

can tradition, the professionalism of judges, and faith in democracy, Frankfurter was never able to articulate a meaningful guide to his decision making. Following the second flag salute case,[50] Frankfurter wrote his friend C. C. Burlingame: "If I said that as a jew I know what religious and racial discrimination are and so am able to spot and declare unconstitutionality, *that* I would regard as bad. But to say with every predisposition to hold an act unconstitutional 'I couldn't do it because that's not my job—to translate my feelings into the Court,' that's something else, that's an emphatic way, a concrete way of putting what is a cardinal canon of constitutional adjudication."[51]

To prove himself capable of disinterested judgment became one of Frankfurter's primary tasks in the 1940s. But without an external standard to measure the application of disinterested judgment, it appeared to many observers to be dependent on personal value choices. As suggested earlier, Frankfurter's view of statesmanship and the judiciary called for judicial enforcement of principles that would aid a progressive society's attainment of shared goals. The determination of which principles were of sufficient primary importance to warrant judicial protection, however, often could not be explained convincingly as a disinterested determination. For example, in cases involving religious freedom, particularly the establishment clause of the First Amendment, the flexibility of Frankfurter's approach permitted him to substitute his judgment for legislative acts designed to foster religious diversity.[52] Frankfurter's rule of deference was often equally absent in cases involving the search and seizure provisions of the Fourth

50. *West Virginia Board of Education* v. *Barnette*, 319 U.S. 624 (1943), raised the same issue as *Gobitis*. Jackson wrote for the majority finding the compulsory flag salute unconstitutional with Black and Douglas filing a short statement explaining their switch from *Gobitis*. Frankfurter began his famous dissent: "One who belongs to the most vilified and persecuted minority in history is not likely to be insensible to the freedoms guaranteed by our Constitution. Were my purely personal attitude relevant, I should wholeheartedly associate myself with the general libertarian views in the Court's opinion, representing as they do the thought and action of a lifetime. But as judges we are neither Jew nor Gentile, neither Catholic nor agnostic."

51. FF to Burlingame, 8/27/43, FFLC 35–600.

52. See e.g., *Everson* v. *Board of Education*, 330 U.S. 1 (1974); *McCollum* v. *Board of Education*, 333 U.S. 203 (1948).

Amendment.[53] Despite long and often passionate attempts, Frankfurter was never able to articulate why his hierarchy of constitutional values, as opposed to that of his adversaries on the Court, was the product of disinterested judicial thought.[54]

Similar considerations compelled Frankfurter to a flexible reading of due process, independent of the Bill of Rights. His understanding of due process was founded on an image of judges as the quintessential experts, capable of understanding and discerning the core principles that united a progressive, democratic state. Although Frankfurter's correspondence with Black suggests a break over the interpretation of due process as early as 1939 and Black's unpublished dissent in *Bridges*[55] and his short dissent in *Betts* v. *Brady*[56] appeared to be further evidence of this break, through the 1941 term Black's interpretation of due process was at best unclear. *Chambers*, despite hints to the contrary, could be seen as consistent with the flexible due process approach. In two confession cases during the 1941 term, *Lisenba* v. *California*[57] and *Hysler* v. *Florida*,[58] Black appeared to confirm his allegiance to the flexible approach.

Four years after his trial and conviction, Hysler contended that

53. See, e.g., *Harris* v. *United States*, 381 U.S. 145 (1947); *United States* v. *Rabinowitz*, 339 U.S. 56 (1950).

54. Frankfurter never publicly admitted that a personal hierarachy of constitutional values was at work in his decision making. Indirectly, however, he did. In a letter to Justice Murphy, he wrote of the Fourth Amendment: "That provision of the Bill of Rights calls for more alert enforcement by this Court, not because it is more important say than the First Amendment but because it is much more likely to be lost in the shuffle. . . . Freedom of speech, of the press, of the exercise of religion, easily summon powerful support against encroachment. But the prohibition against unreasonable search and seizure is normally invoked by those accused of crime and criminals notoriously have few friends" (FF to Murphy, 2/15/47, FFLC 86-1765).

55. *Bridges* v. *California*, 314 U.S. 252 (1941), is discussed at some length in the following chapter.

56. *Betts* v. *Brady*, 316 U.S. 455 (1942), was a right to counsel case decided under the flexible due process approach. Black dissented, noting his belief that the Fourteenth Amendment made the right to counsel provision of the Sixth applicable to the states. During conference, Black raised the point that the Fourteenth incorporates all of the Bill of Rights. See Tinsley Yarborough, "Justice Black, the Fourteenth Amendment and Incorporation," 30 *University of Miami Law Review* 231 (1976).

57. 314 U.S. 219 (1941).

58. 315 U.S. 411 (1942).

the two principal witnesses against him had perjured themselves
as a result of police coercion. Despite the fact that one of the witnesses filed an affidavit to that effect, Florida denied Hysler *coram
nobis* relief. Writing for the Court, Frankfurter affirmed the action of the Florida courts. While agreeing that the knowing use of
perjured testimony violated due process, Frankfurter concluded
that the affidavits failed to establish a sufficiently strong case for
the Court to hold that Florida's denial of relief was itself a violation of due process. Black, joined by Douglas and Murphy, disagreed; it was clear to Black that Florida's position was that even
if Hysler's contentions were true, they did not constitute a violation of due process. In Black's view, the majority had retreated
from the mandate of *Chambers*. "Where as here allegations that
controlling testimony was extorted by third degree methods are
supported by statements and not denied by anyone, a summary
rejection of them without hearing by the court of first instance
would raise serious questions of compliance with the Constitutional requirements of a fair trial."[59]

Black's suggestion that the denial of a hearing on postconviction relief might offend the "fair trial" standard of due process is
striking for its distance from the formal, rigid standards associated with the incorporation theory. The Bill of Rights provides little that might pertain to coerced confessions by witnesses and
postconviction relief, and Black made no effort to construct an argument based on express constitutional provisions. In *Lisenba*,
Justice Roberts, despite evidence of prolonged interrogation and
the enforced absence of counsel, upheld a murder conviction because of a lack of evidence that the police illegalities had a coercive effect on the defendant and thus the introduction of his
statements did not result in fundamental unfairness. Black again
dissented, contending that the facts in *Lisenba* brought it within
the rule of *Chambers* even though the majority emphasized the
"coolness" and "acumen" of the accused. Significantly even in dissent, Black did not contend that the Constitution provided standards to govern police behavior exclusive of the impact on the defendant; nor did he rely on the Fifth Amendment's privilege

59. 315 U.S. at 425.

against self-incrimination or challenge the jurisprudential assumptions of the majority.

Although in *Chambers* and the following confession cases Black appeared to follow the premises of the fair trial approach, when challenged he vehemently denied that he adhered to this traditional notion of due process. In *Buchalter* v. *New York* the Court unanimously upheld the murder convictions of three notorious New York gangsters.[60] Their claim before the Court was founded on the unfair trial interpretation of due process; specifically, they contended that they had been denied due process because of unfair publicity about "Murder Inc." and that the prosecutor had intentionally scheduled their trial during his campaign for mayor. In conference, Frankfurter noted that Black "indicated in a subtle way that the mere presence of error in a criminal trial did not give rise to a federal claim. In a covered way he indicated his view that there can be no violation of due process unless there was a denial of one of the specific provisions of the bill of rights such as the privileges against self-incrimination, etc. etc."[61] At the same time, Frankfurter spoke of his own view of due process:

> It cannot be that a physically extorted confession would upset a conviction but a subtler way of framing a conviction by having the prosecution collaborate with the chief witness of the state in the giv-

60. 312 U.S. 780 (1943). The Court at first voted to deny certiorari with Frankfurter and Roberts wishing to hear the case and Murphy, Jackson, and Rutledge not participating. Roberts had suggested to Frankfurter that although no one error in the record constituted a violation of due process, taken as a whole, the record indicated a trial that did not measure up to due process, particularly in a capital case. On the appellants' petition for a rehearing of the certiorari denial, Frankfurter circulated a memo urging reconsideration, and at conference a dispute broke out when Roberts suggested that Frankfurter's memo might become a dissent to the denial of certiorari. Rutledge then cast a vote to hear the case. With three votes to hear the case, Douglas agreed to change his vote and certiorari was granted. Frankfurter records Black at the conference on the petition for rehearing as stating: "We should leave corrections of error to the state courts and not embark at large on such an unchartered sea as what is fair under the Due Process Clause. Due Process, for me, means the first nine amendments and nothing else" Memo regarding *Lepke* case, bound volume of drafts, FF HLSL, October Term 1942).

61. Joseph Lash, ed., *From the Diaries of Felix Frankfurter* (New York: Norton, 1975), p. 241.

ing of dishonest answers in a vital issue in the case, does not offend our fundamental sense of decency which is the essence of due process. This could only be on the assumption that we cannot trust five members of the highest court of the land to exercise a judgment of whether or not a thing does offend fundamental decency because that would vest too much discretion in a majority of the Court, who, one would suppose, are disciplined by the responsibility of their office and the great tradition of the history of this Court. Are we really prepared . . . to say we are morally impotent to apply due process as historically it has been applied and instead twist and contort in all sorts of funny ways other provisions of the Constitution to accomplish the same result, or at least results that sometimes are desired to be accomplished.[62]

Notwithstanding Frankfurter's often expressed assertion that his construction of the due process clause was founded upon "the glorious history of Anglo-American public law," a firmer basis lay in his belief that judges, as a trained elite, were capable of exercising power in a disinterested manner. Black's political instincts forced him into an opposing position, irrespective of his claims to historical verification. Thus at the very core of the due process debate were not simply differing views of history but two very different understandings of the American democratic tradition.

A few weeks after the commencement of the 1943 term, Frankfurter wrote Black a long letter concerning the problem of due process. In the letter, Frankfurter freely admitted that for years fluctuating majorities on the Court had differed over the meaning and scope of the Fourteenth Amendment. This was to be expected and not a difficulty as long as the members of the Court and the people were aware of the "narrow scope of the Court's power to strike down political action":

My starting point is, of course, the democratic faith on which this country is founded—the right of a democracy to make mistakes and correct its errors by the organs that reflect the popular will—which regards the Court as a qualification of the democratic principle and desire to restrict the play of this undemocratic feature to its narrowest limits. I am aware that men who have power can exercise and too often do—to enforce their own will, to make their will, or if you like their notions of policy, the measure of what

62. Ibid., pp. 242–243.

is right. But I am also aware of the forces of tradition and the habits of discipline whereby men entrusted with power remain within the limited framework of their professed power. More particularly, the history of this Court emboldens me to believe that men need not be supermen to observe the conditions under which judicial review of political authority—that's what judicial review of legislation really amounts to—is ultimately maintainable in a democratic society. When men who had such background and relation to so-called property interests as did, for instance, Waite, Bradley, Moody, Holmes, Brandeis and Cardozo, showed how scrupulously they did not write their private notions of policy into the Constitution, then I am not prepared to say that all that a court does when it adjudicates in these constitutional controversies is an elaborate pretense, and that judges do in fact merely translate their private convictions into decisions and call it the law and the Constitution.

I appreciate the frailties of men, but the War is for me meaningless and Hitler becomes the true prophet if there is no such thing as Law different and beyond the individuals who give it expression.[63]

It is difficult to conceive of any statement less likely to appeal to Black. On almost every level, Black's deepest convictions were contrary to those expressed by Frankfurter. Although for Black as well as Frankfurter, the starting point was a democratic faith, there was little in Black's experience or understanding of the polity which suggested to him that a small group of men could be trusted with power in the manner envisioned by Frankfurter. The suggestion that law existed apart from legislative power was foreign to Black; such a view called forth the Populist image of natural law as the means by which the few controlled the many. To accept Frankfurter's view of due process required Black to renounce his own democratic faith.

The result was that by the 1943 term, Black's approach to the confession cases changed. In a series of cases, *Ashcraft* v. *Tennessee*, *Feldman* v. *United States*, and *Lyons* v. *Oklahoma*,[64] Black sought to tie the result in *Chambers* to the Bill of Rights and, as such, narrowly constrict the sphere of judicial discretion associated with the confession cases. In *Ashcraft*, the conviction of an adult male was set aside because his confession had been secured after being

63. FF to HLB, 11/13/43, FF HLSL 169-2.
64. 322 U.S. 143 (1944); 322 U.S. 487 (1944); 322 U.S. 596 (1944).

questioned by a team of interrogators for thirty-six hours. Black, for the Court, held the confession inadmissible because such circumstances are "inherently coercive" despite the lack of any evidence suggesting physical brutality or special circumstances concerning the defendant. Citing *Chambers*, Black concluded that the Constitution stood "as a bar against conviction of any individual in an American Court by means of a coerced confession." Justice Robert Jackson, joined by Frankfurter, dissented, arguing that any interrogation is inherently coercive. They read *Chambers* as not establishing a hard and fast rule but rather demanding a case-by-case review of whether the interrogation prejudiced the defendant. By emphasizing the status of the defendants in *Chambers*, Black appeared to make each confession case turn on the particular traits of each defendant. *Ashcraft*, in effect, held that such a judgment was constitutionally unnecessary because there was, in the Constitution, a fixed standard to measure a confession irrespective of the nature of the interrogation or the circumstances of the defendant.

Feldman v. *United States* raised the difficult issue of whether testimony given in a state proceeding under a state statute granting immunity would be admissible against the witness in a subsequent federal action. Frankfurter, writing for the Court, held that it was admissible because the privilege against self-incrimination was not operative against the states and there was no suggestion that state officials had secured the testimony at the behest of federal officials. Black dissented not on the basis of "judicially defined concepts of procedural due process or upon judge made rules of evidence"[65] but because the Fifth Amendment governed the proceedings in both federal and state courts. What is striking is Black's dicta repudiating the notion of "judicially defined concepts of procedural due process." As his notes to *Chambers* illustrated, it was just this concept which formed the basis of that decision. A few days later the transformation of *Chambers* was completed. In *Lyons* v. *Oklahoma*, Justice Reed upheld the use of a confession because of a conflict of evidence on the issue of voluntariness. Frank Murphy, joined by Black, wrote in dissent: "Deci-

65. 322 U.S. at 495.

sions of this Court, in effect, have held that the 14th Amendment makes this prohibition [Fifth Amendment privilege against self-incrimination] applicable to the states [citing *Chambers*]."[66]

The Developing Conflict: *Malinski* and *Francis*

The confession cases decided at the end of the 1943 term represent an important turning point for Black. His decision four years earlier in *Chambers* had brought the issue of coerced confessions within the protection of due process through a historical examination of the framers' intent to ensure a fair trial evidenced by enactment of the Fifth Amendment. The linking of the due process clause in the Fourteenth Amendment to the same clause in the Fifth Amendment ensured a degree of flexibility in the Court's review of state criminal procedure.[67] By 1943, however, even "judicially defined concepts of procedural due process" ran afoul of Black's basic inclination to restrict the play of judicial judgment and discretion. The result was an ever-increasing attempt to tie decisions to specific constitutional provisions. Several years later, during the consideration of the *Adamson* case,[68] Justice Wiley Rutledge's clerk sent Rutledge a memo concerning a meeting with Black which illustrated his apparent change of position:

> The other day Black had lunch with the law clerks. We more or less subjected him to a cross-examination on his constitutional views, and the results were a little surprising. He stated, of course, that the bill of rights applies to the states, but he went further than that. He said that independent of the other provisions in the bill of rights, the due process clause in the 5th Amendment, and I assume also in the Fourteenth, had *no* meaning except that of emphasis. In short, Black would never hold that a trial or other proceeding was bad solely for want of process. He would have to find some other specific clause in the Constitution.[69]

66. 322 U.S. at 605.
67. Such an interpretation permitted the privileges or immunities clause to be the vehicle of incorporation. Although Black often spoke of the Fourteenth Amendment taken as a whole as incorporating the Bill of Rights, in *Jackson* v. *Denno*, 378 U.S. 369 (1963), he appeared to settle on privileges or immunities as the source of incorporation.
68. *Adamson* v. *California*, 332 U.S. 46 (1946), is discussed at length below.
69. Memo dated 5/28/47 in Rutledge LC 155.

Of course, the confession cases decided before the 1943 term were evidence of Black holding state criminal proceeding bad for "want of process." Although his later attempts to tie the confession cases to self-incrimination established a certain ideological consistency, they did so at the expense of the historic interpretation of self-incrimination.[70] In these early cases, Black had attempted to confine the flexible due process approach by limiting the scope of judgment to traditional notions of process. By the end of the 1943 term, his public position was that such an interpretation of due process was historically and theoretically unsound.

Between 1939 and 1943 Black and Frankfurter had become increasingly estranged on personal as well as philosophical grounds.[71] In 1940, at the time of *Gobitis*, Frankfurter was the leader of the "liberal" wing of the Court; his great professional prestige as well as his service in aid of liberal causes made him the natural choice. With his unpublished dissent in 1940 in *Bridges*, Black, with Douglas and Murphy, began to question Frankfurter's leadership. By 1942 with *Jones* v. *Opelika*[72] the estrangement was complete. During that period, as Frankfurter continually reminded Black that the task for judges in a democracy was judgment, Black increasingly sought to deny the exercise of that judgment.

In *Malinski* v. *New York*,[73] a complicated and difficult confes-

---

70. In Black's work papers in *Chambers* is a notation to the effect that Wigmore's *Treatise on Evidence* shows the confession rule not based on self-incrimination (HLBLC 256). Thus both the *Chambers* opinion and Black's work product indicate he did not believe the basis of the decision was the privilege against self-incrimination.

71. Although a good deal of this work is based on the belief that personality does not explain ideology, personality is an extremely useful tool in understanding the behavior and interaction of the justices. As Hirsch admirably documents, Frankfurter did not accept ideological differences easily; he constantly sought to "educate" Black to the correct position (*Enigma of Felix Frankfurter*, ch. 5). Although a personality study of Black is beyond the scope of this work, it is clear that he did not suffer these lessons very well. The result was that both men began to emphasize the differences in their approaches, thus making any reconciliation on a middle ground impossible.

72. 316 U.S. 584 (1942). In *Jones* the Court upheld the power of municipalities to tax the sale of literature by Jehovah's Witnesses. Black, Douglas, and Murphy used the case as an opportunity to announce that they had changed their views since *Gobitis* and were prepared to overrule that decision.

73. 324 U.S. 401 (1945).

sion case, the full breadth of the due process debate almost broke into the open. Malinski, with two accomplices, had been convicted of the murder of a police officer. After being arrested, Malinski was taken by the police to a hotel room, where he was stripped naked and confessed. A few days later he confessed a second time. A five-man majority of the Court concluded that the first confession was coerced and thus tainted the conviction. The case was complicated because a co-defendant, one Rudish, was tried with Malinski, and three members of the majority—Douglas, Black, and Frankfurter—found that the use of Malinski's first confession did not prejudice the conviction of Rudish. The result was a 5–4 vote overturning Malinski's conviction and a 7–2 vote affirming Rudish's. Only Rutledge and Murphy voted to reverse both convictions.

Douglas's initial opinion for the Court was to affirm both convictions on the basis that the second uncoerced confession was independent of the first. Black immediately noted his dissent and Frankfurter, at least disposed to find for Malinski, dashed off a note to Douglas: "I think the requirements of 'due process' are an independent constitutional demand and not merely the compendious statement of some of the specific 'ten amendments.' Therefore, for me, the prosecutor's performance and general conduct of a trial may offend, for me, 'due process' even without my considering that such incidents help establish self-incrimination."[74] Douglas soon agreed to change his position, and Black and Frankfurter expressed approval.[75] When Black noted his agreement with Douglas's disposition of the case, he wrote: "Will discuss with you later whether or not I should in this case add the short paragraph about which I talked to you."[76] Although Black never wrote in *Malinski*, it is probable that the content of this proposed paragraph was reflected in a memo later circulated to the Court:

74. FF to Douglas, Douglas LC 104.

75. With respect to Malinski, Douglas concluded that the admission of the first coerced confession tainted the trial. Before he agreed to this change, however, he wrote a note to Rutledge stating that he had searched the record for any evidence of the third degree following the first confession: "I searched the record in vain for it. Malinski's examination by his lawyers failed to produce it. I do not think we can fill it in from the void unless we are to say that illegal detention without more will be presumed to produce an 'inquisition.' We passed that point in Lisenba where I dissented" (Douglas to Rutledge, 1/23/45, Rutledge LC 117).

76. HLB to Douglas, 2/9/45 Douglas LC 274.

Mr. Justice Frankfurter has filed a concurring opinion which con-
strues the Due Process Clause as authorizing this Court to invali-
date state action on the ground of a belief that the state action fails
to set "civilized standards." This seems to me a restoration of the
natural law concept whereby the supreme constitutional law becomes this Court's view of "civilization" at a given moment. Five
members of this Court . . . have expressed their assent to this interpretation of the Due Process Clause.

I disagree with that interpretation. Due Process, thus construed,
seems to me to make the constitution mere surplusage. This Due
Process Interpretation permits the Court to reject all of these provisions of the Bill of Rights, and to substitute its own ideas of what
legislatures can and cannot do. In the past, this broad judicial
power has been used to preserve the economic status quo and to
block legislative efforts to cure its existing evils. At the same time
the court has only grudgingly read into "civilized standards" the
safeguards to individual liberty set out in the Bill of Rights. While
the case under consideration unquestionably involves the admissibility of compelled testimony, the concurring opinion is careful to
point out that this question must not be resolved by reliance upon
the constitutional prohibition against compelled testimony.[77]

Three days after Black's memo was circulated, Frankfurter responded by noting an addition to his *Malinski* concurrence:

In the Bill of Rights, Eighteenth century statesmen formulated
safeguards against the recurrence of well-defined historic griev-
ances. Some of these safeguards, such as the right to trial by a jury
of twelve and immunity from prosecution unless initiated by a
grand jury were built on experience of relative and limited validity.
. . . Others like freedom of the press or the free exercise of religion
or freedom from condemnation without a fair trial, express rights
the denial of which is repugnant to the conscience of a free
people.[78]

The issue was thus joined. Although Douglas's majority opinion
carefully avoided any controversy on the due process issue,
Frankfurter used his *Malinski* opinion as the vehicle for expressing his view of the Fourteenth Amendment, and the themes

77. Memo dated 3/23/45, FFLC 218-4022.
78. A copy of Frankfurter's Memorandum for the Conference, 3/26/45, is in
Stone LC 72.

presented—the inconsistency of the incorporation approach, the feat of straitjacketing state attempts at innovation in criminal procedure, the inescapable necessity of judgment in due process cases—were themes he would reiterate ceaselessly in the ensuing years. Continually he would remind his audience that the issue was not whether the record indicated a technical violation of one of the provisions of the Bill of Rights but rather whether the proceedings, taken as a whole, violated "those canons of justice of English speaking people."[79] When rightly understood, the judgment required by due process was not based upon the "idiosyncracies of merely personal judgment."[80] Frankfurter's political vision called for leadership by elites whose training and background instilled in them an understanding and appreciation of fundamental goals that served to unite the modern state. A similar understanding powered his view of the role of judges. What differentiated elites from masses was primarily a greater understanding of democratic principles; a similar understanding limited the subjectivity and discretion of judges. Nevertheless, as Frankfurter increasingly sought to separate due process from the text of the Constitution, he removed from due process analysis the one objective standard by which judges could structure their "disinterested" analysis of the core principles that united the American polity. Notwithstanding his protests to the contrary, Frankfurter's analysis appeared to leave judges with only their subjective understanding of what was fair and just; as he noted in *Malinski*: "These standards of decency are not authoritatively formulated anywhere."[81]

The debate over the judicial role and its impact on decision making appeared to reach its zenith during the 1946 term. In *Louisiana ex rel Francis* v. *Resweber*, Willie Francis, a young black man, was convicted of murder and sentenced to death.[82] At the moment of electrocution, the electric chair malfunctioned, and the issue before the Court was whether it was a denial of due process for Louisiana to attempt to execute Francis a second time.

79. 324 U.S. at 416, 417.
80. 324 U.S. at 417.
81. Ibid.
82. 329 U.S. 459 (1947).

As Frankfurter noted at conference, this was "not an easy case."[83] The initial vote was 6–3 to permit reexecution with Frankfurter and Black in the majority.[84] During the conference, Frankfurter warned against considering the case against the "technicalities" of double jeopardy and cruel and unusual punishment. The case must be viewed in light of current community standards; as Douglas recorded Frankfurter's words: "Though it is hardly a defensible thing for the state to do, it is not so offensive as to make him puke. Does not shock conscience."[85]

Frankfurter's initial reaction to *Francis* reveals much of the internal constraints his role conception of the judiciary envisioned. He had long opposed the practice of capital punishment, and yet he openly acknowledged that, at least in his view, opposition to capital punishment did not rest upon a principle indispensable to the operation of a modern, progressive state. When Justice Harold H. Burton, who had originally opposed hearing the *Francis* case, drafted a powerful dissent, Frankfurter wrote him:

> I read your opinion in the Willie Francis case and have reflected upon it with sympathy. I have to hold on to myself not to reach your result. I am prevented from doing so only by the disciplined thinking of a lifetime regarding the duty of this Court. . . . Holmes used to express it by saying he would not strike down state action unless the action of the state made him "puke." I have tried to express in more elegant but more ponderous terms the extremely limited nullifying power of the Court vis-a-vis state action in what I wrote in Malinski. . . .
>
> And that being so, I cannot say it so shocks the accepted, prevailing standards of fairness not to allow the state to electrocute . . . that we, as this Court, must enforce that standard by invocation of the Due Process Clause. . . . And when I have that much doubt I must, according to my view of the Court's duty give the state the benefit of the doubt and let the state action prevail."[86]

In Frankfurter's view of Court and society, there were certain core values vital to the development of a progressive people. Fur-

83. Douglas LC 189.
84. Douglas later joined Burton's dissent, making the final tally 5–4.
85. Douglas LC 189.
86. FF to Burton, 12/13/46, Burton LC 171.

thermore, the affairs of state, particularly law enforcement, had to be conducted in a civilized manner. Judgment on such matters ultimately rested with the judiciary, and Willie Francis faced execution because his cause failed to trigger one of the justifications for judicial review.[87] In this sense, Frankfurter's deliberative process did serve as a constraint on the imposition of personal values for in voting to uphold the Louisiana courts, Frankfurter was leaving a closely held personal preference—opposition to capital punishment—to the vagaries of the political process. In another sense, however, Frankfurter's efforts in *Francis* were unsatisfactory because of his inability to articulate meaningful guides for judges in measuring and enforcing community standards and values. Later he wrote to Learned Hand:

> To what extent may a judge assume that his own notions of right moral standards are those of the community? But if it is his job—as you and I believe it to be—to divine what rightly may be the standards of the community by what process is he to make that divination? How and where should he look for the disclosure of the community's mores? I struggled with that problem last year in the Willie Francis case—for I personally deemed it shocking that a state should insist for a second go for a pound of flesh, but I felt confident that while for me it was a barbaric thing to do, that would not be the feeling of the community whether the community be Louisiana or the United States at large—and that, therefore, I had no right to find a violation of the Due Process Clause.[88]

Amid the flurry of opinion writing was a draft of a concurring opinion by Black:

87. For an example of a case that did trigger judicial review, see *Sweezy* v. *New Hampshire*, 354 U.S. 234 (1957), detailed in Chapter 5. In *Rochin* v. *California*, 342 U.S. 165 (1952), the stomach pump case, Frankfurter overcame his reluctance announced in *Wolf* v. *Colorado*, 338 U.S. 25 (1949), to exclude from state proceedings illegally seized evidence. Douglas's conference notes in *Rochin* record that Frankfurter stated that the means of securing the evidence—the pumping of a suspect's stomach—made him "puke." *Rochin* did touch on a fundamental moral choice of the community—the right to privacy Frankfurter found in the Fourth Amendment—and the state's role was not an innocent error but overzealous police behavior. In *Francis*, a fundamental moral choice of the community was not involved and the error was innocent and capable of correction at the executive level. When Frankfurter's visceral reaction coincided with what he believed to be a value of the community, the case was appropriate for judicial review.

88. FF to Hand, 12/6/47, FFLC 64-1239.

I think there is ample support for holding that the Fourteenth
Amendment was intended to and does prohibit states from legal-
izing double jeopardy and cruel and unusual punishment to the
same extent as the Fifth and Eighth Amendments prohibit federal
laws of that kind. But I do not reach that conclusion with reference
to a mystical natural law which is above and beyond the Constitution, and which is read into the due process clause so as to authorize us to strike down every state law which we think is "indecent,"
"contrary to civilized standards," or offensive to our notions of
"fundamental justice."[89]

Black's unpublished concurring opinion in *Francis* foreshadowed
much of what was to come later that term in his famous *Adamson*
dissent. In *Francis*, he began his historical defense of the incorporation position, citing Harry Flack's *The Adoption of the Fourteenth
Amendment* and material from the congressional debates on the
passage of the amendment to prove that the purpose of the
amendment was "to protect all persons from state invasions of the
freedoms guaranteed by the Bill of Rights." He argued that the
flexible approach to due process ultimately left judges without
guidance requiring that they "measure the validity of every state
and federal criminal law by our conception of national 'standards
of decency' without the guidance of constitutional language. . . .
Adoption of one or the other conflicting views as to what is 'decent,' what is right, and what is best for the people, is generally
recognized as a legislative function."[90]

One idea that was present in *Francis* did not explicitly appear in
Adamson. At the outset of the opinion, Black wrote: "Since there is
no contention in this case that petitioner has been denied procedural due process [citing *Chambers*] it is my view, for reasons here-
inafter discussed, that the only basis for decision should be
whether the Eighth Amendment . . . and the Fifth Amendment . . .
have been made applicable to the states and, if so, whether Louisiana's execution of the petitioner would violate either one of
them."[91] In *Francis*, Black returned to the assertion that *Chambers*
rested on procedural grounds other than the privilege against
self-incrimination. But the opinion in *Francis* was never pub-

89. See copy in Rutledge LC 147.
90. Ibid.
91. Ibid.

lished.[92] When Justice Reed agreed to several modifications in his majority opinion, Black joined the opinion. Reed assumed that the double jeopardy provision of the Fifth Amendment and the cruel and unusual punishment provision of the Eighth Amendment governed the case but found no violation of either constitutional safeguard. Reed's willingness to find in the text of the Constitution the principles that controlled the case resulted in the defection of Frankfurter. "In order that there be an opinion of the Court," he wrote in a memorandum,

> I had hoped to join brother Reed's opinion in addition to expressing my own views. The reason I cannot do so, inter alia, is that I do not think we should decide the case even on the assumption that the Fifth Amendment as to double jeopardy is the measure of due process in the Fourteenth Amendment. I do not see why we should make an assumption which is contrary to the whole tenor of [*Palko*]. It makes for nothing but confusion in the consideration of constitutional cases under the Due Process Clause to cite cases that construe the scope of the double jeopardy provision of the Fifth Amendment.[93]

The result was a new concurring opinion by Frankfurter, emphasizing the independence of the Fourteenth Amendment from the Bill of Rights. But in divorcing his analysis from the constitutional text, Frankfurter was left with little save for intuitive assumptions concerning society's response to the issues posed by *Francis*: "I cannot rid myself of the conviction that were I to hold that Louisiana would transgress the due process clause if the state were allowed, in the precise circumstances before us, to carry out the death sentence, I would be enforcing my private view rather than the consensus of society's opinion, which for purposes of due process, is the standard enjoined by the Court."[94]

Francis became for Frankfurter the symbol of his capacity for disinterested judgment. Certainly he was personally disturbed by

---

92. Black apparently never wrote why he did not publish the *Francis* opinion. His important allies, Murphy, Rutledge, and Douglas, were clearly moved by the facts and prepared to dissent. Perhaps because these men, in general sympathetic to Black's view of due process, were in dissent, Black chose to withhold his public defense of incorporation.

93. Memo dated 1/11/47. A copy is in Rutledge LC 147.

94. 329 U.S. at 471.

the facts; he contacted friends in Louisiana in an attempt to secure clemency.[95] Ultimately, however, Francis was executed and
that execution symbolized the vagaries of the flexible due process
approach employed by Frankfurter. By refusing to consider the
values in the Fifth and Eighth Amendments, Frankfurter had di-
vorced himself from the single objective criteria for measuring
the moral choices of the community relevant to the case. By removing the Eighth Amendment from the case, he was free to
frame the issue to be the constitutionality of leaving the decision
concerning clemency to the executive branch of Louisiana, thus
avoiding any meaningful analysis of the issues presented by *Francis* and, in effect, preordaining a conclusion of judicial deference.[96] In striving to distance himself from Black, Frankfurter's
due process analysis appeared increasingly dependent upon idio-
syncratic personal judgment. Yet in his own mind, *Francis* represented the highest form of judicial statesmanship. His role orientation and the process of decision making on which it rested had
severely restricted the operation of his personal value choices in
Francis. Nevertheless, unable to articulate objective criteria for determining the moral sentiments of the community and unwilling
to concede relevance to the constitutional text, Frankfurter was
left with the apparent task of weighing imponderables.

Adamson v. California

Several weeks after *Francis*, the Court announced its
decision in *Adamson* v. *California*,[97] and the depth of the conflict
over the meaning of the Fourteenth Amendment, hitherto largely
limited to the confines of the Court, was presented for public

95. Frankfurter wrote Monte Lehman, a friend and member of the Louisiana
bar, in an attempt to organize support for clemency. He concluded the letter:
"This cause has been so heavily on my conscience that I finally could not overcome
the impulse to write to you. It is difficult for me to believe that clemency would
not be forthcoming whatever may be the machinery of your state for its exercise if
leading members of the bar pressed upon the authorities that even to err on the
side of humaneness in the *Francis* situation can do no possible harm and might
strengthen the forces of good will, compassion and wisdom in society." Frankfurter circulated a copy of the letter to members of the Court. A copy is in Burton
LC 336.
96. See R. Danzig, "How Questions Begot Answers in Felix Frankfurter's First
Flag Salute Opinion," *Supreme Court Review* 27 (1977).
97. 332 U.S. 46 (1947).

view. *Adamson* was a classic case for such a confrontation because it raised the precise issue decided by the Court forty years earlier in *Twining* v. *New Jersey* under the flexible approach.[98] Adamson had been convicted of first degree murder by a California jury. A state statute permitted the prosecution and the trial judge to comment on a defendant's failure to testify and the jury to consider in its deliberations the defendant's failure to explain the evidence against him. Adamson was presented with a difficult choice: to refuse to testify and permit the jury to draw harmful inferences or to testify and give the prosecution the opportunity on cross-examination to bring to the attention of the jury his substantial prior criminal record. Adamson chose not to testify and then challenged his conviction before the Supreme Court on the grounds that the California procedures violated the protections of the Fourteenth Amendment.

At the conference following oral argument, Black's vote was a "pass." Douglas's conference notes show that Black thought the Fifth Amendment applicable under "either *Twining* approach or other approach" but questioned whether the California procedure violated the privilege against self-incrimination. Frankfurter found *Twining* "cloudless" and voted to affirm on that basis. Reed, to whom the opinion was assigned, assumed the Fifth Amendment applicable but found no violation.[99]

Reed's majority opinion, however, did not reflect his position at the conference. Now willing to assume that the California procedure would violate the privileges against self-incrimination found in the Fifth Amendment, Reed affirmed on two different grounds. Relying upon *Palko* and *Twining* as well as the *Slaughterhouse* case, Reed held that the privilege against self-incrimination was not a privilege or immunity of national citizenship guaranteed by the Fourteenth Amendment. Furthermore, although he conceded that the due process clause guaranteed a fair trial,

98. 211 U.S. 78 (1908). *Twining* was a challenge to a New Jersey statute that permitted prosecutors to comment upon and jurors to consider an accused's failure to testify on his own behalf on the ground that the statute violated the accused's privilege against self-incrimination. Justice Moody, for the Court, denied the claim while Justice Harlan dissented, contending that the Fourteenth Amendment made the provisions of the Bill of Rights binding on the states.

99. Douglas LC 217.

Reed, employing the "concepts of ordered liberty" test of *Palko*, held that the privilege, under the circumstances presented, was not a fundamental principle inherent in due process.

Reed's new approach was at least in part attributable to Frankfurter. During the consideration of the case, Frankfurter wrote Reed: "I am not unappreciative of the extent to which you have hewn to what I deem the right lines in the *Adamson* case. But for reasons I cannot hope will commend themselves to you, I deem it important to underline the *Twining* case by deciding the *Adamson* case upon it without further discussion. I deem it all the more important, because, I assume there will be a dissent."[100] Frankfurter hoped to dispose of *Adamson* on the basis of *Twining*, and thus he wrote a two-paragraph concurring statement to the effect that *Twining* represented Supreme Court decision making at its best and should not be "diluted, even unwittingly, either in its judicial philosophy or its particulars."[101] Frankfurter's uncritical acceptance of *Twining* was an important element in his analysis of *Adamson*. A year earlier, when the petition for certiorari in *Adamson* was pending, Frankfurter wrote to Justice Burton: "Twining v. NJ is in my opinion one of the truly great decisions of the Court in modern times."[102] In his zeal to protect the integrity of the reasoning behind *Twining*, Frankfurter undercut one of the principal tenets of the flexible approach. If due process was to be a continual process of inclusion and exclusion dependent upon the underlying mores of the community, then simply relying upon a forty-year-old precedent was to straitjacket the community's development in much the same way as did the incorporation approach.

Ultimately Frankfurter was moved to write a more substantial concurring opinion reflecting much of what he said in *Malinski*, and unquestionably Black was the catalyst. Reed's assumption that the California procedure would violate the Fifth Amendment freed Black of his principal doubt in the case. The result was that *Adamson* became the jurisprudential statement he had hinted at in

100. FF to Reed, 3/27/47, FF HLSL 170-8.
101. A copy is in HLBLC 284. In effect, the original opinion constitutes the first two paragraphs of the published concurring opinion.
102. FF to Burton, 6/1/46, Burton LC 336.

Malinski and *Francis*. Drawing extensively upon the congressional debates during the passage of the Fourteenth Amendment, Black set forth at length his historical argument that the framers of the Fourteenth Amendment intended to extend the safeguards of the Bill of Rights to the citizens of the several states. He attacked the early flexible due process cases—particularly *Twining*—because this historical evidence had not been brought to the attention of the Court. Echoing his memorandum in *Malinski*, he attacked the flexible approach as an "incongrous excrescence on our Constitution." There was, Black asserted, a distinct difference between "looking to the particular standards enumerated in the Bill of Rights and other parts of the Constitution," as he asserted he had done in *Chambers*, and the "application of 'natural law' deemed to be above and undefined by the Constitution." In language reflecting the political vision that stood at the foundation of his judicial philosophy, he wrote:

> I cannot consider the Bill of Rights to be an outworn 18th century "straight jacket" as the *Twining* opinion did. Its provisions may be thought outdated abstractions by some. And it is true they were designed to meet ancient evils. But they are the same kind of human evils that have emerged from century to century wherever excessive power is sought by the few at the expense of the many. In my judgment the people of no nation can lose their liberty so long as a Bill of Rights like ours survives and its basic purposes are conscientiously interpreted, enforced and respected so as to afford continuous protection against old, as well as new, devices and practices which might thwart those purposes.[103]

Adamson has come to be viewed as the quintessential statement of Black's constitutional jurisprudence, and during his lifetime he did nothing to dispel that notion. With *Chambers* and its progeny tied to the letter of the Fifth Amendment, Black's dissent appeared to stand for the proposition that due process in the Fourteenth Amendment meant no more nor no less than the Bill of Rights. Clearly, Justice Murphy, Black's longtime ally on the Court, so read the opinion. Moved to dissent separately, Murphy wrote in his first draft:

103. 332 U.S. at 89, 91.

I agree that the specific guarantees of the Bill of Rights should be carried over intact into the due process clause of the Fourteenth Amendment. But I am not prepared to say that the due process clause is limited by the Bill of Rights. Occasions may arise where a proceeding falls so far short of "conforming to fundamental standards of procedure" [citing *Chambers*] as to warrant constitutional condemnation in terms of lack of due process despite the absence of a specific provision in the Bill of Rights.[104]

When Murphy asked Black for his thoughts on this draft, Black responded:

I think coerced confessions are barred by specific provisions of the Fifth Amendment, as we held in *Ashcraft* following Bram v. U.S. Your opinion indicates that to bar confessions you must go beyond Fifth Amendment. You reserve the point as to whether procedural due process may go beyond the specific prohibitions of the Bill of Rights and in so doing you imply that my opinion has stated the contrary. I have not intended to say that in the *Adamson* opinion, so far as procedural due process is concerned. In other words, I have not attempted to tie procedural due process exclusively to the Bill of Rights. In fact there are other Constitutional prohibitions relating to procedure which I think due process requires to be observed.[105]

Black was, perhaps, drawing a distinction without a difference and avoiding the issue posed by Murphy's dissent. Whether procedural due process is limited to the Bill of Rights or, in addition, includes the relatively few other procedural protections found in the text of the Constitution is, at best, an academic point. The point raised by Murphy, and by Stone years earlier in his *Carolene Products* note, was whether a progressive society might require additional procedural safeguards which, although consistent with the general intent of the framers, could not be linked directly to the constitutional text. In his notes to *Chambers*, Black had employed the text of the Constitution as an indicator of the framers' intent to ensure a fair trial and, armed with this intent, proceeded to find in the Fourteenth Amendment procedural safeguards not

104. HLBLC 284.
105. My thanks to J. Woodford Howard of Johns Hopkins University for bringing these papers from the Murphy collection to my attention. See also Howard, *Mr. Justice Murphy*, pp. 439–443.

contained in the text of the document. His *Adamson* dissent, however, appeared to make the text of the Constitution (and despite
Black's contentions to the contrary, the Bill of Rights) the precise
measure of due process and the Fourteenth Amendment.

Just as the influence of Black had forced Frankfurter to cast his
judicial philosophy so as to maximize the distinctions from the incorporation approach, so, too, did the influence of Frankfurter
work on Black. Coming to the Court with a basic distrust of
judges and judicial review, Black had sought to minimize the element of judgment in constitutional decision making. His opinions
in *Chambers* and the early confession cases were consistent with this
impulse. At the same time, these cases illustrate that Black could
not, and did not, intend to eliminate judgment. Due process did
have an independent meaning for Black, and within the admit-
tedly narrow confines of procedural safeguards, judicial reason
and discretion were integral elements of due process. As the debate with Frankfurter grew in intensity, Black denied even this
minimal but significant aspect of judicial lawmaking. His note to
Murphy concluded with the observation that Murphy's use of the
Chambers opinion suggested that Black had employed the "fundamental justice" standard of *Twining* and *Hurtado* in that case. "I do
not think," Black added, "that the Chambers' opinion supports the
implication in your dissent." As a result of Black's note, Murphy
deleted all references to *Chambers* and due process from his dissent. On the back of the Black note, Murphy wrote to his law clerk:
"It is hard for me to agree with all that Hugo writes. He may be
right but I doubt it."[106]

Aftermath

Throughout this chapter I have tried to illustrate the
extent to which concepts of judicial role shaped the responses of
Hugo Black and Felix Frankfurter to the problems posed by the
due process cases. The task for each man during his early years
on the Court was to fashion a judicial method consistent with the
demands of these concepts of role. One demand, hardly unique,
was that of judicial restraint, and both Black and Frankfurter en-
deavored to restrict the impact of personal attitudes and values

106. Ibid.

on votes. To a degree perhaps unappreciated by those who simply study votes and not process, they succeeded. An understanding of judicial values and attitudes, taken alone, would have served little use in predicting the outcome in *Francis*; in a macabre way, the literalism of Black and the flexibility of Frankfurter were vindicated by the vote in *Francis*.

It is, however, perhaps the essential paradox of the judiciary in America that although a firmly developed process of decision making may spare votes from the vagaries of individual value preferences, that very process and the conceptions of judicial role on which it is based are themselves the product of personalized values and attitudes. Despite the continued attempts of both Frankfurter and Black to justify their "methods" in history and precedent, their conceptions of judicial role were the product of neither historical research nor legal theory but of individualized beliefs concerning the nature of the polity and American constitutional democracy.

In the intense intellectual atmosphere of the Supreme Court, differences in role orientation do not go unchallenged. Although Frankfurter and Black came to the Court with divergent views of the polity, the dynamics of their relationship on the Court resulted in each construing his judicial method in a manner intended to increase rather than decrease the distance from the other. Thus as Black increasingly sought in the constitutional text the solution to the problem of due process, Frankfurter seemingly denied the relevance of that text. The result was that common ground was obscured and the intensity of the debate heightened.

The years following *Adamson* evidence the continuation of these themes. Repudiation of the incorporation position became, for Frankfurter, almost a religious crusade.[107] Judgment in due process cases was inescapable, and the truly disinterested jurist was capable of understanding the subconscious factors at work in any

107. In *Bartkus* v. *Illinois*, 359 U.S. 121 (1959), for example, Bartkus was first tried for bank robbery and acquitted in a federal court. He was then tried on the same facts and convicted in a state court. For a five-man majority, Frankfurter affirmed the state court conviction, rejecting Bartkus's double jeopardy claim. Black was in dissent. During discussion of the case among the majority, Frankfurter urged a strong statement finally putting the incorporation theory to rest. Justice Clark thought that tactic unnecessary, and Frankfurter sought to change his think-

exercise of judgment. In *Haley* v. *Ohio*, the issue was whether the Fourteenth Amendment permitted the use of a confession secured from a fifteen-year-old black after hours of interrogation in which the prisoner was not permitted to see a lawyer, friends, or relatives.[108] In a 5–4 decision overturning Haley's murder conviction, Frankfurter cast the deciding vote. In a separate concurring opinion, Frankfurter wrote of the "humility" keyed to "an alert self-scrutiny so as to avoid infusing into the vagueness of a Constitutional command one's merely private notions."

> It would hardly be a justifiable exercise of judicial power to dispose of this case by finding in the Due Process Clause Constitutional outlawry of the admissibility of all private statements made by an accused to a police officer, however much legislation to that effect might seem to me wise. . . . But whether a confession of a lad of fifteen is "voluntary" . . . or "coerced" . . . is not a matter of mathematical determination. Essentially it invites psychological judgment—a psychological judgment that reflects deep, even if inarticulate, feelings of our society. Judges must divine that feeling as best they can from all the relevant evidence . . . and with every endeavor to detach themselves from their merely private views.[109]

It would be a serious mistake to view such statements by Frankfurter as a public masquerade intended to obscure the imposition of personal values upon judicial votes. Only when Frankfurter was satisfied that a deeply felt personal value was consistent with a fundamental moral choice of the community was he willing to exercise the power of judicial review. (Conversely, one searches in vain for an instance when Frankfurter exercised that power to further a community value he did not share.) Hence Frankfurter found in his judicial method a means for developing an understanding of the impact of personal feelings upon decision making. Immediately after the decision in *Haley*, Frankfurter wrote Reed:

---

ing through a series of notes and memos. Finally Clark capitulated and wrote Frankfurter: "Your present plea to lay to rest the 'incorporation' theory weighs heavy with me. I shall reluctantly join although I do feel it unnecessary to the decision, especially since Hugo barely touches on it. But as I say your plea turns the balance" (Clark to FF, 2/24/59, FF HLSL 107-10).

108. 332 U.S. 596 (1947).

109. 332 U.S. at 603.

"I repeat my suggestion to you that you try your hand, for the sake of your own intellectual conscience, at answering the analysis of the *Haley* case. I am not talking about the result, but I am talking about the true factors that underlie the determination of 'due process' in such a situation."[110]

In *Haley*, Douglas wrote for the Court reversing the conviction. On the back of Douglas's circulation, Black wrote: "This is good writing and I agree. The use of 'standards of decency' is necessary, I suppose, to get our majority. Perhaps previous protests against its use carry over here, at least I intend for them to. But we have been outvoted and for the time being, at least in this case, acquiescence seems to be the better course. My underlying reason here as in other cases is that the defendant was compelled to give evidence against himself."[111]

Although *Adamson* was Black's most eloquent defense of the incorporation theory, it did not present an entirely accurate picture of his jurisprudence. Despite his disclaimers to Murphy, clearly both Murphy and Rutledge read the *Adamson* dissent as attaching to due process a meaning no more nor no less than the provisions of the Bill of Rights. Indeed, during the 1940s Black did little to dispel that impression as he constantly sought to tie *Chambers* and the early confession cases to the privilege against self-incrimination found in the Fifth Amendment. But, as the cases following *Adamson* suggest, the notes to *Chambers* were an amazingly accurate prediction of Black's view of due process. Although Black joined with the gradual process of selective incorporation of the Bill of Rights—a process that gathered momentum following Justice Frankfurter's retirement—at the same time he was hardly reticent about finding in due process procedural guarantees not explicitly found in the text of the document. Thus he concluded that due process was violated by vague and indefinite statutes,[112] by a conviction without evidence,[113] and by judgment rendered by a judge who had an interest in the outcome of the case.[114]

110. FF to Reed, 1/17/48, FFLC 93-1926.
111. Douglas LC 138.
112. *Edelman* v. *California*, 344 U.S. 357 (1953).
113. *Thompson* v. *Louisville*, 362 U.S. 199 (1960).
114. *In re Murchison*, 349 U.S. 133 (1955).

Hence due process for Black, as for Frankfurter, did have a content independent of the provisions of the Bill of Rights. As Frankfurter sought to free due process (and judges) from the confines of the constitutional text, Black found in the text and the intent of the framers the limits to judicial decision making. Judgment was an inescapable factor in due process adjudications, but the judgment employed by Black was substantially different from that used by Frankfurter. At the heart of this difference was not simply diverse understandings of history and precedent but a fundamental disagreement over the nature and role of judges within the political system. As such, the dispute was not limited to due process; it formed the nucleus of their judicial lives and would dictate their responses to a broad range of cases and issues.

5 From *Bridges* to *Dennis*: Free Expression and the Needs of a Democratic State

> It is therefore sufficient to test the constitutionality of this statute by comparing it with the literal language of the First Amendment.
>
> Hugo Black, unpublished concurring opinion, *Cox* v. *New Hampshire*, 1941

> Not every type of speech occupies the same position on the scale of values.
>
> Felix Frankfurter, concurring in *Dennis* v. *United States*, 1951

The numerical position of the First Amendment is indicative of its significance in the development of American political and social thought. The freedoms enumerated in that amendment represent certain core values of the American polity; elites as well as masses easily proclaim the sanctity and importance of freedom of speech and conscience in the nation's political system. This allegiance is, of course, to an abstract ideal; in practice the protection of these freedoms has varied with the temper and passions of the times. Nevertheless, the abstraction has almost universal appeal. Judges, for example, inevitably couple a decision upholding restrictions on free expression with a passionate, if abstract, statement of the importance of the First Amendment to a free society.[1]

Upon initial examination this universal acceptance of the ideal of free expression is hardly surprising for it finds support in both the liberal and democratic traditions in America. In the classical liberal society, free speech and association were an integral part of the market society, the means by which government could be made responsive to the shifting needs of a new economy. In the preliberal society, political goods were dispensed according to a static and ordered understanding of society. Liberalism and the political freedoms inherent in it made government responsive to the needs of a dynamic market economy. Political freedoms, particularly in the realm of speech and association, were critical elements in the middle-class battle against aristocratic privilege.

As C. B. McPherson has noted, there was nothing necessarily democratic about this development.[2] The franchise was limited, and despite a presumption of equality of opportunity in the marketplace, there was little, if any, support for social and political equality. The democratization of liberal society, however, altered these assumptions. Freedom of speech remained an important value to further political education and choice. More significant, however, was that democracy, with its ever-increasing emphasis on equality, viewed man not simply as he was but as what he might become. The result was that freedom of speech gained an added dimension as a means by which man could strive to fulfill his uniquely human potential.[3]

Thus on the surface, the values of the First Amendment appear particularly compatible with the liberal and democratic strains of American thought. Beneath that surface, however, are differing

1. Anyone familiar with the First Amendment decisions of the Supreme Court will have often encountered this judicial technique. For an example, consider *Dennis* v. *United States.*, 341 U.S. 494 (1951), discussed at length in this chapter.

2. C. B. McPherson, *The Real World of Democracy* (New York: Oxford University Press, 1966), p. 9.

3. Although John Stuart Mill had reservations about extending the franchise, he was one of the first to identify in free expression a means by which man could reach his full intellectual and moral development (*On Liberty* [London, 1859], esp. chap. 2).

assumptions and contradictions, which were quickly exposed when Frankfurter and Black confronted the free speech cases of the 1940s. Black's vision of the polity and the role of judges demanded a First Amendment jurisprudence that would severely circumscribe the power of courts and the state in the free exchange of ideas. Generated by a liberal view of man and human nature, this jurisprudence was, in effect, to carve from the whole of community affairs an inviolable area in which the marketplace of ideas could flourish. In the liberal ideal of the free play and clash of ideas, Hugo Black found the democratic means to ensure progress.

Democracy in the mind of Felix Frankfurter was not simply a method of choosing political leaders but the means by which a progressive society and its individual members could achieve common goals and aspirations.[4] Within this broad concept of democracy, freedom of expression assumed a perspective in which speech must be continually measured against democracy's higher purpose; certain speech might hinder, or even preclude, individual as well as communal fulfillment. Thus in Frankfurter's democratic vision not all speech was of equal value, and to judges fell the statesmanlike task of balancing the principle of free expression against the needs of a democratic state.

The Question of Standards

With the commencement of the 1940 term, the Roosevelt majority on the Court was firmly in place. The rule of deference to legislative judgments, long argued in dissent by Holmes, Brandeis, and Stone, appeared to be a shared norm of decision making of the new majority. Within twelve months, however,

---

4. Thus Frankfurter drew a distinction between a "democratic" process and a democracy. The Court, he noted in a letter to Charles Wyzanski, was not a democratic institution, and judicial review was an "undemocratic" process, but this did not mean that the society was not a democracy: "I have said, and I repeat, that this Court is an 'undemocratic' element in our democratic society, just as the House of Lords is an undemocratic element within British democracy. . . . In short, I did not give you a definition of 'democracy.' [Frankfurter had previously defined "democratic" as the selection of rulers by the people and thus popular control over government decisions.] An undemocratic ingredient in a society, let me repeat, does not preclude the society from being a democracy" (FF to Wyzanski, 3/10/58, FFLC 113-2380).

cleavages appeared in the new coalition. The Court was soon confronted by a seemingly endless series of cases which raised difficult and disturbing questions concerning the scope of the protections of the First Amendment and the Court's role in its interpretation. Against the backdrop of World War II and its aftermath, these cases forced the new majority to reexamine and redefine seemingly shared beliefs about the role of the Court in American government. The result was that the Roosevelt Court was soon deeply divided with Felix Frankfurter and Hugo Black at the center of the controversy.

The initial tremors were hidden from public view. In *Cox* v. *New Hampshire*,[5] a group of Jehovah's Witnesses were convicted of parading without a permit. They challenged the permit requirement as a violation of the speech and assembly provisions of the First Amendment. Although the regulation appeared to confer unlimited discretion with the licensing authority, the Court, at least publicly, had little difficulty sustaining the convictions. Chief Justice Hughes, writing for a unanimous Court, emphasized the narrow construction given the regulation by the state courts and concluded that the power to regulate, without discrimination, the time, place, and manner of the use of its streets could not be denied to the state.

Behind the apparent unanimity in *Cox* lay substantial differences over the proper role for the Court in civil liberty cases. In his original draft, Hughes had emphasized the reasonableness of the New Hampshire permit requirement. Although in accord with the result, Black fervently protested the use of the word "reasonable."[6] Indeed, Black was sufficiently upset to draft a concurring opinion to the effect that the major premise of the Hughes opinion—that the Court could consider the reasonableness of statutes and uphold any statute restricting freedom of expression if it was deemed reasonable—was an unwise statement of the proper role of the Court.[7] Black preferred to rest his vote on the "literal language of the First Amendment."

5. 312 U.S. 569 (1941).
6. HLB to Hughes, 3/27/41, HLBLC 262.
7. Draft in HLBLC 262.

Fully realizing the difficulties involved in enforcing observance of
these constitutional privileges in instances where they apparently
clash with exertions of an admitted state power, I am still not per-
suaded that invocation of the word "reasonable" offers a solution to
the problem these difficulties present. Standards of reasonableness
vary according to individual views. The broad and I might say lim-
itless range within the area of differing concepts of the word "reasonable" cause me to fear its use in relation to the cherished privileges intended to be guaranteed by the First Amendment.

The Black opinion remained uncirculated because Hughes
quickly agreed to delete every use of the word "reasonable" in his
opinion. Both Black and Frankfurter agreed to support Hughes's
new opinion. In a revealing note to Hughes, Frankfurter expressed amusement at Black's requested changes. In Frankfurter's view, deletion of a judicially enforced standard of reasonableness gave to the states greater power to restrict personal freedoms
than had Hughes's original opinion.[8]

The importance attached to the word "reasonable" in *Cox* provides a meaningful starting point for examining the differing
views held by Frankfurter and Black concerning the Court's role
in enforcing and construing the First Amendment. Both men
were concerned with the protection of personal freedom in the
modern state. Black, however, feared the discretion and subjectivity inherent in a reasonableness standard. His understanding of
the democratic process required a judiciary whose will and power
were restricted by hard and fast rules. To purge from the judicial
process the vice of subjectivity caused Black, as early as the decision in *Cox*, to look to the literal language of the First Amendment. In juxtaposition was Frankfurter's attempt to find in flexibility and discretion the judiciary's power, albeit limited, to
protect personal freedom. The careful weighing of circumstances
combined with an appreciation of history, tradition, and democratic goals would make the judiciary an important guardian of
both freedom and order. In *Cox* these differing role conceptions
produced an insignificant disagreement. But the docket for the

8. "Why of course I agree to the omissions you have indicated in the opinion
in No. 502 even though it amuses me that as a matter of textual reading, a broader
power is now left to the states to make inroads on 'civil liberties' than in your original phrasing" (FF to Hughes, 3/28/41, FFLC 68–1341).

1940 term contained a case in which these differences would explode into a major confrontation.

Bridges v. *California* and the Doctrine of Preferred Freedoms

Harry Bridges, a West Coast labor leader, had been held in contempt by California courts when he sent to the Secretary of Labor and had published in several newspapers a telegram in which he warned that a strike would ensue if the state courts enforced an "outrageous" decision in a labor case. The state courts found that the publication of the telegram interfered with the orderly administration of justice. On appeal to the U.S. Supreme Court, Bridges argued that the contempt citation abridged his constitutionally protected freedom of speech.[9]

Bridges posed a difficult problem for it pitted the right to a fair trial administered by an independent judiciary against free expression. The case was originally argued during the 1940 term, and the vote was 6–3 to affirm with Black, Douglas, and Reed in the minority.[10] Hughes assigned the opinion to Frankfurter, and his draft majority opinion constituted one of his most thoughtful statements concerning the role of the judiciary and freedom of expression. Acknowledging that freedom of expression was "implicit in the concept of ordered liberty," Frankfurter nonetheless asserted that the measure of any freedom was in the particular nature of that freedom and the means of its alleged curtailment. Hence the first step in considering any free expression case was the realization that it could not be decided by reliance upon any "talismanic formula." If such a mechanical jurisprudence represented the role of the judiciary, "it would hardly call for the labors of Marshall or Taney, of Holmes or Cardozo."[11]

The task was to balance, measure, and mediate. Freedom of expression was not an absolute command but a principle to be delineated within the context and circumstances of each case. Califor-

9. 314 U.S. 252 (1941). The case was consolidated with a similar case involving the *Los Angeles Times*, which, in an editorial, had urged a state court to hand out stiff sentences to two convicted "labor goons."

10. Docket book, Douglas LC 231.

11. A copy is in HLBLC 231. With minor changes, Frankfurter's subsequently published dissent reflects the views set out in the draft.

nia had chosen a historically valid method of curbing the substantive evil of interference with the rational and disinterested administration of justice. To treat freedom of speech as an absolute would preclude courts from mediating its impact on other, equally important values: "But even that freedom [of expression] we all are agreed, is not an absolute and is not predetermined. By a doctrinaire overstatement of its scope and by giving it an illusory absolute appearance there is danger of thwarting the free choice and the responsibility of exercising it which are basic to a democratic society."[12] By carefully limiting any decree to the facts at issue and by exercising a thoughtful respect for the democratic process, courts, particularly the Supreme Court, were capable of fashioning the accommodations necessary to ensure the progress of a modern state.

Throughout the Frankfurter draft opinion (as well as his published dissent) appears a constant sense of the delicate balance between order and freedom. In the liberal state, the absence of the deeply ingrained traditions of older, hierarchical societies or the shared values imposed by a state religion vastly increased the possibility of freedom degenerating into disorder. Frankfurter believed the likelihood of such an event dramatically increased as the principle of freedom of expression took on the attributes of an absolute command. With *Bridges* Frankfurter began a career-long task of reminding his brethren that in the liberal state it fell to the judiciary to perform the statesmanlike task of infusing tradition, culture, and reason into the operation of principle. Judges were different from other political actors not simply because they were unelected anomalies in a democratic state but also because of the delicate and intricate task with which they were charged.

Thus to ensure progress within the constraints of freedom and order required leadership vested with the power to seek solutions in accord with the "felt necessities of the times." In the first instance this power belonged to the democratically chosen representatives of the people; but, if judicial review was to have any

12. HLBLC 231. After tracing the development of the contempt power to its roots in English practice, Frankfurter concluded that the use of the contempt power was appropriate "because historic." Black circled these words on his copy of the Frankfurter draft and wrote "False premise."

place in a modern, progressive state, that power must also be vested in the courts. One manifestation of this view was Frankfurter's refusal to consider the Court's role in free expression cases in terms of mechanistic rules. Another was his often recognized propensity to assign the disposition of disputes to other institutions of government.[13] In *Bridges* he wrote: "By the Constitution of California . . . the citizens of that state have chosen to place in its courts the power, as we have defined it, to insure impartial justice. If the citizens of California have other desires, if they want to permit the free play of modern publicity in connection with pending litigation, it is within their easy power to say so and have their way."[14] A healthy respect for the virtues of federalism and the democratic process no doubt helped trigger these words. An unstated but significant point, however, was that this "easy power" of amendment was continually subject to review by the Supreme Court; it was, as Black noted in *Cox*, always subject to the Court's determination of reasonableness. Nothing Frankfurter wrote in *Bridges* or subsequent free expression cases precluded the power of the Court to scrutinize legislation. Seen in this light, the assignment of the disposition of disputes to other areas of decision making did not serve to limit judicial review but rather to maximize judicial choice and flexibility in the operation of judicial review.

Furthermore, as in *Gobitis*,[15] choice (and hence progress) was maintained through a conscious limiting of the scope of any decision. In *Bridges*, Frankfurter emphasized the limited nature of the holding:

> The question concerning the narrow power we have recognized is—was there a real and substantial threat to the impartial decision by a court of a case actively pending before it? The threat must be close and direct and must be directed towards a particular litigation. The litigation must be immediately pending; and when a case is pending is not a technical lawyer's problem but is to be determined by the substantial realities of the specific situation.[16]

13. See, Louis Jaffe, "The Judicial Universe of Mr. Justice Frankfurter," 62 *Harvard Law Review* 357 (1949).
14. HLBLC 231.
15. See Chapter 4.
16. HLBLC 231.

In short, the Court faced with the next case retained choice. Frankfurter's opinion in *Bridges*, as in many of his judicial efforts in the realm of civil liberties, cannot be understood as precedent in the common law sense of the term; for Frankfurter the command that courts faced with similar cases achieve similar results was less significant than that courts bring to bear on these cases the correct method and process of decision making. That at times this method and process would compel apparently inconsistent results was the inevitable outcome of the delicate role played by the Court in American government.

After Frankfurter's draft majority opinion was circulated, Black set out on a scratch pad his differences with that opinion:

> (1) Are we to judge upon [several words illegible] of a concept of ordered liberty or by construction and enforcement of Amendment 1. He says first—I say latter.
> (2) Must we in considering the comparative qualities and importance of right to exercise liberties guaranteed by first amendment place courts and first amendment on a parity? I say no, Amendment ranks higher—He says opposite.
> (3) Are we to construe an exception to right to free press to exist as to public discussion of matters involved in cases pending before judges? He says yes, I say no.
> (4) Can we reach this conclusion because courts have historically exercised power to punish for contempt by reason of publication while cause pending? He says yes, I say no.
> (5) Can we justify the conclusion upon the grounds that judiciary must remain—
> (a) completely free and independent?
> (b) the restraint of freedom of expression is a narrow one
> (c) courts will exercise it only in flagrant cases with utmost forebearance?
> (d) after all it is a question of the "degree" of abridgement?
> (e) unless exercised we cannot possibly have a [illegible] detached and fearless exercise of judicial duty?[17]

From these notes, Black fashioned his dissent. Like Frankfurter, he found the essence of freedom to be in order.[18] Unlike

17. HLBLC 256.
18. As noted in Chapter 3, Black greatly admired the ancient Greeks. One reason is found in his copy of Hamilton, *The Greek Way*. On p. 295, Hamilton wrote that the Greeks did not develop excesses. "It could not happen to a people who

Frankfurter, however, he was not troubled by the divisive possibilities of free and unrestrained speech. His response to the challenge of reconciling freedom with order was to carve from the whole of community affairs an "inviolable area" of freedom. The boundaries of this sphere were set by the Constitution and, in particular, the First Amendment, and within the sphere the principle of the marketplace of ideas would be at work.[19] Black never conceived of the competition of the marketplace as a means of achieving "truth" for he doubted the existence of an absolute truth in the same way he doubted the existence of an identifiable public interest. He did, however, see the marketplace as the democratic means of accommodating competing truths. The choices made by the majority would serve to define progress; the marketplace would become the democratic safety valve as competition in ideas replaced revolution as a means of social change. Frankfurter ensured freedom consistent with order by placing the search for truth in the hands of disinterested statesman-judges. Black, lacking a faith in either the truth or statesman-judges, found in the vicissitudes of a sharply defined marketplace of ideas the means by which freedom could be reconciled with order. Outside of this sphere, the state retained wide latitude to legislate for the public good. The line defining the sphere was clearly established by the Constitution, and in *Bridges* the contempt citations issued by the state of California clearly fell within the protected area.

Although Black did not characterize the First Amendment as an absolute in his *Bridges* dissent, that conclusion pervades the entire opinion.[20] As his preliminary notes indicated, the first step

knew better than any other that liberty depends on self-restraint, *who knew that freedom is only freedom when controlled and limited*." The emphasis is Black's.

19. The notion of a marketplace of ideas was keyed to Black's view of a polity divided between the few and the many. He believed that the best defense against despotism was the free exchange of ideas. As long as the few did not control the means of communication, ultimate power would remain with the many. He thus fought long and hard as a senator, for example, to prevent utilities from acquiring broadcast permits. See Hugo Black, "No Broadcasting by Utilities," *Public Utilities Fortnightly* 3 (June 13, 1929). See also, Chapter 3, n. 2, above.

20. The opinion is in HLBLC 256. Speaking of Black's majority opinion published the following term, Robert McCloskey stated: "In short, the majority opinion in *Bridges* comes close to saying, though somewhat obliquely, that speech is absolutely immune from governmental interferences" (*The Modern Supreme Court* [Cambridge, Mass.: Harvard University Press, 1972], p. 15).

was to define freedom of expression not as "implicit in our concept of ordered liberty" but as emanating full force from the words of the First Amendment. Whereas Frankfurter sought to make the measure of any principle dependent upon judicial appreciation of both the nature of the principle and the circumstances of its abridgment, Black sought to limit the judicial task to a construction of the basic words of the constitutional text. If Frankfurter found relevance in the fact that the contempt power as exercised by the California courts was in accord with the long history of English practice, Black used the same history as indicative of what the framers intended to *avoid* in drafting the Bill of Rights. In a critical passage, Black wrote:

> The First Amendment was written in the form of a command so unequivocal, and so pervasive in its expression and implication that it is impossible to deny that those who drafted it intended to mark off an inviolable area and dedicate it to the liberties there enumerated. It may be true that there are no such things as absolute liberties. It may be true that newspapers and others take undue and mischievous advantage of the privileges granted them by the Constitution. But even if newspapers were guilty of all the offenses of which they have sometimes been accused it was the theory of those responsible for our Bill of Rights that in the last analysis the solution would lie in censorship by public opinion rather than in censorship by a court of law. [Footnote omitted.][21]

Such a view of the First Amendment did not countenance judicial balancing, at least as suggested in Frankfurter's draft for the majority. Black used the clear and present danger test (and the balancing inherent in that test) but only at the conclusion of his draft dissent after acknowledging that the majority did not accept his view of the First Amendment. Assuming, Black wrote, that the Court did have the wide-ranging powers described in Frankfurter's opinion for the Court, "considering the values of the constitutional liberties that are here abridged, I believe it would be much better to say that state courts should never punish for contempt in such cases unless there was found to be a clear and present dan-

21. HLBLC 256.

ger of an immediate interference which could not be averted without the imposition of punishment."[22]

After the circulation of opinions, Justice Murphy switched his vote, which, along with McReynolds's retirement, meant that the Court was now equally divided in the *Bridges* case. Reargument the following term and the vote of newly appointed Justice Jackson resulted in a majority for reversal.[23] Frankfurter's majority opinion, which painstakingly expressed his view of the role of the Court in free expression cases, now became a dissent. Black wrote for the majority, but his dissent of a year before was put aside in favor of an entirely new opinion. Absent from this draft was any discussion of an inviolable area of freedom established by the First Amendment. Instead, Black focused on developing from clear and present danger a test more protective of First Amendment values. As defined by Black, this test required that the substantive evil "must be extremely serious and the degree of imminence extremely high before utterances can be punished."[24] The burden on the state was perceptibly increased; the interest at stake was not simply Bridges's interest in articulating his point of view but the public interest in timely discussion of controversial events. And there was at least an oblique suggestion that the powers of the Court under the First Amendment did not extend to evaluating the social utility of particular speech.[25]

In fact, Black's interpretation of clear and present danger in *Bridges* was an important step in elevating the First Amendment

22. Ibid.

23. J. Woodford Howard sees Murphy's switch as signifying his change of allegiance from Frankfurter to Black. (*Mr. Justice Murphy* [Princeton: Princeton University Press, 1968], p. 262). Justice Byrnes had assumed Stone's seat (Stone replacing Hughes as chief justice) and voted with Frankfurter.

24. 314 U.S. at 263. Black added that this did not mark "the furthermost constitutional boundaries of protected expression."

25. Black noted that it was a prized American freedom to speak one's mind "although not always with good taste." He quoted from Jefferson: "I deplore . . . the putrid state into which our newspapers have passed and the malignity, the vulgarity and mendacious spirit of those who write them. . . . These ordures are rapidly depraving the public taste. It is however an evil for which there is no remedy, our liberty depends on the freedom of the press, and that cannot be limited without being lost" 314 U.S. at 270 n.16. Cf. Frankfurter's view that newspapers should be measured by what is presented as well as how it is presented (Chapter 2 above).

to a preferred position in the hierarchy of constitutional values. The first steps had been Cardozo's effort in *Palko* and Stone's famous footnote in the *Carolene Products* case.[26] The effort reached its zenith during the 1940s as a further refinement of a jurisprudential assumption that considered judicial deference to legislative judgments in the realm of economic regulation combined with more active review of cases involving personal freedom to be the hallmark of judicial liberalism of the twentieth century.[27] As described by Justice Rutledge, the preference doctrine was a response to an increasing judicial belief that

> our system places [a duty] on this Court to say where the individual's freedom ends and the state's power begins. Choice on that border, now as always delicate, is perhaps more so when the usual presumption supporting legislation is balanced by the preferred place given in our scheme to the great, the indispensable democratic freedoms secured by the First Amendment . . . that priority gives these liberties a sanctity and a sanction not permitting dubious intrusions. And it is the character of the right, not the limitation, which determines which standard governs the choice.[28]

During the mid-1940s, clear and present danger in conjunction with preferred position evolved into a doctrine truly protective of the First Amendment. The result was to place upon the state the burden of establishing the constitutional validity of any restriction of free expression. This shifting of the burden of proof was the single most important step in the First Amendment jurisprudence of Hugo Black. In so doing, Black and his colleagues radically altered the nature of the inquiry demanded by First Amendment cases. The clear and present danger standard was essentially a balancing process.[29] Use of the preference doctrine significantly altered the weights placed in the balance. Under a restricted interpretation of clear and present danger, the individual's right to

26. See Chapter 4, n. 14, above.
27. Martin Shapiro characterizes preferred freedoms as an "excuse for activism" (*Freedom of Speech: The Supreme Court and Judicial Review* [Englewood Cliffs, N.J.: Prentice-Hall, 1966], p. 58).
28. *Thomas* v. *Collins*, 323 U.S. 516, 529, 530 (1945).
29. See Paul Freund, *The Supreme Court of the United States* (Cleveland: World, 1961), p. 44.

free expression was measured against the threat to the health, safety, and welfare of the community. The preference docrine replaced the individual's interest with society's interest in the free and open exchange of ideas. In essence, the individual petitioner no longer represented his particularized claim but the more generalized interest of the community.

The impact of this shift was twofold. It clearly simplified the task of those challenging regulations that restricted free expression; it freed advocates from the constraints of the particular and permitted argument based upon generalized principles. Perhaps more significantly, the preference doctrine severely restricted the ability of courts to treat free expression cases as discrete instances and to fashion, or deny, relief accordingly. Weighing, balancing, and measuring circumstances, as well as deference to legislative will, became largely irrelevant.

Black's majority opinion in *Bridges* made no direct claim for a preferred position for the First Amendment; the necessity of keeping together a fragile majority precluded overt innovation.[30] In 1941 preferred position had not yet become an articulated doctrine; Black's efforts in the early free expression cases were born of his generalized concept of the role of the Court.[31] In the cases following *Bridges*, the development of the preference doctrine took on sharper focus. The evolution of the move from a particularized to a generalized view of the First Amendment, for example, is evidenced by *Martin* v. *Struthers*,[32] which involved the violation by Jehovah's Witnesses of a city ordinance that prohib-

30. In Black's first circulation he quoted from *Palko* to the effect that the First Amendment was "the matrix, the indispensable condition of nearly every other form of freedom." Justice Reed asked him to "soften" this language, and it does not appear in the final draft (page 5 of Reed's return of Black's circulation, HLBLC 266).

31. James Magee in his study of Black and free expression concludes that the consistency achieved by Black in the free speech cases in the 1940s, because of Black's reliance on clear and present danger and not the absolute position, was due to his "devout libertarianism" and not his "constitutional jurisprudence" (*Mr. Justice Black: Absolutist on the Court* [Charlottesville: University Press of Virginia, 1980], p. 81). I disagree; clear and present danger modified by the preference doctrine fit neatly within Black's jurisprudence. It permitted limited flexibility in free expression cases in the same way that *Chambers* (see Chapter 4) indicated Black's desire to retain some flexibility in due process cases.

32. 318 U.S. 141 (1943).

ited the door-to-door distribution of handbills. Black originally
authored an opinion for a five-man majority sustaining the statute. He then changed his vote and wrote for a new majority inval-
idating the regulation. In his original opinion, Black announced
the Court's task to be "weighing the conflicting interests of the appellant in the civil rights she claims and of the community in the
protection of the interests of its citizens." He concluded that the
regulation was not a disguised attempt to regulate the content of
speech, emphasized the substantial state interest in regulating
door-to-door solicitation, and conceded to the community the
right to choose rational means to protect that interest. These interests were discounted in the new majority opinion because the
state's interest was ultimately measured against "the freedom to
distribute information to every citizen whenever he desires . . .
[which] is so clearly vital to the preservation of a free society." The
issue was now articulated as "weighing the conflicting interests of
the appellant in the civil rights she claims, *as well as the right of the
individual householder to determine whether he is willing to receive her
message*, against the interests of the community which by this ordinance offers to protect the interests of all its citizens."[33] The
state interest had remained the same; the particularized interest
of the appellant, however, had given way to a more generalized
societal interest in the exchange of ideas.

Years later, after Black had moved to an absolute reading of
the First Amendment, he would explain the obvious balancing at
work in decisions like *Struthers* as appropriate because the regulation was aimed at conduct and only indirectly a regulation of
speech.[34] This explanation should not obscure the degree to
which the preferred position doctrine was a product of Black's
role conception of the Court in American government. The first
effort in *Struthers* followed the Frankfurter view of First Amendment adjudication: a particularized evaluation of competing inter-

33. 318 U.S. at 143 (emphasis added). Copies of Black's draft opinions and
those of the other justices as well as an interesting memorandum written by Frankfurter entitled "The Story of Struthers" can be found in FF HLSL, October Term
1942, bound volume of drafts.
34. See *Cox* v. *Louisiana*, 379 U.S. 536 (1965) (Black, J. concurring and dissenting).

ests, a ready acknowledgment of the state's right to choose reasonable means to further its interest, and an assumption of the constitutional validity of the regulation. In the second opinion, a particularized interest was replaced by a generalized societal interest in the First Amendment. Not only did this new interpretation significantly raise the stakes in any First Amendment case, but it also restricted the Court's freedom to evaluate speech based on social utility. This latter point would become a matter of contention between Frankfurter and Black in the following years.

The "mischievous phrase"

By the conclusion of World War II, the libertarian quartet (the "Axis" as Frankfurter called them) of Murphy, Rutledge, Douglas, and Black constituted a solid block in favor of the preferred position approach. The result was inevitably four votes in favor of the First Amendment claim. Although his initial efforts in *Cox* and *Bridges* strongly evidenced a literal approach to the First Amendment, Black found it unnecessary to pursue that line of thought. In the hands of Murphy, Rutledge, Douglas, and Black the preferred position doctrine appeared to satisfy the need to restrict judicial discretion while ensuring the necessary flexibility in the unlikely event that particular utterances did pose an imminent threat to the public order. In many respects, the preferred position was similar to balancing with one critical difference: one weight in the balance—the value of free expression—remained constant despite the nature of the claim, the societal value of the speech, or the extent of the alleged restriction. Thus over a wide range of cases involving the free speech provisions of the First Amendment the generalized societal interest in free expression was measured against the state's claim that particular utterances threatened the health, welfare, and safety of the community.

While substantially increasing the burden on the state, the preference doctrine did not preclude the state from sustaining that burden in extraordinary circumstances. To retain similar flexibility within the literal or absolute approach, however, required the creation of seemingly arbitrary exceptions which served to undercut doctrinal consistency.[35] Flexibility was further maintained under the preference doctrine by the removal of certain categories of speech from the protections of the First Amendment. In *Chaplinsky* v. *New Hampshire*[36] Justice Murphy held for a unanimous Court that "fighting words" were not protected by the First Amendment; in dicta, he added libel, slander, profanity, and obscenity to the excluded list. Black saw defining the content of the First Amendment as a judicial task and judgment as inescapable; there was, in his view, a qualitative difference between setting the limits to the First Amendment at the definitional stage and expanding and contracting that meaning on a case-by-case basis.[37]

Even though under preferred freedoms a limited categorization of speech was undertaken, Frankfurter considered it a "mischievous phrase."[38] During the years following World War II he waged a relentless campaign to liberate free speech analysis from what he considered the mechanical jurisprudence of the preference doctrine and to substitute a form of ad hoc balancing. In this effort, Frankfurter's conception of the judge as "democratic factfinder" most clearly manifested itself.[39] The progressive tradition of which Frankfurter was a part envisioned progress defined by commonly held goals. The task of leadership was to direct society to the attainment of those goals. Progress could not be assured through the unsupervised clash of all views; some ideas were more important than others. Thus the task of leadership was to ensure that the appropriate views were presented in the appropriate manner. It was naive to believe that all speech was of the same

35. Thus as Magee points out, when Black moved to the absolute position, flexibility was destroyed and Black found it necessary to carve out exceptions, albeit somewhat hidden, from his reading of the absolute protection of free speech (*Mr. Justice Black*, chap. 5).

36. 315 U.S. 568 (1942).

37. "Freedom of speech . . . could be greatly abridged by a practice of meticulously scrutinizing every editorial, speech, sermon or other printed matter to extract two or three naughty words on which to hang charges of 'group libel.' The *Chaplinsky* case makes no such broad inroads on First Amendment freedoms" (*Beauharnais* v. *Illinois*, 343 U.S. 250, 273 [1952] [Black, J. dissenting]).

38. *Kovacs* v. *Cooper*, 336 U.S. 77, 90 (1949) (Frankfurter, J. concurring).

39. The phrase was used by Jacobsohn to characterize Roscoe Pound (*Pragmatism, Statesmanship and the Supreme Court* [Ithaca, N.Y.: Cornell University Press, 1977], p. 79). Shapiro has connected balancing to Pound's jurisprudence (*Freedom of Speech*, pp. 99–101).

intrinsic worth and, furthermore, speech which in some circumstances would be beneficial (or at least harmless) in other circumstances might be worthless (or at worst dangerous). In the last analysis, to judges fell the statesmanlike task of weighing and balancing. Under Frankfurter's view of the polity, each free speech case presented a discrete instance to be carefully measured against the needs of a progressive state. Order and freedom could be ensured only by a judiciary performing such a task freed from the constraints of dogma and absolutes.

The opening salvo in his campaign against the preference doctrine was fired in his dissent in the second flag salute case.[40] There he invoked Holmes to support his contention that the rule of deference to legislative judgment applied regardless of the nature of the legislation before the Court. This repudiation of a hierarchy of constitutional values has been viewed by at least one commentator as symbolizing a significant change in his constitutional jurisprudence.[41] Frankfurter in *Barnette*, however, was not disclaiming his belief in the scaling of constitutional rights but rather the judicial process established by Black and the preference doctrine. Later he wrote to Justice Reed:

> I fully understand all that Stone meant to convey by his wholly irrelevant footnote 4 in the *Carolene Products* case. . . . Before Stone wrote that footnote, I spelt out in some detail the different considerations that come into play when passing on "legislation attempting economic readjustments as against legislation restricting freedom of utterance." See, Frankfurter, *Mr. Justice Holmes and the Supreme Court*, pp. 61–62. And that I take it is the intrinsic meaning of loose talk about rights having a "preferred position." A conventional way of expressing this idea is to say that certain statutes are to be "liberally" construed. There is nothing new about this. . . . As you know, I have attached the greatest possible importance to the Fourth Amendment but it would never occur to me to say it has a "preferred position." . . . I understand, of course, that in construing a particular provision, one of the considerations to be taken into account is that freedom of speech is involved. . . . That is a matter of relevance in construction.[42]

40. *West Virginia v. Barnette*, 319 U.S. 624 (1943).
41. H. N. Hirsch concludes that this change evidenced Frankfurter's denial of his "belief in fundamental values and hardening his concept of judicial deference" (*The Enigma of Felix Frankfurter* [New York: Basic Books, 1981], p. 174).
42. FF to Reed, 2/7/56, FF-HLSL 170–19.

Throughout his career, Frankfurter retained this understanding of the hierarchy of constitutional values. His objection to the preferred position doctrine was that it substituted mechanical jurisprudence for the type of judgment he described to Reed.[43] The fact that important constitutional rights were at issue should not, in Frankfurter's view, change the nature of the judicial process; disinterested jurists were capable of weighing the significance of the right involved within the process described by Frankfurter. But this was only one factor to be considered with many others in reaching final judgment.

One of these factors was the social value of challenged speech, and it was this factor, perhaps more than any other, which separated Frankfurter from Black. As the preference doctrine evolved during the 1940s, Black categorically refused to measure the value of particular speech. In *Winters* v. *New York*[44] Justice Reed, writing for the Court, struck down a New York statute restricting the distribution of magazines devoted to bloodshed and violence. Admitting that the magazines were of little social value, Reed nevertheless concluded they were entitled "to the protection of free speech as the best of literature." Although *Chaplinsky* had suggested that the lewd and the profane were outside the protection of the First Amendment, Reed, in the best tradition of preferred freedom analysis, refused to permit either a legislature or a court to construe these categories broadly.

"Not to make the magazines with which this case is concerned part of the Court's opinion," wrote Frankfurter in dissent, "is to play 'Hamlet' without Hamlet."[45] Although the majority had ultimately reversed on the grounds of vagueness, Frankfurter could not let Reed's assertion go unchallenged. Because the speech lacked any social value, it was not protected by the First Amendment; in effect, Frankfurter read the First Amendment out of the case. This determination was not based upon the category of speech into which these publications purportedly fell but upon a

43. "The objection to summarizing this line of thought by the phrase 'preferred position' is that it expresses a complicated process of constitutional adjudication by a deceptive formula" (*Kovacs* v. *Cooper*, 336 U.S. at 97).
44. 333 U.S. 507 (1948).
45. 333 U.S. at 527.

judicial weighing of the value of the publications.[46] In the first instance this power remained with the state legislature; but under Frankfurter's conception of the role of the Court, it was part of the Court's power in judicial review of First Amendment cases.

Later, in *Beauharnais* v. *Illinois*,[47] Frankfurter extended the weighing of the social merits of speech to political utterances. An Illinois statute made it unlawful for any person to publish writing that "portrays depravity, criminality, unchastity or lack of virtue of a class of citizens of any race, color, creed, or religion . . . [or] exposes the citizenry of any race, color, creed or religion to contempt, derision, or obloquy which is productive of breach of the peace or riots." Beauharnais, the leader of a white supremacy group, petitioned the mayor and city council of Chicago "to halt the further encroachment, harassment and invasion of white people, their property, neighborhoods and persons by the Negro." Copies of the petition were distributed on street corners by members of the organization.

Without question this was a form of political speech. Nevertheless, Frankfurter, writing for a five-man majority, concluded that it was not a First Amendment case. Citing *Chaplinsky*, Frankfurter noted that libel was a category of speech unprotected by the First Amendment. If libel of the individual was unprotected, then it followed that libel of a group was similarly unprotected. But, as Black argued in dissent, for purposes of the First Amendment the two were entirely different. Criminal libel, as narrowly and historically defined, centered on purely private disputes; to extend the same treatment to group libel was to ensure that a form of political speech, albeit vile, would be unprotected. This, for Frankfurter, was a distinction without a difference; in both cases the speech was not essential to the exposition of ideas critical to the American polity. To respond to Black's position, Frankfurter instructed his law clerk to draft an additional paragraph to be added to the opinion to the effect that free speech as protected

46. During consideration of *Winters*, Frankfurter asked Sheldon Glueck, a Harvard criminologist, for the results of any research linking such literature to crime. Glueck replied that there was no proven causal connection (Glueck to FF, 11/22/47, 11/17/47, FF HLSL 21–8).

47. 343 U.S. 250 (1952).

by the Fourteenth Amendment must always be considered in light of the federal system and the need to preserve the states as laboratories for new social legislation. The law clerk, however, urged Frankfurter not to include the additional paragraph. The opinion, he noted, rested on the historical fact that the First Amendment could not be interpreted as restricting even the power of Congress in the area of libelous publications. "By adding this paragraph," he warned, "we permit Black to draw us onto his ground." Frankfurter agreed. He handwrote on the clerk's memo: "In my more rational moments of reflection I had reached precisely your conclusion. Thank you."[48] For Felix Frankfurter, the First Amendment was simply not at issue in the *Beauharnais* case.

Beauharnais forcefully illustrates the differing conceptions of the role of the Court held by Felix Frankfurter and Hugo Black. Conceding that the power to punish for group libel could be abused, Frankfurter emphasized that as long as "this Court sits" it retained the power and authority to review prosecutions to determine whether freedom of expression had been denied. Black could not let such an assertion pass unchallenged. At the conclusion of his powerful and eloquent dissent he responded:

> We are told that freedom of petition and discussion are in no danger "while this Court sits." This case raises considerable doubt.

48. FF HLSL 48–10. The law clerk was Abraham Chayes, and the paragraph and footnote read as follows: "Some thirty years ago, Mr. Justice Holmes gave expression to a profound admonition against judicial disregard of the social implications of our federal system. 'There is nothing that I more deprecate,' he said, 'than the use of the Fourteenth Amendment beyond the absolute compulsion of its words to prevent the making of social experiments that an important part of the community desires, in the insulated chambers afforded by the several states, even though the experiments may seem futile or even noxious to me and to those whose judgment I respect.' *Truax* v. *Corrigan*, 257 U.S. 312, 344.[1] *Cf.* Letter of Madison to Edward Livingston, July 10, 1822, IX Writings of James Madison 100 (Hunt ed. 1910). It is never untimely to recall that warning."

"1. Lest it be urged that he sought this latitude for the States only in the sphere of 'economic' legislation, it should be remembered that in his famous *Gitlow* dissent Justice Holmes remarked that the 'general principle of free speech' which must be taken to be included in the Fourteenth Amendment may be accepted with a somewhat larger latitude of interpretation than is allowed to Congress by the sweeping language that governs or ought to govern the laws of the United States. *Gitlow* v. *New York*, 268 U.S. 652, 672."

Since those who peacefully petition for changes in the law are not to be protected "while this Court sits," who is? I do not agree that the Constitution leaves freedom of petition, assembly, speech, press or worship at the mercy of a case-by-case, day-by-day majority of this Court. I had supposed that our people could rely for their freedom on the Constitution's commands, rather than on the grace of this Court on an individual case basis. To say that a legislative body can, with this Court's approval, make it a crime to petition for and publicly discuss proposed legislation seems as farfetched to me as it would be to say that a valid law could be enacted to punish a candidate for President for telling the people his views. I think the First Amendment, with the Fourteenth, "absolutely" forbids such laws without any "ifs" or "buts" or "whereases." . . .

If there be minority groups who hail this holding as their victory, they might consider the possible relevancy of this ancient remark: "Another such victory and I am undone."[49]

Dennis v. *United States* and the Art of Balancing

Justice Black's opinions in *Bridges* foreshadowed two developments that would significantly influence the Court during the ensuing decade: the dominance of the preference doctrine as the judicial standard in free expression cases and the emergence of Black as the leader of the "libertarian" wing of the Court. The deaths of Frank Murphy and Wiley Rutledge within two months of each other in 1949, however, served as a somber prelude to a new decade.[50] By the early 1950s, Black and Douglas were often in lonely dissent, the preference doctrine was soon replaced by ad hoc balancing, and leadership appeared to shift to Frankfurter. If *Bridges* represented the free speech decisions of the 1940s, then *Dennis* v. *United States*[51] represented the new decade.

At issue in *Dennis* were the provisions of the Smith Act that made it a crime to teach or advocate the overthrow of the government or to help organize or be a member of any group advocating or teaching such overthrow.[52] Although never previously ap-

49. 343 U.S. at 274, 275.

50. Tom Clark replaced Murphy, and Sherman Minton replaced Rutledge. Frankfurter went to great lengths to cultivate these men as well as Chief Justice Vinson. See Hirsch, *Enigma of Felix Frankfurter*, pp. 188–190.

51. 341 U.S. 494 (1951).

52. The background to the Smith Act is set out in Dennis O'Brien, "*Dennis* v. *U.S.*: The Cold War, the Communist Conspiracy and the FBI," (Ph.D. dissertation, Cornell University, 1979).

plied to members of the Communist party, these provisions had
been tested twice before in cases against dissident groups during
World War II.[53] By 1948 the political climate had changed; the
Soviet Union was no longer an ally, the Cold War had begun, and
the government obtained indictments against twelve members of
the Central Committee of the Communist party charging a conspiracy to violate the advocacy and organizing provisions of the
Smith Act.

The trial, before Judge Harold Medina in the Southern District
of New York, lasted more than six months and was marked by
continuing controversy between the trial judge and defense counsel.[54] In a jury verdict the defendants were found guilty, and the
convictions were affirmed on appeal in a decision authored by
Learned Hand. To sustain the convictions, Hand found it necessary to restate the clear and present danger test: "In each case
[courts] must ask whether the gravity of the evil, discounted by its
improbability, justifies such invasion of free speech as is necessary
to avoid the danger."[55] The likelihood of an overthrow of the government in 1948 as a result of the teaching of the doctrines of
Marxism-Leninism was highly remote. Nevertheless, the inherent vagueness of the Hand test permitted both him and Chief Justice Frederick M. Vinson (Vinson's opinion for the Court substantially followed the Hand test) to inflate the evil while, in effect,
disregarding the probability. Moreover, the trial judge had not
permitted the issue of clear and present danger to go to the jury,
ruling as a matter of law that there was sufficient danger to satisfy
the test. Hand found that, in the first instance, the weighing of
the evil and the value of free speech belonged to the legislature.
Because it was often impossible for legislatures to undertake such

53. The first was a successful prosecution of several Trotskyites. See *Dunne* v.
United States, 138 F.2d 137 (8 Cir. 1943). Black, Murphy, and Rutledge voted to
grant certiorari. Douglas did not because he believed he lacked the fifth vote to reverse on the merits. It was a vote he was later to regret (William O. Douglas, *The
Court Years* [New York: Random House, 1980], pp. 94–95). The second was an
unsuccessful prosecution of twelve native fascists and isolationists. See O'Brien,
"Dennis v. U.S.," chap. 4.

54. This controversy resulted in contempt citations which found their way to
the Court. See *United States* v. *Sacher*, 343 U.S. 1 (1952).

55. *United States* v. *Dennis*, 183 F.2d 201 (2 Cir. 1950).

balancing in specific circumstances, it was correct for the court (and not the jury) to act in place of the legislature.[56]

"The amazing thing about the conference in this important case," wrote Douglas in his conference notes, "was the brief nature of the discussion. Those wanting to affirm had minds closed to argument or persuasion. The conference discussion was largely pro forma. It was more amazing because of the drastic revision of the clear and present danger test which affirmance requires."[57] The problems in *Dennis* were many. The Court had limited its grant of certiorari to the constitutional issues, thus precluding a review of the evidence.[58] This evidence consisted basically of the introduction of Marxist-Leninist tracts available in any large library. There was no evidence of overt acts or of the specific advocacy of immediate violence or the use of force; the lower courts had used the slippery notion of intent to bridge the gap between advocacy and action. The interpretation of clear and present danger by Hand had eliminated the idea of "clear," emasculated any meaning of the requirement of "present," and satisfied the demand that the evil be serious through reliance on judicial notice.[59] Douglas was substantially correct; to affirm did require a drastic revision of the clear and present danger test.

Not surprisingly, Black at conference voted to reverse on the simple grounds that clear and present danger was not satisfied. More surprising was the reaction of Frankfurter. Although stating that he would affirm, Douglas recorded that he raised four points that the Court had to consider:

1) status of a c & p since Gitlow
2) how imminent must the substantive evils be?

56. 183 F.2d at 211–212.
57. Douglas LC 310.
58. Only Black refused to vote to limit the grant of certiorari. Minton voted to deny (Docket book, 1950 Term, Burton LC).
59. Thomas Emerson, *The System of Freedom of Expression* (New York: Random House, 1970), p. 114. Judicial notice is a means by which the party charged with the burden of proof may satisfy that burden without the formal presentation of evidence. Typically it is used when all reasonably intelligent members of the community know the fact (e.g., the sun rose on March 27, 1947) or the fact is ascertainable by authoritative books of record (e.g., the population of the United States).

3) should clear and present danger be submitted to jury? In
Holmes and Brandeis opinions it is a question of fact.
4) can we take judicial notice of existence of the evil and danger?

The points raised by Frankfurter cut to the heart of the problems in *Dennis*. The government's basic position was that *Gitlow*
controlled because the Smith Act was similar to the New York
statute challenged in *Gitlow*; in both cases the legislature had outlawed not a generalized evil but a specific type of utterance, and
thus the only issue for the courts was the sufficiency of the evidence.[60] Although *Gitlow* had not been specifically overruled,
subsequent cases had eroded its value, and it would be impossible
to rule on *Dennis* without going beyond *Gitlow*.[61] The question of
imminence appeared unanswerable; few believed a coup possible
either in 1948 or 1951. Moreover, Holmes and Brandeis had made
clear and present danger a factual determination to be decided in
each particular case; in *Dennis*, lacking any evidence of the defendants' connection to a worldwide conspiracy, the convictions
could be affirmed only by disregarding the test of substantial evil
or satisfying it through judicial notice.

Despite his vote to affirm, *Dennis*, for Frankfurter, once again
represented the folly of replacing judgment with formula. In
the 1940s he had attacked the members of the "libertarian Axis"
for their automatic invalidation of legislation touching speech
through the use of the preference doctrine. With a new Court,
the results might be different but the failure of analysis and process the same. His frustration with an apparent result-oriented jurisprudence that substituted conclusions for the proper analysis
erupted during the *Dennis* deliberations against the mild-man-
nered Reed. Reed joined Vinson's opinion, affirming on the basis
of the restated clear and present danger test. In response to
Frankfurter's queries pointing out the weaknesses of that analysis,
Reed took the position that seditious speech was not entitled
to the protections of the First Amendment. "Which is it," Frankfurter exploded,

60. See Brief for the Respondents, *Dennis* v. *United States*. *Gitlow* is discussed in
Chapter 1, above.
61. Both the majority opinion of Vinson and the concurring opinion of Frankfurter conceded as much.

a free speech case, and as such to be tested by the clear-and-present-danger or . . . not a free speech case at all? It seems of profound importance to me to decide what it is. Just as the past talk of clear-and-present-danger has built up difficulties which now have to be evaded and averted, so a new opinion regarding clear-and-present-danger adjusted to meet the circumstances of this case will beget difficulties for cases having very different circumstances coming here in the future.

It is this that makes me say what doubtless will not please you that it makes all the difference in the world whether you start this case with a problem or an answer.[62]

Frankfurter wrote in *Dennis* out of an equal frustration with the legal method of Black and Douglas in dissent and Vinson for the Court. The conflict of interests in *Dennis* and ultimately any free expression case could "not be resolved by a dogmatic preference for one or the other, not by a sonorous formula which is in fact only a euphemistic disguise for an unresolved conflict." The process of adjudication required a careful and disinterested weighing of interests by judges freed from a mistaken, formalistic conception of decision making. "Free speech," he reminded his colleagues, "is subject to prohibition of those abuses of expression which a civilized society may forbid."[63]

He began the process by articulating the state's interest in security. The jury was free to find from the facts presented that the American Communist party was not an ordinary political party. Its credo was the overthrow of the government by force and violence. Furthermore, the Court was free to take judicial notice of world events in which communist doctrines "are in ascendancy in powerful nations who cannot be acquitted of unfriendliness to the institutions of this country." With this perspective "the Congress was not barred by the Constitution from believing that indifference to such experience would be an exercise not of freedom but of irresponsibility."[64]

Measured against the nation's security was a weighty interest in free expression. Thee was a public interest "in granting freedom to speak their minds even to those who advocate the overthrow

62. FF to Reed, 3/14/51, FF HLSL 40–3.
63. 341 U.S. at 519, 523.
64. 341 U.S. at 547, 548.

of the government by force." Within the defendants' call for revolution were trenchant criticisms of defects in American society. Free expression was the "well-spring of our civilization," and the sobering fact was that any limitation of the defendants' speech would adversely affect the free exchange of ideas.

How could these interests be balanced? Faced with the weighing of imponderables, Frankfurter appeared to revert to the reasonableness test of *Gitlow*: "It is not for us to decide how we would adjust the clash of interests which this case presents. . . . Congress has determined that the danger created by advocacy of overthrow justifies the ensuing restriction on freedom of speech."[65] As he articulated it, the Frankfurter balancing test appeared a sham; it was impossible to formulate a common ground of measurement and a standard of reference to measure interests of the magnitude of national security and freedom of expression.

Nevertheless, balancing did take place. Early in his opinion, Frankfurter almost casually noted that "not every type of speech occupies the same position on the scale of values."[66] This measure determined the outcome of the case; Frankfurter's conception of the role of judges and his understanding of the First Amendment demanded that judges measure the social utility of challenged speech. In future cases in which the competing interests appeared to be similar to that in *Dennis* but the social utility of the speech was of greater value, the result was reversed.[67] In *Dennis* however, Frankfurter determined that "on any scale of values which we have hitherto recognized, speech of this sort ranks low."[68] When the preference doctrine held sway, this was a judgment that could not be made; with its demise, this was the judgment that sealed the fate of the defendants.

In contrast to Frankfurter's long concurring opinion, Black's dissent was a mere three pages. Even for Black, such brevity was unusual. His frustrations were evidenced by his explanation that no useful purpose could be served by an extended discussion be-

65. 341 U.S. at 550–551.
66. 341 U.S. at 544.
67. See discussion of *Sweezy* v. *New Hampshire*, below.
68. 341 U.S. at 545.

cause his disagreement with the Court stemmed from "a fundamental difference in Constitutional approach."[69]

His differences with Vinson were substantial. On Black's copy
of the opinion of the Court are marginal notes which almost ridi-
cule Vinson's efforts. When the chief justice construed the Smith
Act as aimed at "advocacy" and not "discussion," Black wrote,
"What is the difference?" When Vinson argued that the protection from "armed internal attack" justified restriction of speech,
Black commented, "Now puts 'speech' and 'armed internal attack'
in same category." To Vinson's attempt to distinguish the decisions of Holmes and Brandeis by emphasizing the increased
threat posed by worldwide communism, Black caustically wrote,
"The goblin'll get you." And when Vinson adopted the Hand slid-
ing scale restatement of clear and present danger, Black replied,
"In other words, courts can approve suppression of free speech at
will and despite 1st Amendment."[70]

Although he protested the demise of clear and present danger
in his dissent, he left the bulk of the argument to the dissent of
Douglas, using his own dissent to pose an indirect challenge to the
majority of the Court. Frankfurter, as well as Vinson, had retained the power of judicial review in First Amendment cases
while stripping that amendment of any real substantive content.
Not only did this use offend Black's most basic political instincts
but after *Dennis* it appeared to demand an answer to an obvious
question: if the Court was to continue to exercise the power of judicial review in First Amendment cases, what was the measure of
that review? Thus he wrote:

> So long as this Court exercises the power of judicial review of legis-
> lation, I cannot agree that the First Amendment permits us to sus-
> tain laws suppressing freedom of speech and press on the basis of
> Congress' or our own notions of mere "reasonableness." Such a
> doctrine waters down the First Amendment so that it amounts to
> little more than an admonition to Congress.[71]

69. 341 U.S. at 579.
70. HLBLC 306.
71. 341 U.S. at 580.

Under the preference doctrine, the exercise of judicial review was tied to an almost literal reading of the First Amendment. *Dennis* signaled the demise of the preference doctrine; indeed, Black concluded his notes on Vinson's draft majority opinion with the assertion, "Five years ago very few would have thought such convictions possible."[72] Years earlier in *Adamson* Black had responded to the flexible approach to due process by publicly proclaiming that due process meant no more nor no less than the Bill of Rights. Now in response to the balancing of First Amendment rights he would follow a similar strategy. "I think the First Amendment, with the Fourteenth," he would soon declare, "'absolutely' forbids such laws without any 'ifs' or 'buts' or 'whereases.'"[73]

Aftermath

Thus within a year of *Dennis*, Black began to move toward an absolute reading of the First Amendment. Although such a position easily squared with his larger political vision and although its roots are found in his original *Bridges* dissent, the move to absolutism was, in many ways, a response to Frankfurter. In both due process and First Amendment cases, Black originally sought to limit sharply but not eliminate judicial judgment. As Frankfurter increasingly sought to expand the sphere of discretion and judgment, Black increasingly reverted to the textual commands of the Constitution. In the incorporation debate, Black lost the battle but won the war when the Court relied upon selective incorporation to bring the critical provisions of the Bill of Rights within the scope of the Fourteenth Amendment. In the First Amendment debate, the results are harder to assess. To a great degree Black's move to absolutism was a reaction to Frankfurter and designed to force the Court to delineate the scope of judicial review under the First Amendment. Nevertheless, ad hoc balancing remained the "test" of a majority of the Court at least through the 1969 decision in *Brandenburg* v. *Ohio*.[74]

The similarity between Black's move to incorporation and his

72. HLBLC 306.
73. *Beauharnais* v. *Illinois*, 343 U.S. at 275 [Black, J. dissenting]).
74. 395 U.S. 444 (1969).

advocacy of a literal reading of the First Amendment is further evidenced by the attempt to escape the confines of both. Judgment *was* inescapable in due process cases,[75] and to ensure freedom within order required more than a literal reading of the First Amendment. This was particularly evident during the 1960s, when symbolic protest became an important method of communicating ideas.[76] The preference doctrine permitted judicial intervention when freedom of expression appeared to threaten disorder; on its face, absolutism precluded such flexibility. Unwilling to abandon the absolute approach, Black was faced with the difficult task of remaining faithful to the absolute position while retaining the flexibility lost with the demise of the preference doctrine.

"In giving absolute protection to speech," he wrote in 1968, "I have always been careful to draw a line between speech and conduct."[77] As easy as this distinction might be to articulate, it was difficult to put into practice; as his opinion in *Struthers* indicated, certain conduct was constitutionally protected. Thus another dichotomy was created between direct and indirect regulation of speech; regulations directly restricting speech must fall, but those intended to regulate conduct and only indirectly impinging on speech were subject to a balancing test.[78] But again, despite the ease with which these exceptions could be expressed, their application hinged on precisely the judgment and discretion the absolute position was intended to inhibit.[79]

Throughout the 1950s, Frankfurter's ad hoc balancing occupied the middle ground between the absolutism of Black and Douglas and the apparent abnegation of Tom Clark and Harold Burton. Frankfurter and John Harlan became critical swing votes.[80]

75. See Chapter 4.
76. See A. E. Dick Howard, "Mr. Justice Black: The Negro Protest Movement and the Rule of Law," 53 *Virginia Law Review* 1030 (1967).
77. Hugo Black, *A Constitutional Faith* (New York: Knopf, 1968), p. 53. See, e.g. *Tinker* v. *Des Moines Indep. Comm. School Dist.*, 393 U.S. 503 (1969) (Black, J. dissenting).
78. See *Cox* v. *Louisiana*, 379 U.S. 536 (1965) (Black, J. dissenting).
79. A review of Black's free speech decisions of the 1960s is beyond the scope of this work. The contradictions within Black's absolute position and their impact on these cases are set out in Magee, *Mr. Justice Black*, pp. 144–181.
80. One indication of this alignment is that from 1955 through 1958 in the more than twenty cases coming to the Court involving internal security, Frank-

During the difficult days of the McCarthy era, Frankfurter and
Harlan provided leadership in disposing of cases based on procedural grounds or statutory interpretation rather than broad constitutional pronouncements sure to arouse the wrath of powerful
political forces.[81] Despite this attempt, decisions narrowly construing national and local attempts to investigate subversives resulted in a congressional backlash;[82] in the face of this threat to
the Court, the votes of Frankfurter and Harlan proved critical
in reversing the Court's direction and sustaining congressional
power.[83]

Frankfurter could easily occupy the swing position on the
Court: indeed, his role conception appeared to demand that he
do so. But ad hoc balancing of constitutional claims did not always
tilt in favor of the state. In *Sweezy* v. *New Hampshire*,[84] the attorney general of the state, operating under a resolution of the state
legislature, began an investigation to determine whether the state
subversive activities act was being violated. Sweezy, a professor at
the state university, was called to testify. He described his past associations at length and denied being a member of the Communist party. He refused, however, to answer questions concerning
the Progressive party. At a later hearing he also refused to answer
questions concerning a lecture he had given at the university. He
was found in contempt, and the state courts affirmed the conviction.

---

furter dissented only twice. See Clyde Jacobs, *Justice Frankfurter and Civil Liberties*
(Berkeley and Los Angeles: University of California Press, 1961), pp. 131–132.

81. See, e.g., Frankfurter concurring in *Joint Anti-Fascist Committee* v. *McGrath*,
341 U.S. 123 (1951). In *Watkins* v. *United States*, 354 U.S. 178 (1957), Chief Justice
Earl Warren raised serious constitutional questions concerning the scope and
power of congressional committees. Frankfurter in a brief concurring opinion focused on procedural irregularities. On receiving Warren's draft opinion, Frankfurter struck every reference to the First Amendment and tried to convince Warren that this was not a First Amendment case (FFLC 220–4048). Frankfurter's
political instincts were sharp; *Watkins* became a rallying point for those who sought
to curb the power of the Court. See Walter F. Murphy, *Congress and the Court*
(Chicago: University of Chicago Press, 1962).

82. See, e.g., *Pennsylvania* v. *Nelson*, 350 U.S. 497 (1956); *Yates* v. *United States*,
354 U.S. 298 (1957).

83. Compare, e.g., *Watkins* with *Barenblatt* v. *United States*, 360 U.S. 109 (1959).

84. 354 U.S. 234 (1957).

A six-man majority of the Court reversed. Chief Justice Warren, writing for Black, Douglas, and William Brennan, avoided
the First Amendment issue by holding that the failure of the state
legislature to specify in its grant of authority to the attorney general that it desired the type of information those questions were
designed to elicit violated due process. Frankfurter, joined by
Harlan, found ruling on the First Amendment issue inescapable.
As in *Dennis*, the case presented the difficult task of weighing the
state's right to self-protection against the values of the First
Amendment. In *Sweezy*, the balance was struck in favor of the
First Amendment. The reasons are not hard to discern: "Whatever, on the basis of massive proof and in the light of history of
which this Court may well take judicial notice, be the justification
for not regarding the Communist Party as a conventional political
party, no such justification has been afforded in regard to the
Progressive Party."[85] The party of Henry Wallace was simply not
the same as the party of Josef Stalin.

An additional judgment had to be made regarding the intrinsic
worth of Sweezy's speech. Although academic freedom was obviously an important value to Frankfurter, it was not simply a personal value but critical to the progress and development of the
modern state. He found Sweezy's lecture (regardless of the content) qualitatively different from the rhetoric of Eugene Dennis
and his cohorts:

> Progress in the natural sciences is not remotely confined to findings
> made in the laboratory. Insights into the mysteries of nature are
> born of hypothesis and speculation. The more so is this true in the
> pursuit of understanding in the groping endeavors of what are
> called the social sciences, the concern of which is man and society.
> The problems that are the respective preoccupations of anthropol-
> ogy, sociology and related areas of scholarship are merely depart-
> mentalized dealing, by way of manageable divisions of analysis with
> interpenetrating aspects of holistic perplexities. For society's good
> —if understanding be an essential need of society—inquiries into
> these problems, speculations about them, stimulation in others of
> reflection upon them, must be left as unfettered as possible.[86]

85. 354 U.S. at 266.
86. 354 U.S. at 261.

Ad hoc balancing in the hands of Frankfurter meant measuring the social worth of any activity. Such judgment was critical to his view of the polity and progress; indeed, throughout his opinion in *Sweezy* are constant references to the needs of a "progressive society." The judge as democratic fact-finder was an important and vital participant in that society. Frankfurter concluded *Sweezy* with words that summed up his entire vision of the role of the Supreme Court in American government: "But in the end, judgment cannot be escaped—the judgment of this Court."[87]

87. 354 U.S. at 267.

Conclusion

The Founders knew that Law alone saves a society
from being rent by internecine strife or ruled by
mere brute power however disguised. . . . To that end
they set apart a body of men, who were to be the
depositories of law, who by their disciplined training
and character and by withdrawal from the usual
temptations of private interest may reasonably
be expected to be "as free, impartial, and independent
as the lot of humanity will admit."

> Felix Frankfurter, *United*
> *States v. United Mine Workers*
> 330 U.S. 250, 308 (1947)

The Chief [Earl Warren], [William] Brennan, Bill
Douglas, Arthur [Goldberg], Thurgood [Marshall],
are usually going to do the right thing. They're kind
of like Marcus Aurelius. While they're around we'll
generally get just judgment. But when they're gone
and we get a McReynolds type he's free to let go with
his bad sense of right and wrong. I believe we've got to
tie the judges of this Court . . . even if we've got to
sacrifice doing some good through the federal courts.

> Hugo Black, recounted by his
> son, Hugo Black, Jr., *My Father*

The Dilemma of the American Judiciary

The study of the decision making of Felix Frank-
furter and Hugo Black forcefully illustrates the impact of political
environment on judicial behavior. The democratic culture and

values of America demand a judiciary professing allegiance to restraint, and, although this expression of self-denial is a source of
judicial power, it also reveals the ambiguous role played by a "coequal" branch devoid of the legitimacy conferred by popular sovereignty in a culture with a strong democratic ethos. The very political setting in which American judges toil places powerful
constraints upon their conduct. Despite frequent scholarly attempts to study judges in a manner similar to the study of other
political actors,[1] judges are different and studies of judicial behavior must account for these differences.

A theme that has resounded throughout these pages is the
ever-present tension between majority rule and judicial review.
To place in an elite clothed in judicial robes the power to oversee
the decisions of popularly elected branches has evoked an uneasi-
ness in both the populace and the judiciary. Further complicating
the judicial role are the constant yet often discordant demands of
liberalism and democracy. Although we often speak of the liberal
democratic tradition in describing American politics and thought,
the two components of that tradition are often at odds, and nowhere is this conflict more apparent than in the decisions of the
Supreme Court. The Court has been characterized by men as diverse as Brooks Adams and Robert Jackson as the spokesman of
"conservative" and "privileged" classes; it is perhaps testimony to
the imprecision of labels in American politics—as well as the wisdom of Louis Hartz—that the words of both Adams and Jackson
were evoked by a Court whose principal failing was an unyielding
attachment to the liberalism of John Locke.[2] The Court, as many
have suggested, may well be the guardian of principles and values
that transcend the clash of day-to-day politics, but the question of
which values and principles still remains.

1. For example, Glendon Schubert described the critical question in judicial
research: "When men play political roles, to what extent are their public acts influenced by their personal beliefs?" (*The Judicial Mind* [Evanston: Northwestern University Press, 1965], p. 15). None other than the founder of political jurisprudence, C. Herman Pritchett, has warned against overlooking jurisprudence in the
haste to understand the political in the study of political jurisprudence ("The Development of Judicial Research" in Joel B. Grossman and Joseph Tanenhaus, eds.,
Frontiers of Judicial Research [New York: Wiley, 1969]).

2. Brooks Adams, *The Theory of Social Revolutions* (New York: Macmillan,
1913), p. 33; Robert J. Jackson, *The Struggle for Judicial Supremacy* (New York:
Knopf, 1941), p. 187.

The clash of these discordant themes finds expression in the expectation that American judges will reach the right substantive result while adhering to the correct judicial method. Courts are not superlegislatures, and judges, acutely aware of this political truth, must constantly strive to distinguish their decision making from that of other political actors who are more directly accountable.[3] At the same time courts have assumed enormous responsibility in the formation and implementation of public policy and, as such, are often judged by the consequences of their decisions. The result is that judges in America must serve two masters. On the one hand, they must strive to remove from their decisions the appearance of ad hoc judgment and develop a method of decision making freed from the vagaries of personal will and discretion. On the other, these decisions are often measured against the dominant political impulses of the day. In starkest terms, the dilemma of the American judiciary is the inevitable truth that correct judicial methods do not inexorably lead to correct political results.[4]

Frankfurter, Black, and the Judicial Role

Hugo Black and Felix Frankfurter arrived on the Supreme Court with a deep-seated faith in the wisdom of judicial restraint and a belief that the failure of their predecessors lay in their disregard for this fundamental norm of judicial behavior. In retrospect, despite Frankfurter's extensive knowledge of the

3. By the late 1950s a growing body of scholarly literature criticized the Warren Court for failing to keep this distinction in mind. See, e.g., Herbert Wechsler, "Toward Neutral Principles of Constitutional Law," 73 *Harvard Law Review* 1 (1959); Alexander Bickel, *The Least Dangerous Branch* (Indianapolis: Bobbs-Merrill, 1962); Philip Kurland, "Toward a Political Supreme Court," 37 *University of Chicago Law Review* 19 (1969). A review of these critiques and an attempt to place them within the context of American legal thought appears in G. Edward White, "The Evolution of Reasoned Elaboration: Jurisprudential Criticism and Social Change," in G. Edward White, *Patterns of American Legal Thought* (Indianapolis: Bobbs-Merrill, 1978).

4. This same recognition of the judicial dilemma implicitly appears in Bickel, *Least Dangerous Branch*. Bickel's celebration of the "passive virtues"—judicial techniques for disposing of cases without reaching the merits—is a recognition that right methods do not always lead to right results. Rather than sacrificing either, Bickel called for increased use of standing, ripeness, and so forth as a means of disposing of cases. His frustration with the Warren Court's failure to heed this advice appears in his *The Supreme Court and the Idea of Progress* (New Haven: Yale University Press, 1978).

Court and Black's political experience, this was a naive understanding. Roosevelt had transformed the Court not by replacing
activists with those believing in restraint but by replacing eighteenth-century liberals with twentieth-century liberals. Frankfurter and Black, as well as the judges of an earlier era, accepted
the Horatio Alger image of advancement in America. The justices
of the Stone Court, however, differed from their predecessors in
their faith in the state as the means for returning to this liberal
ideal. In this way, their dominant political and economic values,
for the most part, coincided with those of the New Deal, and a position of judicial deference to popularly elected branches appeared to join the appropriate judicial method with the correct
substantive results. World War II and the subsequent Cold War
paranoia shattered this consensus and forced a reexamination of
the relationship between right results and right methods. For an
earlier generation of justices, a faith in restraint failed to protect
essential property rights from the perceived excesses of the democratic process. For Frankfurter and Black, a similar faith in restraint left the liberal values of personal freedom and autonomy
similarly undefended. Once again the dynamic tension between
liberal values and the democratic process found expression in the
workings of the Supreme Court.

At the heart of this tension is the basic fact that restraint, like
many words in the American political lexicon, means different
things to different people. To give flesh to the bare bones of such
a term requires an appreciation of why it is a necessary and accepted norm. Hence scholarly disputes over judicial review rest,
more often than not, on the competing authors' differing views of
the dynamics of the American political system.[5] The same is true
for judges; a judge's perception of his role is inexorably shaped
by his larger political education and values. To understand the
former, one must appreciate the latter.

Through a detailed study of the background and writings of

5. Cf. Henry Steele Commager, *Majority Rule and Minority Rights* (New York:
Oxford University Press, 1943), and Eugene Rostow, "The Democratic Character of
Judicial Review," 66 *Harvard Law Review* 193 (1952). For Commager, the distin-
guishing element of American democracy is majority rule, whereas Rostow main-
tains that a democracy need not be marked by the election of all officials who exercise critical authority. From this basic disagreement, the authors derive very
different approaches to judicial review.

Frankfurter and Black, I have attempted to develop a richer, more precise picture of the political values of these two men than is possible through merely descriptive and ambiguous labels such as liberal and conservative. From these political values each man developed a role orientation that guided his career on the Court. By concentrating on the work product as opposed to published opinions or recorded votes, it was possible to illustrate the operation of role orientation in the judicial process. In the case of Frankfurter and Black, role did not directly determine judicial votes but rather dictated the process of decision making employed to reach those votes. This conclusion at once illustrates the value of role research in judicial studies and the difficulty of developing a truly predictive model of decision making.[6] Role orientation controlled how Frankfurter and Black perceived cases, and the resulting method of decision making governed which of the many stimuli presented by a constitutional case could be properly considered and assigned normative weights to those stimuli deemed appropriate. Thus the ultimate vote in any case was rarely the direct expression of an individualized value but rather a far more complex process in which role and process intervened between values and votes. The votes of Frankfurter and Black to permit the reexecution of Willie Francis, for example, were not the judicial expression of similar attitudes toward capital punishment or the rights of the accused. Indeed, the evidence presented here illustrates that these votes were the product of very different understandings of the role of judges; Frankfurter and Black voted to affirm for very different reasons that were only indirectly related to the substantive issues posed by the case. To focus simply upon votes in the study of judicial behavior is to fail to appreciate the important, if often difficult to perceive, impact of process and jurisprudence.

The role and process of Frankfurter and Black illustrated in this

---

6. James Gibson, "The Role Concept in Judicial Research," 3 *Law and Police Quarterly* 291 (1981), suggests other reasons for the failure to link role concepts to voting behavior but acknowledges that role's primary impact is on process and not votes. This may explain a gap in the most recent empirical work on role theory. J. Woodford Howard has found in his study of U.S. courts of appeals judges a strong correlation between political values and role conception coupled with a significantly lower correlation between role and voting outcome (*Courts of Appeals in the Federal Judicial System* [Princeton: Princeton University Press, 1981]).

study in two areas of civil liberty cases were at work across a broad spectrum of issues. In *United States* v. *Darby*,[7] a case upholding the Fair Labor Standards Act which Black had supported as a senator, Justice Stone wrote for the Court overruling *Hammer* v. *Dagenhart*[8] and broadly defining Congress's power under the commerce clause. In his original draft, Stone noted that a minimum wage of $600 for a year's work could hardly be judged unfair or oppressive. In a response recalling his objections to Hughes's effort in *Cox* v. *New Hampshire*,[9] Black refused to accept any suggestion of a judicially enforced standard of reasonableness. "So far as the due process clause of the Fifth Amendment is concerned," he wrote Stone, "I am unable to see its application to an act properly coming within the commerce power."[10] When Stone deleted the passage, Black enthusiastically supported the opinion. Indeed, although Black viewed the commerce clause as vesting sweeping powers in Congress, he was predictably reluctant to find in that clause a source of judicial power to control state legislation affecting national commerce: "Both the commerce clause and the due process clause serve high purposes when confined in their proper scope. But a stretching of either outside its sphere can paralyze the legislative process rendering the people's legislative representatives impotent to perform their duty of providing rules to govern this dynamic civilization. Both clauses easily lend themselves to inordinate expansions of this Court's power at the expense of legislative power."[11]

Although Frankfurter might easily agree with these sentiments, he nonetheless was far more willing to find in the commerce clause a source of judicial power.[12] Implicit was a belief that although the primary responsibility of governing fell to the states, the states did not always govern wisely. In the absence of congres-

---

7. 312 U.S. 100 (1941).

8. 247 U.S. 251 (1919).

9. See text accompanying note 5, Chap. 5.

10. Alpheus Mason, *Harlan Fiske Stone: Pillar of the Law* (New York: Viking, 1956), p. 554.

11. *H. P. Hood and Sons* v. *Du Mond*, 336 U.S. 525 (1949) (Black, J. dissenting). See also *Dean Milk* v. *Madison*, 340 U.S. 349 (1951); *Southern Pacific* v. *Arizona*, 325 U.S. 761 (1945).

12. Louis Henkin, "Voice of Modern Federalism," in Wallace Mendelson, ed., *Felix Frankfurter: The Judge* (New York: Reynal, 1961).

sional action, the Court could act as Congress's surrogate, making the necessary adjustments to ensure economic progress. As in due process and free expression cases, judgment was inescapable, requiring not "absolutes" but a judiciary "striking a balance between competing interests."[13]

The commerce clause cases were further examples of the continuing impact of the distinct role orientations of Frankfurter and Black. They also illustrate the imprecision of activism and restraint as categories of judicial behavior. A similar example can be found in the search and seizure cases. "There isn't a man on this Court who has as deep a conviction as I have against 'unreasonable searches and seizures,'" Frankfurter wrote Chafee in 1955, and in the fifteen "pure" Fourth Amendment cases decided during his twenty years on the Court, he voted to exclude the evidence in every case but one.[14] In the same cases, the "activist" Black took a narrow view of the Fourth Amendment, voting with unusual frequency to uphold the government's position.

Explaining this anomalous voting behavior illustrates the subtle interaction of values and process. Although Frankfurter openly admitted his attachment to the values protected by the Fourth Amendment and commentators have sought to explain Black's voting as an expression of personal preference,[15] a more profitable enterprise would be to consider the individual role orientations and process of decision making in the context of search and seizure. A fundamental explanation of the voting in search and seizure cases on the part of Black and Frankfurter is that the Fourth Amendment prohibits only "unreasonable" searches and

13. *H. P. Hood and Sons* v. *Du Mond*, 336 U.S. 525 (1949) (Frankfurter, J., dissenting). See also *Freeman* v. *Hewitt*, 329 U.S. 249 (1946); *McLeod* v. *J. E. Dilworth Co.*, 322 U.S. 327 (1944).

14. FF to Chafee, 10/25/55, FFLC 42-751. A "pure" Fourth Amendment case is one in which the federal government is a party and the case turns on the application of the Fourth Amendment. My thanks to Robert Swidler, student at Cornell University Law School, for bringing these facts to my attention.

15. Explanations run from Black's dislike of "ordinary" criminals to his days as prosecutor in Jefferson County to his conflicts with federal courts in his attempts to secure evidence for his Senate investigations. See Sylvia Snowliss, "The Legacy of Justice Black," 187 *Supreme Court Review* (1973); Gerald T. Dunne, *Hugo Black and the Judicial Revolution* (New York: Simon and Schuster, 1977); Charlotte Williams, *Hugo Black: A Study in the Judicial Process* (Baltimore: Johns Hopkins University Press, 1950).

seizures, and that word triggered very different responses on the part of the two men. A reasonable standard, in the hands of Frankfurter, was another source of judicial power, and with little hesitation he sought to tie that standard to a wide-ranging protection of privacy. "It makes all the difference in the world," he wrote Justice Sherman Minton, "whether one recognizes as the central fact about the Fourth Amendment that it was a response to abuses felt by the colonies to the extent of being one of the potent causes of the Revolution or one thinks of it merely as a requirement for a piece of paper."[16] In 1947 he wrote Frank Murphy of his understanding of the Court's Fourth Amendment decisions: "This Court, unlike several of the state courts, has jealously applied the protection of privacy which the experience with lawlessness of the framers of the Bill of Rights led them to secure by the prohibitions of unreasonable searches and seizures."[17] The result was a jurisprudence in which the provisions of the Fourth Amendment became the means of furthering the liberal value of personal privacy.

As Frankfurter found in the Fourth Amendment a broad mandate for judicial protection of privacy, Black sought to confine its scope. He freely acknowledged that the Fourth Amendment called for judicial judgment,[18] but he exercised that judgment with a constant fear of its potential for abuse. Throughout the 1940s and 1950s Black voted to uphold the power of the national government to search, narrowly confining the scope of the Fourth Amendment and the discretion of the Court under the reasonableness standard. Moreover, he rebelled against finding in the Fourth Amendment a judicially enforced right of privacy which extended the Court's power beyond the narrow confines he found in the Fourth Amendment. Years after Frankfurter's death he wrote:

> With this decision the Court has completed, I hope, its rewriting of the Fourth Amendment which started only recently when the Court began referring incessantly to the Fourth Amendment not so

16. FF to Minton, 1/25/50, FFLC 84-1721.
17. FF to Murphy, 2/15/46 FFLC 86-1765.
18. Hugo Black, *A Constitutional Faith* (New York: Knopf, 1968).

much as a law against *unreasonable* searches and seizures as one to protect an individual's privacy. . . . Few things happen to an individual that do not affect his privacy in one way or another. Thus, by arbitrarily substituting the Court's language, designed to protect privacy, for the Constitution's language, designed to protect against unreasonable searches and seizures, the Court has made the Fourth Amendment its vehicle for holding all laws violative of the Constitution which offend the Court's broadest concept of privacy. . . .

No general right is created by the Amendment so as to give this Court the unlimited power to hold unconstitutional everything which affects privacy. Certainly the Framers, well acquainted as they were with the excesses of governmental power, did not intend to grant the Court such omnipotent lawmaking authority as that. The history of governments proves that it is dangerous to repose such power in courts.[19]

Challenges to state convictions based on illegally seized evidence produced different results. Black's understanding of the judicial role demanded that both federal and state cases be decided under the provisions of the Fourth Amendment.[20] For Frankfurter, the state cases were a distinct issue; the applicable standard was no longer the reasonableness of the challenged search and seizure but the "shocks the conscience" test of the Fourteenth Amendment. In *Wolf* v. *Colorado*[21] he had little difficulty in concluding that privacy was a "concept of ordered liberty" protected by the

19. *Katz* v. *United States*, 389 U.S. 347 (1967) (Black, J. dissenting).

20. The troublesome issue for Black was whether the exclusionary rule was a constitutional command and thus binding on the states. Since *Weeks* v. *United States*, 232 U.S. 383 (1914), illegally seized evidence was inadmissible in federal courts. In *Wolf* v. *Colorado*, 338 U.S. 25 (1949), the Court per Frankfurter held that a state did not deny a defendant due process simply because evidence had been obtained in a manner that would have made it inadmissible in a federal court. The Court emphasized that the exclusionary rule of *Weeks* was not based on the requirements of the Fourth Amendment. Justice Rutledge's conference notes in *Wolf* indicate that Black originally voted to reverse because "the 14th takes in the 4th," presumably including the exclusionary rule. Following Frankfurter's statement at the conference, Black switched his vote to a "pass" because he was "waiting to see what 4 Amend. means in fed. const." Black later voted with Frankfurter in *Wolf* and filed a concurring opinion to the effect that although the Fourteenth Amendment incorporated the Fourth, the exclusionary rule was not part of the Fourth Amendment (Rutledge LC 173). By *Mapp* v. *Ohio*, 367 U.S. 643 (1961), Black had moved to the position that the Fourth and Fifth Amendments, taken together, required the exclusion of illegally seized evidence in state proceedings.

21. See note 20, above.

Fourteenth Amendment, but he refused to hold that states must exclude all illegally seized evidence from state proceedings. In a subsquent letter to Justice Clark he underscored the inherent discretion vested in the courts in determining when such evidence must be excluded:

> The decision in the *Wolf* case, it cannot be too often repeated, was strictly limited to the holding that a state conviction is not invalidated under the Fourteenth *merely* because some evidence in a state court would have to be excluded by virtue of the Fourth Amendment in a federal prosecution and by reason of that fact would invalidate a federal conviction. The controlling circumstance in this case as in *Rochin* is that there was conduct by the police in obtaining this evidence which went beyond merely not having a search warrant for the assailed evidence.[22]

The search and seizure cases further illustrate the impact of process on values and judicial votes. Frankfurter cared deeply about protection of privacy, and his understanding of the judicial role permitted, for the most part, judicial protection of this value in the federal context.[23] At the same time, role and process served to limit the operation of this value in federal review of state searches and seizures. In the case of Black, role and process resulted in a limited reading of the apparently flexible standards of the Fourth Amendment and a more confident implementation of constitutional commands that appeared to require little judicial discretion.

22. FF to Clark, 12/29/53, FFLC 45-497. The letter was written during consideration of *Irvine* v. *California*, 347 U.S. 128 (1954), in which the state police had made repeated illegal entries into Irvine's house to install a listening device. The majority found the police behavior abhorrent but followed what they believed to be the holding of *Wolf* and refused to exclude the evidence. Frankfurter was sufficiently outraged that he believed the evidence inadmissible following *Rochin* (see Chapter 4, n. 87). Black dissented on the grounds that the evidence had been seized in violation of the Fifth Amendment. *Irvine* again illustrates Frankfurter's refusal to be tied to literal standards. If the police had made a mere technical violation, the evidence would not be excluded; if their behavior shocked the conscience, it would.

23. It is interesting to recall Frankfurter's reaction to Black's request to remove "reasonable" from the *Cox* opinion, i.e., that civil liberties would be better protected if the Court were free to proceed under a reasonableness standard. See text accompanying notes 5–8, Chapter 5.

Personality and Judging

Throughout this study I have avoided any sustained discussion of psychological factors that may have led Frankfurter and Black to arrive at their political values. As suggested earlier, there may well have been psychological factors at work that compelled Frankfurter's expansive reading of the commands of the Fourth Amendment. The present study, however, is directed at a broader understanding of how Frankfurter and Black understood the role of courts and judges within the polity and the effect of this understanding on their decision making. To further this end, the two men were considered as parts of larger intellectual movements shaped by a particular social setting rather than as particular personality types.

Although the use of psychology has yet to be established as a reliable tool in understanding judicial ideology, it is useful in understanding judicial behavior. H. N. Hirsch's portrait of Frankfurter coupled with what we know of Hugo Black (a psychological study of Black may now be impossible, given the guarded and limited extent of his personal writing) compels a conclusion that, despite disclaimers to the contrary, the relationship between the two men was marked by tension.[24] This tension, in turn, affected their behavior on the Court. As described in Chapters 4 and 5, each man began with basic differences concerning his understanding of the Court and American government, and the dynamics of their personal relationship compelled them to maximize the differences in their approaches. Although it is impossible to point to conclusive evidence to establish this point, this hypothesis, particularly in the case of Black, fits with the evidence uncovered in this study.

That evidence points to the conclusion that despite the professed literalism of Black, it is highly questionable whether he actually intended to define the due process clause of the Fourteenth Amendment as meaning no more nor no less than the Bill of Rights or that he viewed the free expression provision of the First Amendment as an absolute command prohibiting judicial judgment. Rather, the evidence shows that Black did believe that due

24. H. N. Hirsch, *The Enigma of Felix Frankfurter* (New York: Basic Books, 1981).

process had an independent meaning, albeit limited, and that only when the intensity of Frankfurter's "lessons" on the correct interpretation of the Fourteenth Amendment increased did Black's public position begin to harden. A similar movement can be seen in the First Amendment cases; the switch from the preference doctrine to the absolute position followed the ascendancy of the ad hoc balancing position of Frankfurter. Although less apparent, Frankfurter continually sought to expand the sphere of judicial judgment while Black sought to decrease it.

In short, these men began with two distinct role orientations, but how these role perceptions manifested themselves over the course of their careers was influenced by personality and personal relations.[25] Personality unquestionably plays a role in judicial behavior; in the highly charged atmosphere of the Supreme Court, it also influences the development and expression of American law.

Felix Frankfurter, Hugo Black, and the American Judicial Tradition

A basic conclusion of this work is that despite the powerful position assumed by the judiciary in American life, a judge's perception of his role is often shaped by doubt and uncertainty. The framers' decision to remove judges from popular accountability in the name of judicial independence has worked as a serious constraint upon judicial power. Lacking the legitimacy conferred by popular sovereignty, judges must continually strive to justify, to themselves and to the populace, the exercise of judicial authority. The result is that judges have become our political philosophers, not simply because of the complexity of the issues

25. Several scholars have concluded that Black became more conservative in his decision making during his later years. One example will suffice. Glendon Schubert suggests that this turnaround was the result of old age—a biological explanation of judicial voting (*The Constitutional Polity* [Boston: Boston University Press, 1970], pp. 118–129). In reaching this conclusion, Schubert assigns no significance to Black's jurisprudence and his understanding of the Court's function in American government. From this latter perspective, however, Black remained remarkably consistent; the variable was not Black but the nature of the issues coming to the Court in the 1960s and early 1970s. Nevertheless, assuming that Black's voting behavior did change, it is interesting that this change coincided almost precisely with Frankfurter's retirement from the Court.

they are called upon to decide but also because of their continual need to reexamine and rearticulate core principles of American government as a prerequisite to their authority.

The net effect is that the American judicial tradition is marked by ambiguity. Principally this is the case because we are a nation that is at once liberal and democratic, and we expect judges to be faithful to both traditions. It is, perhaps, an unrealistic expectation, and thus it is hardly surprising that after two hundred years the judiciary is still a subject of intense controversy and debate. In the final analysis, the judicial role remains ambiguous for judge and citizen alike.

Frankfurter and Black are symbolic of that tradition. Fearful of judicial tyranny, each sought in highly developed role orientations with roots deep in American political and social thought the means to ensure disinterested decision making. Each continually sought to harmonize judicial review with its democratic setting, and each strove to remove from the judicial process the vagaries of personal preference. Each ultimately was guided in his task by a single-minded devotion to the Constitution and the ideal of the rule of law. In the end, perhaps that is all we can reasonably expect of our judges.

A Note on the
Archival Sources

Many collections of private papers were consulted during the preparation of this manuscript. Those found at the Library of Congress are designated LC preceded by the name of the collection and followed by the box number. Thus Rutledge LC 131 signifies box 131 of the Rutledge collection at the Library of Congress. Felix Frankfurter and Hugo Black are abbreviated FF and HLB respectively. In the case of the Frankfurter collection a file number is also included and this follows the box number. Thus FFLC 55-1049 represents file 1049, box 55, of the Frankfurter collection at the Library of Congress.

A second Frankfurter collection is housed at the Harvard University Law School Library. Material from this collection is designated FF HLSL followed by box and file number.

Selected Bibliography

ABRAHAM, HENRY. *Freedom and the Court*. New York: Oxford University Press, 1977.

———. *Justices and Presidents*. New York: Penguin, 1974.

ADAMS, BROOKS. *The Theory of Social Revolutions*. New York: Macmillan, 1913.

AUERBACH, JEROLD S. *Unequal Justice*. New York: Oxford University Press, 1977.

BALL, HOWARD. *The Vision and the Dream of Hugo Black*. Tuscaloosa: University of Alabama Press, 1975.

BECKER, THEODORE. *Political Behavioralism and Modern Jurisprudence*. Chicago: Rand McNally, 1964.

BENTLEY, ARTHUR. *The Process of Government*. Cambridge, Mass.: Belknap Press, 1967.

BERGER, RAOUL. *Government by the Judiciary*. Cambridge, Mass.: Harvard University Press, 1977.

BERMAN, DANIEL M. "The Political Philosophy of Hugo L. Black." Ph.D. dissertation, Rutgers University, 1957.

BICKEL, ALEXANDER. *The Least Dangerous Branch*. Indianapolis, N.Y.: Bobbs-Merrill, 1962.

———. *The Supreme Court and the Idea of Progress*. New Haven: Yale University Press, 1978.

BIDDLE, FRANCIS. *Justice Holmes, Natural Law and the Supreme Court*. New York: Macmillan, 1961.

BILLINGTON, MONROE LEE. *The Political South in the 20th Century*. New York: Scribners, 1975.

BLACK, CHARLES. *The People and the Court*. New York: Macmillan, 1960.

BLACK, HUGO. *A Constitutional Faith*. New York: Knopf, 1968.

———. "Reminisces." 18 *Alabama Law Review* 3 (1963).

BLACK, HUGO, JR. *My Father: A Remembrance.* New York: Random House, 1975.

BLOOMFIELD, MAXWELL. *American Lawyers in a Changing Society.* Cambridge, Mass.: Harvard University Press, 1976.

CASH, W. J. *Mind of the South.* New York: Knopf, 1946.

CHALMERS, DAVID M. *Hooded Americanism.* New York: Doubleday, 1965.

COMMAGER, HENRY STEELE. *Majority Rule and Minority Rights.* New York: Oxford University Press, 1943.

CONGRESSIONAL QUARTERLY. *Guide to the Supreme Court.* Washington: Congressional Quarterly, 1978.

COOPER, JEROME A. "Mr. Justice Hugo L. Black: Footnotes to a Great Case," 24 *Alabama Law Review* 1 (1972).

CORWIN, EDWIN. *Liberty against Government.* Baton Rouge: Louisiana State University Press, 1948.

———. "The Supreme Court and the Fourteenth Amendment." 7 *Michigan Law Review* 643 (1909).

———. *The Twilight of the Supreme Court.* New Haven: Yale University Press, 1934.

COVER, ROBERT. *Justice Accused: Antislavery and the Judicial Process.* New Haven: Yale University Press, 1975.

CURRENT, RICHARD. *Secretary Stimson.* New Brunswick, N.J.: Rutgers University Press, 1954.

DANELSKI, DAVID. "Values as Variables in Judicial Decision Making: Notes toward a Theory," 19 *Vanderbilt Law Review* 721 (1966).

DANZIG R. "How Questions Begot Answers in Felix Frankfurter's First Flag Salute Opinion." 1977 *Supreme Court Review* (1977).

DAVIS, HAZEL BLACK. *Uncle Hugo.* Privately published, 1965.

DAWSON, NELSON L. *Louis D. Brandeis, Felix Frankfurter and the New Deal.* Hamden, Conn.: Archon Press, 1980.

DEAN, HOWARD. *Judicial Review and Democracy.* New York: Random House, 1966.

DILLARD, IRVING. *The Spirit of Liberty: Papers and Addresses of Learned Hand.* 3d ed. New York: Knopf, 1963.

DOUGLAS, WILLIAM O. *The Court Years.* New York: Random House, 1980.

DUNNE, GERALD T. *Hugo Black and the Judicial Revolution.* New York: Simon and Schuster, 1977.

ELMAN, PHILIP, ed. *Of Law and Men: Papers and Addresses of Felix Frankfurter.* New York: Harcourt, Brace, 1956.

ELY, JOHN HART. *Democracy and Distrust.* Cambridge, Mass.: Harvard University Press, 1980.

EMERSON, THOMAS. *The System of Freedom of Expression.* New York: Random House, 1970.

FORCEY, CHARLES. *The Crossroads of Liberalism: Croly, Weyl, Lippman and the Progressive Era, 1900–1925.* New York: Oxford University Press, 1961.

FRANK, JOHN. *Mr. Justice Black: The Man and His Opinions.* New York: Knopf, 1949.

FRANKFURTER, FELIX. *Mr. Justice Holmes and the Supreme Court.* Cambridge, Mass.: Belknap Press, 1961.

———. *The Public and Its Government.* New Haven: Yale University Press, 1930.

FREEDMAN, MAX, ed. *Roosevelt and Frankfurter: Their Correspondence.* Boston: Little, Brown, 1967.

FREIDEL, FRANK. *FDR and the South.* Baton Rouge: Louisiana State University Press, 1965.

FREUND, PAUL. "Mr. Justice Black and the Judicial Function." 14 *UCLA Law Review* 467 (1967).

———. *The Supreme Court of the United States.* Cleveland: World, 1961.

FULLER, LON. "An Afterword: Science and the Judicial Process." 79 *Harvard Law Review* 1604 (1966).

GABIN, SANFORD. *Judicial Review and the Reasonable Doubt Test.* Port Washington, N.Y.: Kennikat Press, 1980.

GIBSON, JAMES. "Judges' Role Orientations, Attitudes and Decisions: An Interactive Model." 72 *American Political Science Review* 911 (1978).

———. "The Role Concept in Judicial Research." 3 *Law and Policy Quarterly* 291 (1981).

GILMORE, GRANT. *The Ages of American Law.* New Haven: Yale University Press, 1977.

GOLDMAN, ERIC. *Rendezvous with Destiny.* New York: Vantage, 1958.

GOODWYN, LAWRENCE. *The Populist Movement.* New York: Oxford University Press, 1980.

GRAHAM, OTIS, JR. *Encore for Reform: The Old Progressives and the New Deal.* New York: Oxford University Press, 1967.

GREEN, JOHN RAEBURN. "The Bill of Rights, the Fourteenth Amendment and the Supreme Court." 46 *Michigan Law Review* 869 (1948).

GROSSMAN, JOEL B. "Role-Playing and the Analysis of Judicial Behavior: The Case of Mr. Justice Frankfurter." 11 *Journal of Public Law* 285 (1962).

———, and Tanenhaus, Joseph, eds. *Frontiers of Judicial Research.* New York: Wiley, 1969.

HACKNEY, SHELDON. *Populism to Progressivism in Alabama.* Princeton: Princeton University Press, 1969.

HAIGH, ROGER. "Defining Due Process: The Case of Mr. Justice Hugo Black." 17 *South Dakota Law Review* 1 (1972).

HAMILTON, VIRGINIA. *Hugo Black: The Alabama Years.* Baton Rouge: Louisiana State University Press, 1972.

HAND, LEARNED. *The Bill of Rights.* Cambridge, Mass.: Harvard University Press, 1958.

HARTZ, LOUIS. *The Liberal Tradition in America.* New York: Harcourt, Brace and World, 1955.

HAWLEY, ELLIS W. *The New Deal and the Problem of Monopoly.* Princeton: Princeton University Press, 1974.

HIRSCH, H. N. *The Enigma of Felix Frankfurter.* New York: Basic Books, 1981.

HOFSTADER, RICHARD. *The Age of Reform.* New York: Random House, 1955.

———. *The American Political Tradition.* New York: Vintage, 1974.

——. *The Progressive Historians: Turner, Beard and Parrington*. New York: Vintage, 1970.

HOLLINGER, DAVID. *Morris R. Cohen and the Scientific Ideal*. Cambridge, Mass.: MIT Press, 1975.

HOLMES, OLIVER W. *The Common Law*. Boston: Little, Brown, 1963.

HORWITZ, MORTON. *The Transformation of American Law, 1780–1860*. Cambridge, Mass.: Harvard University Press, 1977.

HOWARD, A. E. DICK. "Mr. Justice Black: The Negro Protest Movement and the Rule of Law." 53 *Virginia Law Review* 1030 (1967).

HOWARD, J. WOODFORD. *Courts of Appeals in the Federal Judicial System*. Princeton: Princeton University Press, 1981.

——. *Mr. Justice Murphy*. Princeton: Princeton University Press, 1968.

HUBBARD, PRESTON J. *Origins of the TVA*. Nashville: Vanderbilt University Press, 1961.

HUNTINGTON, SAMUEL P. "Paradigms of American Politics: Beyond the One, the Two and the Many." 89 *Political Science Quarterly* 1 (1974).

HURST, WILLARD. *Law and Conditions of Freedom in Nineteenth Century United States*. Madison: University of Wisconsin Press, 1958.

JACKSON, ROBERT J. *The Struggle for Judicial Supremacy*. New York: Knopf, 1941.

JACOBS, CLYDE. *Justice Frankfurter and Civil Liberties*. Berkeley and Los Angeles, Calif: University of California Press, 1961.

JACOBSOHN, GARY. *Pragmatism, Statesmanship, and the Supreme Court*. Ithaca, N.Y.: Cornell University Press, 1977.

JAFFE, LOUIS. "The Judicial Universe of Mr. Justice Frankfurter." 62 *Harvard Law Review* 357 (1949).

JAMES, DOROTHY B. "Role Theory and the Supreme Court." 30 *Journal of Politics* 160 (1968).

KADISH, SANFORD. "Methodology and Criteria in Due Process Adjudication: A Survey and Criticism." 66 *Yale Law Review* 319 (1957).

KALVIN, HARRY. "Upon Rereading Mr. Justice Black on the First Amendment." 14 *UCLA Law Review* 428 (1966).

KEY, V. O. *Southern Politics*. New York: Random House, 1947.

KONEFSKY, SAMUEL. *Chief Justice Stone and the Supreme Court*. New York: Macmillan, 1946.

——. *The Legacy of Holmes and Brandeis: A Study in the Influence of Ideas*. New York: Macmillan, 1956.

KRAMNICK, ISAAC. "Equal Opportunity and 'The Race of Life.'" *Dissent* 178 (Spring 1981).

KURLAND, PHILIP, ed. *Felix Frankfurter on the Supreme Court*. Cambridge, Mass.: Belknap Press, 1970.

——. *Mr. Justice Frankfurter and the Constitution*. Chicago: University of Chicago Press, 1971.

——. "Toward a Political Supreme Court." 37 *University of Chicago Law Review* 19 (1969).

LASH, JOSEPH, ed. *From the Diaries of Felix Frankfurter*. New York: Norton, 1975.

LASKI, HAROLD. "Mr. Justice Brandeis." *Harper's*, January 1934.

LAWLOR, REED. "Personal Stare Decisis." 41 *Southern California Law Review* 73 (1967).

LEUCHTENBURG, WILLIAM. *Franklin D. Roosevelt and the New Deal.* New York: Harper & Row, 1963.

LEVINSON, SANFORD. "The Democratic Faith of Felix Frankfurter." 25 *Stanford Law Review* 430 (1973).

LEVY, LEONARD, ed. *American Constitutional Law: Historical Essays.* New York: Harper & Row, 1966.

———, ed. *Judicial Review and the Supreme Court.* New York: Harper & Row, 1967.

LLEWELLYN, KARL. *Jurisprudence: Realism in Theory and Practice.* Chicago: University of Chicago Press, 1962.

LUSKY, LOUIS. *By What Right?* Charlottesville, Va.: Michie, 1975.

MCCLOSKEY, ROBERT. *American Conservatism in the Age of Enterprise 1865–1910.* New York: Harper & Row, 1951.

———. *The American Supreme Court.* Chicago: University of Chicago Press, 1960.

———. *The Modern Supreme Court.* Cambridge, Mass.: Harvard University Press, 1972.

MCCURDY, CHARLES W. "Justice Field and the Jurisprudence of Government-Business Relations: Some Parameters of Laissez-Faire Constitutionalism, 1863–1897." 61 *Journal of American History* 970 (1975).

MACLEISH, ARCHIBALD, and PRICHARD, E. F., JR., eds. *Law and Politics: Occasional Papers of Felix Frankfurter, 1913–1938.* New York: Harcourt, Brace, 1939.

MCPHERSON, C. B. *The Real World of Democracy.* New York: Oxford University Press, 1966.

MAGEE, JAMES. *Mr. Justice Black: Absolutist on the Court.* Charlottesville: University of Virginia Press, 1980.

MASON, ALPHEUS. *Brandeis: A Free Man's Life.* New York: Viking, 1946.

———. *Harlan Fiske Stone: Pillar of the Law.* New York: Viking, 1956.

MAYER, MARTIN. *Emory Buckner.* New York: Harper & Row, 1968.

MEADOR, DANIEL. *Mr. Justice Black and His Books.* Charlottesville: University Press of Virginia, 1974.

MENDELSON, WALLACE. *Capitalism, Democracy and the Supreme Court.* New York: Appleton-Century-Crofts, 1960.

———, ed. *Felix Frankfurter: A Tribute.* New York: Reynal, 1964.

———, ed. *Felix Frankfurter: The Judge.* New York: Reynal, 1961.

———. *Justices Black and Frankfurter: Conflict in the Court.* Chicago: University of Chicago Press, 1961.

———. "Mr. Justice Frankfurter and the Process of Judicial Review." 103 *University of Pennsylvania Law Review* 295 (1954).

MILLER, PERRY, ed. *The Legal Mind in America.* Garden City, N.Y.: Anchor, 1962.

———, ed. *The Life of the Mind in America.* New York: Harcourt, Brace and World, 1965.

MURPHY, BRUCE ALLAN. *The Brandeis/Frankfurter Connection: The Secret Political Activities of Two Supreme Court Justices.* New York: Oxford University Press, 1982.

MURPHY, WALTER F. *Congress and the Court.* Chicago: University of Chicago Press, 1962.

NOONAN, JOHN T. *Persons and Masks of the Law.* New York: Farrar, Straus, Giroux, 1979.

O'BRIEN, DENNIS. "Dennis v. U.S.: The Cold War, the Communist Conspiracy and the FBI." Ph.D. dissertation, Cornell University, 1979.

PARRISH, MICHAEL E. *Felix Frankfurter and His Times: The Reform Years.* New York: Free Press, 1982.

PAULSEN, MONRAD G. "The Fourteenth Amendment and the Third Degree." 6 *Stanford Law Review* 411 (1954).

PHILLIPS, HARLAN, ed. *Felix Frankfurter Reminisces.* New York: Reynal, 1960.

PIERCE, NEAL R. *The Deep South States of America.* New York: Norton, 1974.

POLLAK, LOUIS H. "Mr. Justice Frankfurter: Judgment and the Fourteenth Amendment." 67 *Yale Law Review* 304 (1957).

POUND, ROSCOE. *The Formative Era of American Law.* Boston: Little, Brown, 1938.

———. *An Introduction to the Philosophy of Law.* New Haven: Yale University Press, 1922.

PRITCHETT, C. HERMAN. *The Roosevelt Court.* New York: Macmillan, 1948.

PURCELL, EDWARD. *The Crisis of Democratic Theory.* Lexington: University of Kentucky Press, 1973.

RAUH, JOSEPH. "Felix Frankfurter: Civil Libertarian." 11 Harvard Civil Rights–Civil Liberties Law Review 496 (1976).

RICE, ARNOLD. *The Ku Klux Klan in American Politics.* Washington: Public Affairs Press, 1962.

RICE, CHARLES. "Justice Black, the Demonstrators and a Constitutional Rule of Law." 14 *UCLA Law Review* 454 (1967).

ROGAT, CHARLES. "Mr. Justice Holmes: Some Modern Views. The Judge as Spectator." 31 *University of Chicago Law Review* 213 (1964).

ROHDE, DAVID, and SPAETH, HAROLD. *Supreme Court Decision Making.* San Francisco: W. H. Freeman, 1976.

ROSTOW, EUGENE. *The Sovereign Prerogative: The Supreme Court and the Quest for Law.* New Haven: Yale University Press, 1962.

ROSENFIELD, LENORA, ed. *Portrait of a Philosopher: Morris R. Cohen in Life and Letters.* New York: Harcourt, Brace and World, 1962.

RUMBLE, WILFRED E. *American Legal Realism: Skepticism, Reform and the Judicial Process.* Ithaca, N.Y.: Cornell University Press, 1968.

SCHMIDHAUSER, JOHN R. *Judges and Justices.* Boston: Little, Brown, 1979.

SCHUBERT, GLENDON. *The Constitutional Polity.* Boston: Boston University Press, 1970.

———. *The Judicial Mind.* Evanston: Northwestern University Press, 1965.

———. *The Judicial Mind Revisited.* New York: Oxford University Press, 1979.

SELIGMAN, JOEL. *The High Citadel: The Influence of Harvard Law School.* New York: Houghton, Mifflin, 1978.

SHAPIRO, MARTIN. *Freedom of Speech: The Supreme Court and Judicial Review.* Englewood Cliffs, N.J.: Prentice-Hall, 1966.

SHELDON, CHARLES. *The American Judicial Process.* New York: Dodd, Mead, 1974.

SHULMAN, HARRY. "The Supreme Court: Attitude toward Liberty of Contract and Freedom of Speech." 41 *Yale Law Journal* 262 (1931).

SNOWLISS, SYLVIA. "The Legacy of Justice Black." 187 *Supreme Court Review* (1973).

SPAETH, HAROLD. "The Judicial Restraint of Mr. Justice Frankfurter—Myth and Reality." 8 *Midwest Journal of Political Science* 22 (1964).

STEEL, RONALD. *Walter Lippmann and the American Century.* Boston: Little, Brown, 1980.

STEPHENS, OTIS, JR. *The Supreme Court and Confessions of Guilt.* Knoxville: University of Tennessee Press, 1973.

STERNSHER, BERNARD. *Consensus, Conflict, and American Historians.* Bloomington: Indiana University Press, 1975.

STRICKLAND, STEPHAN PARKS, ed. *Hugo Black and the Supreme Court.* New York: Bobbs-Merrill, 1967.

SUTHERLAND, ARTHUR. *The Law at Harvard.* Cambridge, Mass.: Belknap Press, 1967.

SWISHER, CARL. *Stephen J. Field: Craftsman of the Law.* Hamden, Conn.: Archon, 1963.

TANENHAUS, JOSEPH. "The Cumulative Scaling of Judicial Decisions." 79 *Harvard Law Review* 1583 (1966).

THAYER, EZRA. *Legal Essays.* Boston: Riverdale Press, 1980.

THAYER, JAMES BRADLEY. "The Origin and Scope of the American Doctrine of Constitutional Law." 7 *Harvard Law Review* 129 (1893).

THOMAS, HELEN SHIRLEY. *Felix Frankfurter: Scholar on the Bench.* Baltimore: Johns Hopkins University Press, 1960.

TINDALL, GEORGE BROWN. *The Emergence of the New South.* Baton Rouge: Louisiana State University Press, 1967.

TRIBE, LAURENCE. *American Constitutional Law.* Mineola, N.Y.: Foundation Press, 1978.

ULMER, SIDNEY. "The Longitudinal Behavior of Hugo Lafayette Black: Parabolic Support for Civil Liberties, 1937–1971." 1 *Florida State Law Review* 131 (1974).

WECHSLER, HERBERT. "Toward Neutral Principles of Constitutional Law." 73 *Harvard Law Review* 1 (1959).

WESTIN, ALAN F. "The Supreme Court, the Populist Movement and the Campaign of 1896." 15 *Journal of Politics* 1 (1953).

WHITE, G. EDWARD. *The American Judicial Tradition.* New York: Oxford University Press, 1978.

——. *Patterns of American Legal Thought.* Indianapolis: Bobbs-Merrill, 1978.

WHITE, MORTON. *Social Thought in America*. New York: Oxford University Press, 1976.

WIGDOR, HARRY. *Roscoe Pound: Philosopher of the Law*. Westport, Conn.: Greenwood, 1974.

WILLIAMS, CHARLOTTE. *Hugo Black: A Study in the Judicial Process*. Baltimore: Johns Hopkins University Press, 1950.

YARBROUGH, TINSLEY. "Justice Black, the Fourteenth Amendment and Incorporation." 30 *University of Miami Law Review* 231 (1976).

———. "Mr. Justice Black and Legal Positivism." 57 *Virginia Law Review* 375 (1971).

Index of Cases

Adams v. Tanner, 46
Adamson v. California, 155, 162, 164–169, 202
Ashcraft v. Tennessee, 153–154, 168
Avery v. Alabama, 135

Barenblatt v. United States, 204
Barron v. Baltimore, 34
Bartkus v. Illinois, 170
Beauharnais v. Illinois, 193–195, 202
Betts v. Brady, 149
Bram v. United States, 137
Brandenberg v. Ohio, 202
Bridges v. California, 149, 179–185, 189, 195, 202
Brown v. Mississippi, 137, 140, 142
Buchalter v. New York, 151

Chambers v. Florida, 137–142, 150–151, 153–155, 162, 167–169
Chaplinsky v. New Hampshire, 190, 192–193
Charles River Bridge v. Warren Bridge, 32
Connecticut General Life Ins. Co. v. California, 133
Cox v. Louisiana, 188, 203
Cox v. New Hampshire, 177–178, 181, 189, 212, 216

Dartmouth College v. Woodward, 32
Dean Milk Co. v. Madison, 212

Dennis v. United States, 175, 195–202
Dred Scott v. Sanford, 33, 37
Dunne v. United States, 196

Edelman v. California, 172
Everson v. Board of Education, 148

Feldman v. United States, 153–154
Fletcher v. Peck, 32
Fox v. Washington, 47
Freeman v. Hewitt, 213

Gitlow v. New York, 47–49, 194, 200

Haley v. Ohio, 171–172
Hammer v. Dagenhart, 212
Hamn v. City of Rock Hill, 14
Harris v. United States, 149
Hood & Sons, H.P. v. DuMond, 212
Humphrey's Executor v. United States, 85
Hurtado v. California, 131, 169
Hysler v. Florida, 149–150

Irvine v. California, 216

Jackson v. Denno, 155
Joint Anti-Fascist Refugee Committee v. McGrath, 204
Jones v. Opelika, 156

Katz v. United States, 215
Kovacs v. Cooper, 146, 190, 192

Lisenba v. *California*, 149–150
Lochner v. *New York*, 41–42, 46, 68
Louisiana ex rel. Francis v. *Resweber*, 159–164
Louisville Joint Stock Land Bank v. *Radford*, 85
Lyons v. *Oklahoma*, 153–154

Malinski v. *New York*, 156–159
Mapp v. *Ohio*, 215
Martin v. *Struthers*, 187–189, 203
Maxwell v. *Dow*, 131
McCollum v. *Board of Education*, 148
McLeod v. *J. E. Dilworth Co.*, 213
McNabb v. *United States*, 137
Minersville School District v. *Gobitis*, 143–148, 181
Minnesota Rate Case, 37
Mooney v. *Holohan*, 132
Morehead v. *New York ex rel. Tipaldo*, 25
Mugler v. *Kansas*, 48
Muller v. *Oregon*, 45, 68
Munn v. *Illinois*, 36
Murchison, In re, 172

NLRB v. *Jones & Laughlin Steel Corp.*, 25
New York Central Railroad v. *Winfield*, 45

Ogden v. *Saunders*, 32
Osborn v. *Bank of the United States*, 30

Palko v. *Connecticut*, 132, 141, 165, 186
Patterson v. *Colorado*, 47
Pennsylvania v. *Nelson*, 204
Pierce v. *United States*, 47
Pierre v. *Louisiana*, 137
Piqua Branch of State Bank v. *Knoop*, 32
Powell v. *Alabama*, 132

Quaker City Cab Co. v. *Pennsylvania*, 244

Rochin v. *California*, 161

Schechter Poultry Corp. v. *United States*, 85, 121
Slaughterhouse Cases, 34–36, 165
Smyth v. *Ames*, 37
Snyder v. *Massachusetts*, 137
Southern Pacific Co. v. *Arizona*, 212
Sturges v. *Crowinshield*, 32
Sweezy v. *New Hampshire*, 161, 200, 204–206

Thomas v. *Collins*, 186
Thompson v. *Louisville*, 172
Tinker v. *Des Moines Indep. Comm. School Dist.*, 203
Twining v. *New Jersey*, 131, 165–166, 169

United States v. *Butler*, 124
United States v. *Carolene Products Co.*, 134–136, 138, 141, 144, 186
United States v. *Darby*, 212
United States v. *Rabinowitz*, 149
United States v. *Sacher*, 196

Watkins v. *United States*, 204
Weeks v. *United States*, 215
West Coast Hotel v. *Parrish*, 25
West Virginia State Board of Education v. *Barnette*, 148, 191
Winters v. *New York*, 192–193
Wolf v. *Colorado*, 161, 215–216
Wynehamer v. *New York*, 33–34, 37

Yates v. *United States*, 204

General Index

Adams, Brooks, 208
Alabama, University of, 96–97
Ames, James Barr, 56
Arnold, Thurman, 73

Baker, Newton, 63
Bankhead, John, 116–118
Bentley, Arthur, 52
Biddle, Francis, 44
Bisbee Report, 63
Black-Summers Bill, 123
Borah, William, 121
Bradley, Joseph, 34–36, 40, 43
Brandeis, Louis, 43–50, 60–62, 84–86, 123, 198, 201
Brennan, William, 205
Bryan, William Jennings, 97
Buckner, Emory, 57, 64
Burlingame, C. C., 88, 148
Burton, Harold, 160, 203
Butler, Pierce, 43, 49
Byrnes, James, 185

Cardozo, Benjamin, 49, 84, 86–87, 132–135, 141, 186
Chafee, Zechariah, 78, 146
Clark, Tom, 170–171, 195, 203, 216
Cohen, Morris, 56, 73, 86, 88
Court Packing Plan, 25, 86–87, 123–125

Cover, Robert, 29
Croly, Herbert, 60–61, 64, 79–80

Davis, John W., 44, 103, 105
Dennison, Winfred, 60
Dodge Lecture, 78–84
Douglas, William, 25, 137, 144, 151, 157, 160, 163, 165, 172, 179, 189, 195, 197, 199, 201, 203, 205
Durr, Clifford, 103, 117

Field, Stephen, 34–37, 40–41, 43, 49, 51–52, 129
Flack, Harry, 162
Fraenkel, Osmond, 145
Frank, Jerome, 19, 72–75, 78
Frank, John, 107, 120
Gilmore, Grant, 43
Glueck, Sheldon, 193
Goodnow, Frank, 52
Goodwyn, Laurence, 93–94
Grey, John Chipman, 56

Hamilton, Alexander, 26, 91, 107–108
Hamilton, Edith, 111, 182
Hand, Learned, 64, 161, 196–197
Harlan, John Marshall I, 42, 165
Harlan, John Marshall II, 203–205
Hartz, Louis, 25, 29, 208
Harvard Law School, 56–57, 63–64, 96

Heflin, Thomas, 113–118
Hirsch, H. N., 85, 145, 147, 191, 217
Holmes, Oliver Wendell, 41–51, 60, 71,
    84, 86–88, 198, 201
Hoover, Herbert, 78, 114
Horwitz, Morton, 29
Houston, Charles, 102
Hughes, Charles Evans, 49, 79, 123,
    134, 136–137, 142, 144, 177–
    178, 212
Hurst, Willard, 29
Hutchins, Robert, 76–77

Jackson, Robert, 151, 154, 185, 208
Jacobsohn, Gary, 65–66, 71–72
Jefferson, Thomas, 27, 91, 107–109,
    124

Kent, James, 28
Kolb, Reuben, 94
Ku Klux Klan, 101–107, 117, 136, 142

La Follette–Costigan Bill, 91, 119
Laski, Harold, 43
Lehman, Monte, 164
Lippmann, Walter, 59, 81–84
Llewellyn, Karl, 67
Lowell, A. Lawrence, 66

Magee, James, 187, 190
Manning, Joseph, 94–95
Mansfield, Lord, 29
Marshall, John, 30–32, 41, 71
McPherson, C. B., 175
McReynolds, James, 49, 185
Medina, Harold, 196
Mill, John Stuart, 110
Minton, Sherman, 195, 214
Mooney, Tom, 64
Morgenthau, Henry, 63
Murphy, Frank, 145, 149, 151, 154,
    157, 163, 167–169, 172, 185, 189,
    195, 214
Muscle Shoals, 113, 122

NIRA, 85, 121
Norris, George, 113, 122

Parrington, Vernon, 107–108, 111, 123
Peckham, Rufus, 41–42
Pegler, Westbrook, 84
Percy, Lord Eustace, 60
Pound, Roscoe, 30, 52, 64, 66, 68, 72–
    73
Pritchett, C. Herman, 17

Raskob, Jacob, 113
Reed, Stanley, 25, 154, 163, 165–166,
    179, 191–192, 198
Roberts, Owen, 49, 80, 150
Roosevelt, Franklin Delano, 14, 24–25,
    84–87, 113, 120–125, 128, 142
Roosevelt, Theodore, 58–63
Rutledge, Wiley, 151, 155, 157, 163,
    172, 186, 189, 195, 215

Sampson, William, 28
Sanford, Edward T., 48–49
Schubert, Glendon, 17, 208, 218
Smith, Adam, 107, 112, 119
Smith, Al, 78, 83–85, 113–115
Smoot-Hawley Tariff, 91
Stimson, Henry, 58–60, 62–63, 69
Stone, Harlan Fiske, 25, 49, 133–137,
    141, 144–146, 186, 212
Story, Joseph, 28
Sutherland, George, 49

Taft, William Howard, 43, 59, 79
Taney, Roger, 31–33, 41
Thayer, James Bradley, 22, 38–40, 89,
    129
Tocqueville, Alexis de, 109–111

Underwood, Oscar, 105–106

Valentine, Robert, 60
Van Devanter, Willis, 24, 43, 49, 123
Vinson, Fred, 196, 198–199, 201–202

Warren, Earl, 204–205
Wheeler, Burton, 121
Wheeler-Rayburn Act, 122
White, G. Edward, 30
Wilson, Woodrow, 61

Library of Congress Cataloging in Publication Data

SILVERSTEIN, MARK, 1947–
  Constitutional faiths.

  Bibliography: p.
  Includes index.
  1. Frankfurter, Felix, 1882–1965. 2. Black, Hugo
LaFayette, 1886–1971. 3. Judges—United States—
Biography. 4. Judicial process—United States.
5. Political questions and judicial power—United States.
I. Title.
KD8744.S56 1984   347.73'2634 [B]   83-45946
ISBN 0-8014-1650-7 (alk. paper)   347.3073534 [B]